如何策划行之有效的英语课堂活动

The Standby Book
Activities for the language classroom

Seth Lindstromberg 编

外语教学与研究出版社
FOREIGN LANGUAGE TEACHING AND RESEARCH PRESS
剑桥大学出版社
CAMBRIDGE UNIVERSITY PRESS
北京 BEIJING

京权图字：01-2009-4609

图书在版编目（CIP）数据

如何策划行之有效的英语课堂活动：英文／（美）林德斯特伦伯格（Lindstromberg, S.）编. — 北京：外语教学与研究出版社，2009.8（2024.12 重印）
（Learning in Doing · 剑桥英语课堂教学系列）
书名原文：The Standby Book: Activities for the language classroom
ISBN 978-7-5600-8941-6

I. 如… II. 林… III. 英语－课堂教学－教学参考资料 IV. H319.3

中国版本图书馆 CIP 数据核字 (2009) 第 154574 号

出 版 人　王　芳
责任编辑　刘　佳
封面设计　袁　璐
出版发行　外语教学与研究出版社
社　　址　北京市西三环北路 19 号（100089）
网　　址　https://www.fltrp.com
印　　刷　北京盛通印刷股份有限公司
开　　本　650×980　1/16
印　　张　16.75
版　　次　2009 年 9 月第 1 版　2024 年 12 月第 17 次印刷
书　　号　ISBN 978-7-5600-8941-6
定　　价　34.00 元

如有图书采购需求，图书内容或印刷装订等问题，侵权、盗版书籍等线索，请拨打以下电话或关注官方服务号：
客服电话：400 898 7008
官方服务号：微信搜索并关注公众号"外研社官方服务号"
外研社购书网址：https://fltrp.tmall.com

物料号：189410001

总　序

外研社从剑桥大学出版社出版的"Cambridge Handbooks for Language Teachers"中选出10本，结成"Learning in Doing·剑桥英语课堂教学系列"，在中国大陆出版发行。

应外研社要我为这套丛书写一个总序的要求，我通读了全部10本书，同时看了原系列其他书的书名。我发现，在所有这些书都涉及外语教学中的重要问题的同时，编者选出目前这10本来先期出版发行，是有道理的。

首先，从这10本书的书名就可看出，它们都是关于当前外语教学中的一些最关紧要的问题。读这套书的教师朋友们会发现，它们是如此切合我们国家当前外语教学（尤其是基础阶段外语教学）所面临的突出问题，用一句俗语说，它们是如此符合我国的"国情"：大班教学、以学生为中心突出个性化教学、课堂设计、口语教学、词汇教学、如何利用多媒体教学手段等等，方方面面，不一而足。似乎这些内容还不够，《如何策划行之有效的英语课堂活动》（*The Standby Book: Activities for the language classroom*）则提供了各种课堂活动的案例达110个之多。老师们"手到擒来"，直接可以拿到课堂中去用。我在通读各册书时越来越觉得好似剑桥大学出版社是专门为我们中国外语老师们量身定做出版这套书的。

其次，这套书的作者们，全是具有丰富课堂教学经验的一线教师。说实话，他们若不是亲尝过外语课堂教学中的各种酸甜苦辣，是写不出如此实用的书的。同时，每一本书又都是以应用语言学、尤其是它的重要内容——外语教学法为理论根据的，对外语教学法作了深入浅出的阐述和扩展。它们体现了以解决实际问题为目的的理论与实践的完美结合。

第三，我之所以在上文中用了"深入浅出"这个词语，是因为这10本书所涉及到的应用语言学理论是深刻的，但各书的行文，却由于它们密切联系教学实际并且以解决教师实际问题为目的而使用了简洁明晰的语言。全套书中绝无国外某些所谓理论语言学著作中的那种故弄玄虚的晦涩语言。尤其是，由于众多案例都是根据课堂教学实际编写的，其中的语言本身，就可以由老师们搬用在自己的课堂教学中。

第四，这套丛书，涉及到各种课堂教学内容，包括口语教学、语法练习、泛读材料的课堂活动、词汇学习、利用词典进行的活动、语法讲解以及多媒体手段在课堂教学中的运用等。可以说，外语课堂教学的各个方面，在这10本书中都得到了阐述。

第五，如上所说，这10本书的一个共同特点，就是作者使用的工作语言实用、简明、贴近课堂实际。因此，阅读和运用这10本书，不仅可以大大改进我们的课堂教学质量，同时也有助于提高自己的英语语言掌握和课堂用语水平，其中包括在教学中常用的词汇和语句、教材中涉及的学生社会生活的各个方面所需的话语以及组织学生完成各种课堂活动所需要的用语等。

第六，上文中提到的各册书中的众多案例，总的来说，都是以"任务型教学法"为形式的。我们知道，在教育部颁布实施的国家《英语课程标准》中，是推介"任务型教学"这一外语教学法的新发展的。在这10本书中，众多的教学活动的案例，都是根据"任务型教学"来设计的，都强调了"用语言做事情"（Do things with words）和"在用中学"（Learning in doing）的理念。换言之，这10本书所介绍的有关外语教学的各种理念、方法、活动若能为广大教师们所接受并在教学中实施，将会对提高我们外语课堂教学的质量起很大的作用。

最后，这套丛书的另一个共同特色，就是它以"以学生为中心"这个教育的根本理念为出发点。这不仅在10本书中的《如何开展个性化课堂教学》（*Personalizing Language Learning*）一书中集中体现出来，而且贯穿在整套书的其他各册中。这符合我们当前所倡导的素质教育的思想。

总结以上所谈到的这套丛书的各种特色，可以用一句话来表述：这是一套符合我国外语教学的具体情况、有助于外语教师上好课的好书。

我乐于推荐它。

读者老师们可能已经注意到，我在《总序》的开篇第一段中说了这样的话："编者选出目前这10本来先期出版发行，是有道理的。"其中"先期"一语，透露了我一个小小的心愿：盼望外研社在不久的将来，会将原系列其他作品作为这套丛书的续集置于全国外语教师们的案头。

下面，我简略介绍一下这10本书各自的特色，以便教师读者们对这套丛书的全貌有一个概括的了解。

一、《如何教好大班英语课》（*Teaching Large Multilevel Classes*）

这套丛书，本无先后排列。我之首先介绍这一本，是因为"大班教学"是我国基础教育阶段英语教学的主要"国情"之一。而且，班一大，水平必然高低不齐。

本书一反常规，不是抱怨班上学生太多、水平不齐，而是首先提出大班的有利之处：交流机会多、信息多、想法多、意见多、不同背景多，因而可谈论的生活花样多、"小老师"多、兴趣类型多、迫使教师必须以各种手段和方式教学……何等新意！

当然，本书也提出了大班对教师的挑战。作者为教师们概括了11条应对这些挑战的心态和举措：

1．不要气馁，要永远充满信心；
2．教学活动更要多样化；
3．不要心急，要有节奏；
4．始终坚持兴趣第一原则；
5．贯彻师生合作，学生合作；
6．更要注意每个学生的个性；
7．鼓励学生自己负起责任；
8．鼓励对课堂活动各自有自己的结局（"开放式答案"）；
9．明确地使学生在课堂活动中有法可循；
10．尽量使课堂教学活动能覆盖每一个学生；

11．多提出能激发学生兴趣的问题（甚至包括老师自己也没有明确答案的问题）。

有趣的是，在西方国家"大班"的含义是30人左右。当然，这并不妨碍我们在本国七八十人的大班中尝试书中提出的建议。

二、《如何巧妙设计英语课堂》（*Planning Lessons and Courses: Designing sequences of work for the language classroom*）

我紧接着就介绍这本书，是因为我们教师上课前必做的第一件事就是写好教案（Lesson Plans）。作者在这本书中为我们提出一个好教案的11条标准，和设计教案的8个步骤。

好教案的标准是：

1．按这个教案上课，师生都感到舒服、没有压力；
2．能增加师生间相互的了解；
3．明确此前已学过什么；
4．本课主要要学习什么；
5．用什么教学方法能使学生学得最好；
6．能在教学中调动学生的直觉、灵感、动机、兴趣、文化需求、甚至乐感等等；
7．在课堂上进行最有效的活动；
8．使学生信服的确值得学习这些东西；
9．教师能主动作出决策，有正确的判断；
10．有助于学生形成良好的学习习惯；
11．教师有"随机应变"的空间。

写好教案的步骤是：

1．全面分析学生情况；
2．决定教学内容的时间分配；
3．明确这课书主要应做什么事；
4．从确定学生应如何学来确定教师应如何教；
5．利用什么教学资源、教具等；
6．确定灵活运用何种多样化教学手段；
7．具体写出教案；
8．确定教师自己在执行此教案中有什么"规矩"和"自由"。
真是再具体不过了！

三、《如何开展个性化课堂教学》(*Personalizing Language Learning*)

正如教师读者们所熟知的，教育部颁布的国家《英语课程标准》提出，学生要通过5个方面来学习掌握综合英语运用能力，其中第一个方面就是个人的情感态度（其他4个方面分别是语言技能、语言知识、学习策略和文化意识）。而这本书正好着重强调：教师应将学生的个人生活经历、情感、知识、价值观以及对生活和周边事物的见解融入教学之中。并且指出，许多课本正是缺少这方面的内容，谈的都是别人的事情。因此这本书为教师们提供大量人性化的、具创造性的课堂活动案例。有两点格外打动了我，那就是，书中特别提到：一，在个性化课堂活动中，教师应当把自己也摆进去，与学生交流个人的情感态度；二，在个性化学习活动中，要尊重学生，不应涉及他们的隐私（privacy）。这是何等的真知灼见啊！这才是真正的素质教育！

四、《如何设计课堂泛读活动》(*Extensive Reading Activities for Teaching Language*)

按照一般的概念，"泛读"主要是通过大量阅读来提高阅读能力。但本书作者告诉我们，在课堂上可以用泛读材料来进行一百多种生动有趣的语言活动。同时，作者还为我们提出泛读课程的10条原则，它们是：

1. 对基础教育阶段来说，泛读内容主要应是简易读物，包括名著的简写本等；
2. 泛读内容应当广泛，包括多种文体和题材；
3. 学生应自主选择自己爱读的东西，这也是"个性化学习"的一个方面；
4. 泛读量要大，要有大量语言输入，以量取胜；
5. 应学习快读、略读、重点读、浏览等阅读技巧，在有限时间内尽量扩大接触范围；
6. 要为兴趣、信息和提高语感而读；
7. 主要是默读；
8. 一般设有读后的家庭作业；
9. 教师应当帮助学生选择读物并就读物内容给予指导；
10. 最好教师本人给学生做出广为涉猎的榜样。

有趣的是：全书的最后一节，作者设想了一些教师们可能会提出的具体问题，并就个人意见予以解答。例如：不同年级的学生应该读哪样的书、到哪里去找这些书、如何安排学生轮流读教师提供的书、怎样能知道学生读懂与否、如何考查……等等。给教师读者们考虑得何等周到！

五、《如何组织课堂会话活动》（*Dialogue Activities*）

本书首先从理论角度将"对话"这一普遍运用的教学形式作了理论的阐述，指出：任何真实的语言使用（书面或口头的），其主要形式就是对话，因为语言就是为相互间表达情感或意向用的。同时指出，早自16世纪起，"情景对话"（situational dialogue）就已经成为语言教学的主要活动，而且是以教授功能和语法为主的。

当然，本书主要篇幅是为教师提供大量可以在课堂中使用的案例，而且十分详尽具体。例如，我们一般在课堂中广泛运用的"成对活动"（pair work），在书中就得到大大的发展：

封闭对（Closed Pairs）——全班学生分别按座位成对，同时操练，互不干扰；

开放对（Open Pairs）——各对轮流站起来操练，其他学生听后评论；

背靠背对（Back-to-Back Pairs）——如各处课堂一角，模拟打电话；

对面排立对（Line Dance Pairs）——安排学生排两队对面站立，操练一次后，其中一队队首学生换至队尾，与不同学生换练；

并向圈对（Dyadic Circle）——学生站成内外两个圆圈，面对面对话后分别按顺时针和逆时针方向移步；目的也是与不同学生操练；

随意组合对（Milling）——学生站起来自己随意选对操练；

退远对（Ever-widening Gap）——相对而立，边说话边退，直至要大声喊叫。

可以看出，这里又有"国情"了：咱们的课堂里哪有这样的空间进行如此活泼的教学活动呢？但这些理念还是可以给我们以启发的。例如，有些英语课可不可以在操场里上呢？

六、《如何通过课堂活动教语法》（*Grammar Practice Activities: A practical guide for teachers*）

本书企图打破"教语法只能是很枯燥的"这一误区，为教师们提供各种有趣的、生动的、通过有意义的上下文来进行的语法实践活动。作者把各种语法点按字母顺序列出（从以字母a开头的adjective到以字母u开头的短语used to），分别提供各种教学案例。概而言之，就是把语法教学交际化，有时甚至是游戏化。

例如：在教"被动式"（The Passive Voice）这个一般来说比较枯燥的语法项目时，老师选择"旅馆"这个情景，问学生：

What is done in a hotel?

并给出一个回答：Guests are welcomed. 然后要学生模仿说出类似的答案，如：

Prices are listed.

Meals are served.

Breakfast is provided.

Rooms are cleaned every day.

Credit cards are accepted.

Sheets are changed at the guest's request.

这样，就把语法教学生活化，交际化了。学生一点也不会觉得枯燥。

七、《如何提高词汇教学成效》（*Working with Words: A guide to teaching and learning vocabulary*）

这是一本如何教与学词汇的指南。它指出，在许多外语课堂中，词汇教学没有得到应有的重视，或者是教学方法不当。本书从理论出发，阐述了关于字词的理论——词的形和意，包括同义词、反义词、成语、搭配等，以及词汇的课堂教学原则。作者试图帮助教师学会选择教材中最恰当的词语来学习，并提供操练的形式和方法。要指出的是：书中所给案例都是从真实读物中选出的，而不是作者杜撰的。

关于记忆单词的问题，书中举出一个语言学习的小实验：把同样的30个单词给了两组学生。第一组的学生被告知要记住这些单词并要参加一个单词记忆测试。另一组学生被告知设想自己被困在一个孤岛上，要从这30个词的词义上分列出哪些单词是可以利用来使自己脱离困境的，哪些是与此目的无关的。过了同样一段时间，两组学生被投入同样的单词记忆测验，结果第二组的学生成绩优于第一组学生。这说明词汇必须在有意义的使用中才能学会。

八、《如何指导学生有效使用词典》（*Dictionary Activities*）

本书的主题是：一本好词典不仅能提供词义，而且还是可以用来进行各种课堂活动的好资料。作者为我们列出至少8种利用词典进行的活动：

1. 建立信心活动：从不善于使用词典，到掌握熟练使用它的技巧——例如怎么在长长的词条中找到你所需要的词义和用法；
2. 词汇积累活动：怎样通过不同词的词义间的内在关联科学地、系统地学习词汇；
3. 语法学习活动：通过词形和词义变化学语法；
4. 语音学习活动：如学习有韵的谚语，绕口令等来练习语音并学习词语；
5. 读写活动：如掌握正式和非正式文体等；
6. 快速阅读：通过在不同上下文中大量接触来正确理解词义；
7. 电子词典的使用：这是目前流行的趋势；
8. 专项词典的使用：如图解词典，短语词典等。

总之，本书作者旨在指导我们如何使词典成为一种活的学习资料。

九、《如何使用影像材料进行课堂教学》（*Using Authentic Video in the Language Classroom*）

本书不仅从理论上说明了真实影像资料（指在电影院、电视中和DVD光盘上所载的故事片、纪录片、电视新闻、各种电视节目等）在外语课堂教学中的实用性，并提供了多达150项案例来据实说明它们在课堂中的使用方法。

我们且不说故事片等这些已为教师较多使用的资料，而以目前中外电视节目中日益流行的人物专访栏目为例。作者指出：在教师选定某一个人物专访节目作教材时，其教学程序可如下述：

1. 要求学生未看节目前，先以不同方式（如查阅书面材料、上网、访问相关人员等）预先了解一下这个人物的情况，包括家庭背景、个人简历、举止外貌、个性特征、生活态度、点滴事例等；
2. 观看节目；
3. 按节目内容进行各种生动活泼的口语活动，例如：学生可分别假扮记者和受访者，以"脱口秀"（Talk Show）形式来谈论已看过的节目中的人物，甚至可以涉及受访者曾经有过的与该人物的个人接触和相关感受；这之后可以在班上作报告。在高年级还可以就对这个人的评价进行辩论等；
4. 在口头活动基础上、做各种笔头活动、包括写作文、投板报稿、给报纸写文章等。

这样的活动会激发学生极大的学习兴趣。试想，当我们利用前不久去世的世界著名流行歌手迈克尔·杰克逊的生平录像作为此类课堂活动的材料，会起到多么良好的教学效果！

十、《如何策划行之有效的英语课堂活动》（*The Standby Book: Activities for the language classroom*）

可以说，这是为教师提供的一盒"万金油"。它包含各种课堂教学活动的实用案例，教师们可以"各取所需"。这些活动，又适用于采用不同教学方法（语法法、交际法、功能意念法、词汇入门法、题材教学法等）的教师以及不同教学目的的班级（应试班、速成班、口语突击班和正规课程班）。这里要特别提到的是，本书是由来自十几个不同国家和各类型学校的33位英语教师共同撰写成的，各自就其特定教学领域写出自己的心得，可以说是一本"集思广益"的教学指导书。

以上我简要介绍了一下这套丛书各书的内容和特色。

最后，我要借此机会，给各位教师朋友提一个小小的建议：在阅读任何一本书时，首先仔细读一下它的序言（或简介），并浏览一下目录，了解此书的大概内容，然后再开始阅读正文。在阅读中，应时时结合自己的教学实际和体会对内容加以咀嚼消化，并得出自己的结论。

好，话说多了，就此打住。

北京外国语大学

陈琳

Contents

Introduction   1

1   Warm-ups, breaks and fillers 1: Short energisers   8
Introduction
Seth Lindstromberg
1.1   Chair swapping for names   9
        Tessa Woodward
1.2   One chair missing   10
        Pierre Jeanrenaud
1.3   Balloon chase   12
        Paul Sanderson
1.4   I say, you do   14
        Tessa Woodward
1.5   Newspaper bash!   16
        Jane Revell
1.6   Staccato start   18
        Tessa Woodward
1.7   Singing start   19
        Tessa Woodward
1.8   Computer talk   20
        Denny Packard
1.9   Bizarre riot   22
        Tessa Woodward

2   Warm-ups, breaks and fillers 2: Speaking   24
Introduction
Seth Lindstromberg
2.1   By the way   25
        Seth Lindstromberg
2.2   How do you say ...?   26
        Seth Lindstromberg
2.3   Make them say it   27
        Tessa Woodward
2.4   Whatever's in my bag   30
        Tessa Woodward

Contents

2.5   You guess their adjectives   32
Tessa Woodward

2.6   Think of ten, five, or three things   33
Tessa Woodward

2.7   Links with music   34
Clem Laroy

2.8   A proverb a day   36
Seth Lindstromberg

2.9   Making stress physical   42
Tessa Woodward

3   Reviewing   45
Introduction
Seth Lindstromberg

3.1   Vocabulary brainshower   46
Sheila Levy

3.2   Do you know this word?   47
Hanna Kryszewska

3.3   Recycling   49
Adriana Diaz

3.4   Student-produced vocabulary reviews   50
Andrew Glass

3.5   Vocabulary on slips   52
Sheelagh Deller

3.6   True-false student-student dictation   53
Sheelagh Deller

3.7   Student-produced reference booklets   55
Tessa Woodward

3.8   Hidden shape in the puzzle   57
Adriana Diaz

3.9   Guess who grammar quiz   60
Denny Packard

4   Communicative pot-pourri   63
Introduction
Seth Lindstromberg

4.1   The books on the shelf   63
Adriana Diaz

4.2   ETs and earthlings   65
Adriana Diaz

4.3   Live classroom   66
Adriana Diaz

4.4	The Tower of Babel	68
	Adriana Diaz	
4.5	Two part discussion	70
	Seth Lindstromberg	
4.6	Guess my story	72
	Herbert Puchta	
4.7	The movies you've seen	74
	Rick Cooper	
4.8	A radio drama	75
	Adriana Diaz	
4.9	Brothers and Sisters	77
	Clem Laroy	
4.10	Stories that share the past	79
	Mario Rinvolucri	
4.11	Your life in the cards	81
	Clem Laroy	

5   Working with a coursebook   84
Introduction
Seth Lindstromberg/Peter Grundy/Lindsey Gallagher

5.1	Judge the book by its cover (but not only . . .)	86
	Hanna Kryszewska	
5.2	What shall I leave in?	87
	David Cranmer	
5.3	Supplementing coursebooks with authentic materials	89
	Peter Grundy	
5.4	Coursebook recall	93
	Hanna Kryszewska	
5.5	Personalising coursebooks	94
	Steve Gilbride and Peter Grundy	
5.6	Stories in your coursebook	95
	Hanna Kryszewska	
5.7	Reconstructing a patch on a page	96
	Seth Lindstromberg	
5.8	Alternative coursebooks	98
	Lindsey Gallagher and Peter Grundy	

6   Using magazines and newspapers   100
Introduction
Seth Lindstromberg

6.1	Who can take notes best?	101
	Hanna Kryszewska	

Contents

6.2   Meet the demand   102
       Hanna Kryszewska
6.3   That's news to me!   108
       Hanna Kryszewska
6.4   Spot it!   109
       Hanna Kryszewska
6.5   Looking in from outside   111
       Mario Rinvolucri

7   Theme texts, affective texts, stories   113
Introduction
Seth Lindstromberg
7.1   Stories with opposite messages   114
       Mario Rinvolucri
7.2   Flip the frame   116
       Mario Rinvolucri
7.3   Milk bottles and dustbins   119
       Mario Rinvolucri
7.4   Creative criminality   121
       Mario Rinvolucri
7.5   Are you a worthy owner?   123
       Mario Rinvolucri
7.6   Inseparable   127
       Mario Rinvolucri
7.7   Correcting the teller   129
       Günter Gerngross and Herbert Puchta
7.8   Comparing texts – a person-related way   131
       Peter Grundy
7.9   Discussion from key words   138
       Seth Lindstromberg

8   Writing   140
Introduction
Seth Lindstromberg
8.1   Be my scribe   141
       John Morgan
8.2   Lyrical letters   143
       Joe Buckhurst
8.3   From novelists to publishers   147
       Adriana Diaz

8.4   From doodling to writing   149
        Adriana Diaz
8.5   Squalid things   151
        Mario Rinvolucri
8.6   L1 poem to English prose   153
        Bryan Robinson
8.7   As if a wild animal   155
        Tessa Woodward
8.8   Letters to literary characters   156
        David Cranmer
8.9   Sentences about countries   158
        Seth Lindstromberg
8.10   Creative plagiarism: manipulating a text   159
        James Banner
8.11   End of course certificates   161
        Hanna Kryszewska

9   Language through literature   163
Introduction
Colin Evans/Seth Lindstromberg
9.1   Dialogue from a poem   164
        John Morgan
9.2   Copycats   167
        John Morgan
9.3   This is how it ends!   168
        Andy Rouse
9.4   Signing as a character   172
        David Cranmer
9.5   A walk through the seasons   173
        David Cranmer
9.6   Façade: exploring rhythm and rhyme in nonsense poetry   176
        David Cranmer
9.7   Identifying with characters   179
        Colin Evans
9.8   Completion   184
        Colin Evans
9.9   Collective fairy tale   186
        Colin Evans
9.10   Enactment   187
        Colin Evans

10   Music and imagination   190
Introduction
Clem Laroy/Seth Lindstromberg
10.1   Story in the music   191
        David Cranmer
10.2   Silent film mimes   192
        Clem Laroy
10.3   Silent film sequels   193
        Clem Laroy
10.4   Silent film scripts   194
        Clem Laroy
10.5   Musical constructions   196
        Clem Laroy
10.6   My home   198
        Clem Laroy
10.7   Paintings and music   199
        Clem Laroy
10.8   Inside the painting   202
        Clem Laroy

11   Not just for business people   205
Introduction
Seth Lindstromberg
11.1   Advertise your own job   206
        Marcus Child
11.2   The ideal job   207
        Denny Packard
11.3   Marketing a new product   210
        Denny Packard
11.4   Decision makers   211
        Satish Patel
11.5   Selling power   213
        Satish Patel
11.6   Vendor analysis   214
        Satish Patel
11.7   Bad meetings   216
        Chris Dalton
11.8   Concept word pictionary   217
        Marcus Child
11.9   Icon farrago race   218
        Marcus Child
11.10 Market icons   222
        Marcus Child

11.11   Gifts to professionals   225
        Mario Rinvolucri

12 Grammar and register: practice, reflection, review   226
Introduction
Seth Lindstromberg
12.1   The news in our town   227
        Viviana Valenti
12.2   I see . . . You see   229
        John Morgan
12.3   Transposed questionnaires   230
        Mario Rinvolucri
12.4   Crazy fortune   231
        Adriana Diaz
12.5   Gossips   233
        Adriana Diaz
12.6   Talking to the board   235
        John Barnett
12.7   A translation task   236
        Bryan Robinson
12.8   The register of replies   238
        Graham Butler
12.9   Dependency dictation   240
        Jon Carr

Bibliography   244
Index   246

Acknowledgements

The authors and publishers are grateful to the authors, publishers and others who have given permission for the use of copyright material identified in the text. It has not been possible to identify the sources of all the material used and in such cases the publishers would welcome information from copyright owners.

Lufthansa for the text and logo on p. 48; Nicholas D. Kristof/New York Times; Marion Molteno for the extract on p. 121 from *A Language in Common*, published by The Women's Press (also available in several Asian languages); The Cambridge Town Crier for the text on p. 123; Faber and Faber Ltd and The Putman Publishing Group for the extract on p. 125 from *An Artist of the Floating World* by Kazuo Ishiguro; Martine Virgo-Dubois for the text on p. 127; The Guardian for the text and photograph on p. 129, text and photo © The Guardian; Hit & Run Music (Publishing) Limited for the text on p. 147 © 1989 Philip Collins Ltd/ Hit & Run Music (Publishing) Ltd. International Copyright Secured. All rights reserved. Used by Permission; Oxford University Press for the lists on p. 153 from *The Pillow Book of Sei Shonagon*, translated by Ivan Morris, published by Oxford University Press, 1967; Leon Szkutnik for the poems on p. 167; the poem on pp. 178–9 is from *Collected Poems* by Edith Sitwell, published by Sinclair-Stevenson; Reed Consumer Books for the poem on pp. 181 and 183 from *The Complete Poems* by C Day Lewis published by Sinclair-Stevenson (1992). Copyright © 1992 in this edition The Estate of C Day Lewis; Laurence Pollinger Ltd, the Estate of Frieda Lawrence Ravagli and Viking Penguin for the poem on p. 184 from *The Complete Poems of D. H. Lawrence*, edited by V. de Sola Pinto and W. Roberts. Copyright © 1964, 1971 by Angelo Ravagli and C. M. Weekley, Executors of the Estate of Frieda Lawrence Ravagli. Used by permission of Viking Penguin, a division of Penguin Books USA Inc.; Carcanet Press Limited and Oxford University Press Inc. for the poems on p. 186 and pp. 189–90 from the *Complete Poems* by Robert Graves; Eurocentres UK for the questionnaire on p. 231.

We have been unable to trace the copyright owners of the articles on pp. 104–7 and pp. 135–8 and would be grateful for any information which will enable us to do so.

Introduction

The Standby Book in a nutshell

This book describes 110 different classroom activities, most of which can easily be adapted for use in teaching any foreign language. Some of the activities are intended to make up just part of a lesson. Others (see especially some in Chapter 7) are prefabricated chains of activities which make up a complete lesson, or even two – depending on how long your lesson periods are.

Virtually all the activities have been written for adult and older teenage general English classes. There is a chapter of activities for business and professional groups but these too are usable with some general English classes. There are also several activities which work admirably with young learners. (See the Index.) We believe you will find most of these activities substantially new and unrepeated elsewhere. Where more or less familiar language teaching techniques and activities do appear, it is generally because they have been extended or varied in an interesting way or because their underlying rationale might be unexpected.

The Standby Book is intended to be a bank of activities which can be used to supplement a coursebook on a longish non-intensive course, regardless of whether the course is exam-oriented, specialised (e.g. for business people or literature students) or not. That is, the activities here can be accommodated within syllabuses of various kinds (structural, notional/functional, lexical, thematic, etc.). The activities can also be used to create a short intensive course whose participants' principal aims are to become more fluent, to enlarge their vocabularies on a broad front and to have an interesting, lively time with plenty of opportunity for social contact. That is, this book includes activities which could figure in a 'communicative activities syllabus' (Stern 1992: 177–204).

The Standby Book does not present activities in the order you are supposed to do them. Some do dovetail nicely in this or that sequence (as will be noted in the text), but none is absolutely necessary as preparation for any other.

Books like this one have a number of features in common with the average cookbook, which is why they are sometimes called 'recipe books'. For example, they contain step-by-step outlines of procedure;

1

lists of necessary ingredients and equipment, and indications of hoped-for results. As the average cookbook, groups recipes, the activities in *The Standby Book* are grouped, by theme, into chapters which are presented in an order that reflects the compiler's personal preference rather than any practical or theoretical necessity. So, 'Fish' before 'Poultry'? 'Writing' before 'Business'? You can start reading where you like.

The approach

The Standby Book is a moderately eclectic anthology of activities which are broadly 'communicative'. Thus, many of the activities are designed to encourage students to read, write or listen to texts which are intrinsically interesting. Students are also encouraged to express opinions, offer solutions, recount experiences and so on.

Many of the activities involve two assumptions – firstly, that it is good for students to find out about each other as people, and secondly that it is good to try to build learners' confidence. In other words, the majority of the activities in this book are more or less 'humanistic' without moving into the realm of classroom psychologising.

Additionally, there are activities which focus on grammar or pronunciation. Generally, these too encourage communicative use of language during at least one stage of the activity and/or involve some element of fun.

What this book takes for granted

There are further, background similarities between a book like this and a cookbook. Eating brings about biological growth (or, at least, maintenance); teaching (one hopes) brings about linguistic growth. Not all of what is eaten is metabolised; not all of what is read or heard is remembered. What is learned must be integrated into a pre-existing body of knowledge. Thus, in language teaching as in cooking, it's important to operate with a sense of system and principle. A cook should have some knowledge of, or instincts about, nutrition. A teacher should understand that language learners need to see how new vocabulary or features of language relate to what has already been learned. Cooks should know that dining and digestion proceed best when patrons, guests or family have a pleasant atmosphere. Teachers should know that much the same applies to learning. In editing this book, I have assumed that its users take such basic facts about good learning into account when planning and teaching. (Your cooking will have to look after itself.)

Regarding manner of use, there is a further analogy between a cookbook and a resource book of classroom activities. That is, authors and editors of both cookbooks and teachers' resource books assume that users already know how to carry out certain basic procedures. Few cookbooks, for example, bother to repeat the steps involved in stirring a liquid:

> 'Find a longish, thin object – but not one of your fingers. Spoons or knives are usually suitable. The object must be clean and also small enough to fit easily into the container you are using. Hold one end and poke the other end into the liquid so that it nearly touches the bottom of the container. Now move it in a circle, one way or the other, so that it . . . '

Likewise, in editing this book I have assumed that readers know what is meant by such instructions as 'Circulate and answer any questions about vocabulary'. I have also assumed that readers will know without being explicitly told when and how to use such fundamental techniques as drilling, pairwork and so on.

In short, this book has been written for teachers with some teaching experience, who have been through some kind of language teacher training course and have used and got to know at least a couple of coursebooks.

Planning with *The Standby Book*

Let's suppose, for a moment, that you make regular use of a coursebook. Let's presume also that you feel that your coursebook is basically good for your class but not ideal in all respects. Try this:

1. Choose a unit that you have already used with the class. Mark the parts that worked well and the parts you weren't happy with.
2. Look at the parts that didn't work well.
   a) Decide if you could make them work better next time without going outside the coursebook for help. Maybe you didn't follow the instructions in the teacher's book. Well, try to next time. Or maybe you did. Can you see how to alter the stipulated procedure in a way that might make things go better in future?
   b) Or maybe you ought to look for help outside the coursebook. Ask yourself . . .
      – whether this or that section of the coursebook needs to be replaced with something quite different

    – whether to keep a certain section but precede it with an introductory activity of some kind

    – whether to keep it but add some kind of extension.

3. In your book, mark where the lesson breaks actually fell as you worked through the unit. Did you have to rush through any activity because of time constraints? Did you spend too much time on one section (mainly to kill time) because you knew you didn't have enough time to get through the following section in the time available in that lesson?

4. Look at the unit in your coursebook that you plan to cover next. On the basis of what happened with the unit you've just thought about, see if you can predict: dull bits (texts or exercises your students won't take to), unstimulating lead-ins and uninteresting follow-ons.

5. Guess where the lessons breaks will most naturally fall. Sometimes, to avoid rushing through a task you almost (but don't quite) have time for, you should postpone it till the following lesson. However, each time you take this decision, you create a chunk of extra time in the lesson from which an activity has been cut. And this means you will need a filler (or a warm-up).

6. Look through a couple of coursebooks and resource books to see if you can find what you need. (Don't forget to ask your colleagues for tips.) If you're lucky, you may find an activity with aims similar to those of the longer activity you have postponed. Or perhaps your students might in fact best profit from doing a review activity (see Chapter 3). Or perhaps after a long battle with one topic it might actually be more appropriate to change to something completely different.

The initial advantage of grafting the use of a resource book onto the use of a coursebook is that this helps you retain a sense of system which will enable you to avoid leading your class through a series of disjointed one-off activities. As you become familiar with several coursebooks and resource books, a sense of system should increasingly become second nature to you. As a result, you'll be able to knit together activity sequences more and more quickly for classes of various levels and interests. You'll also be able to rely more and more on your own ideas and materials (if you're not at this stage already). You'll be able more quickly and more and more flexibly to adapt what you find in coursebooks, the media and elsewhere. You may even start creating whole new activities that are better suited to your classes and to your way of working than any you can find in a published source. We think this book can play a part in this process.

    A few final thoughts on planning ... The language teaching establishment (i.e. senior teachers, trainers, educators) can often seem quite dogmatic about what can be a legitimate starting point in planning. (Always assuming that one has got to know one's students' level, needs, wishes, and learning styles.) Thus, when deciding what to do in a given lesson teachers are often told that there is a very small set of legitimate starting points. That is, in order to avoid being pedagogical heretics, teachers are often obliged to choose from a list not very much longer than this one:

a) a grammar structure (up to three or so maximum)
b) one or two or a small set of fixed expressions like *Could you . . . ?*
c) a set of vocabulary items and the aim of teaching them for production (or sometimes just for recognition)
d) a small set of postulated reading or listening sub-skills such as scanning, skimming, guessing the meanings of unfamiliar words in context, and so on.

On the fringe, there are the advocates of more or less natural language acquisition in the classroom (e.g. Stephen Krashen and N. S. Prabhu) who say, 'No, thank you' to the above starting points, that lesson planning should start with a choice of:

e) a content area such as long division, seaside geography or making tortillas . . . (e.g. Krashen, 1982).
f) a task or two (Prabhu 1987).

Points (e) and (f) widen things out considerably. But actually teachers start to plan lessons from many more points than (a) to (f). For example:

- They've found a text that's interesting or funny.
- They have a class that's flaccid and somnolent and needs waking up, or is divided into cliques.
- Some of the students have said they want to do a particular song.
- Nobody knows anything about the countryside around the town the course is taking place in.

And so on.
Are teachers wrong when they start planning from observations and desires like these? To say yes would be a bit like saying you can only get to London from six villages. Yes, you do need to plan a sensible route towards the destination you choose. And yes, you should have good reason to believe that your passengers want to go there with you. But there are literally scores, if not hundreds, of useful lesson structures and even more points at which you can enter into one of these structures in order to plan and teach a useful lesson. We hope that using this book will stimulate your inventiveness in this regard as well.

Who wrote this book?

All the activities in this book are ones I received from 1989 to 1993. They come from:

- 33 different EFL teachers
- more than a dozen countries
- private language schools, universities, secondary schools, British Council schools, and company training centres.

The majority of the contributors have, at one time or another, taught at the Pilgrims summer school at the University of Kent, Canterbury. Some of the other contributors had used an earlier, different collection of recipes from Pilgrims teachers (e.g. Sion 1985, Sion 1991, Lindstromberg 1990) and, feeling some kinship with the approach, they decided to send their ideas to Pilgrims and see what might happen. This is how Adriana Diaz (Santa Fe, Argentina) came to figure so prominently in this volume. A couple of other contributors were recommended to me by Mario Rinvolucri, himself a prominent contributor. For example, of Colin Evans (then at the University of Cardiff) Mario said, 'Write him. He does great stuff.'

Information provided for each activity

For each activity you will find information on:

- **level** of students: e.g. elementary to intermediate.
- **time**: a minimum and a maximum are given where relevant.
- **focus**: what is to be practised or learned. Aspects of focus that follow from the chapter title may not be repeated at individual activities. Thus activities in the chapter on writing do not bear the specific note that they involve writing.
- **materials**: what is needed apart from pen and paper for students, and a black/white board for the teacher.
- **requirement** for the class, if any: e.g. a minimum number of students; age.
- **preparation**, if any.
- a brief **note** about the activity the purpose of which is to orientate you about rationale and other useful background information.
- **procedure**: the steps to follow in class.
- **extensions**, if any.
- **variations**, if any: variations for one-to-one teaching are clearly labelled.
- **comments**: e.g. how this has worked in class.

- supplementary notes or statement of rationale.
- **acknowledgement** of sources, except in the cases of teaching ideas which have been around for some time and ideas whose source has been forgotten.
- **worksheet**, if any. These include the wording '© Cambridge University Press' and may be photocopied.

Thanks

I would like to thank everyone who either left recipes hanging on the Pilgrims recipe board or who sent them to me direct. Additional thanks to:

- Mario Rinvolucri for comments on an early draft and for his many contributions.
- Peter Grundy and co-authors at the University of Durham for their contributions to Chapter 5.
- Hanna Kryszewska for much of Chapters 5 and 6.
- Colin Evans for much of Chapter 9 including much of the chapter introduction.
- Clem Laroy for most of Chapter 10.
- Adriana Diaz for her numerous delightful contributions.

I have tried to ensure that each activity is fairly novel in at least one important respect. Where appropriate, the authors and I have tried to acknowledge sources of ideas that have been adapted or extended. Please let us know if we have overlooked anything in this area.

Seth Lindstromberg
Canterbury, 1997

1 Warm-ups, breaks and fillers 1: Short energisers

This chapter contains nine activities for waking people up. All can be used at various times in a lesson, though, by and large, the authors use them as warm-ups at the beginning of a lesson. Beyond being energisers, these activities are quite varied.

- 'Chair swapping for names' (1.1) gets students moving from chair to chair and, along the way, learning or reviewing each other's names. Or, again, you can revamp this into an activity which reviews vocabulary rather than names.
- 'One chair missing' (1.2) is a lively adaptation of the well-known children's party game 'musical chairs' (but without the music). It too doubles as a review activity.
- 'Balloon chase' (1.3), another one that doubles as a review activity, has people batting a balloon around the room.
- 'I say, you do' (1.4) is meant primarily to be repeated from lesson to lesson. It's lively, potentially fun and immensely useful in language learning.
- 'Newspaper bash!' (1.5) is a circle game that involves the person in the centre hitting classmates on the head with a rolled up newspaper. You needn't feel guilty about the hilarity because it's all in the name of vocabulary review.
- 'Staccato start' (1.6) is pure fun. And you can learn a bit about people's natures too.
- 'Singing start' (1.7) is just what it sounds like. Just find a simple song that can be sung as a round (there's one provided) and you're ready to go.
- 'Computer talk' (1.8) gets students doing something zany at the same time as they concentrate on message and grammatical accuracy. It's a great closer in a small class or a good activity for end of term in a largish one.
- Finally, comes 'Bizarre riot' (1.9), which can't be described in a nutshell. No, it won't make your students riot, but it will make them laugh.

1.1 Chair swapping for names

Level
Beginner–Advanced

Materials
None

Time
5–10 minutes

Requirement
At least five students

Focus
First names; asking someone their name

This is a fun activity to use near the start of a course to consolidate name learning.

Procedure

1. Form a circle of chairs, one for each participant. If you have more than 15 people, form two circles. If more than 30, form four circles.
2. Try to remember the name of someone else sitting in the circle. Say it out loud, for example, 'Anna!'. If Anna remembers your name, she says it out loud too, 'Tessa!' Immediately, you swap chairs.
3. Encourage Anna to call out someone else's name. If they can't remember a name, they can ask. (That goes for the rest of the activity.) The person named calls out 'Anna!' and they both briskly swap chairs.
4. Ask people to call out another person's name and swap chairs. Ask them to do this as quickly and as often as possible, all at once. As people get going, a noisy, active and somewhat chaotic feeling builds up. The noise will hide individual queries about names and so the uncertainty and embarrassment are masked in the general fun and commotion.
5. Stop when everyone has had a chance to call out the names of all the other students.

Variations

i) Instead of calling out people's names, students call out:

   - infinitives and past tenses (e.g. 'go' → 'went')
   - antonyms (e.g. 'hot' → 'cold')
   - comparatives (e.g. 'good' → 'better')

- words of the same stress pattern (e.g. 'vegetable' → 'comfortable') or of different stress patterns (e.g. 'bored' → 'sleepy')
- a colour and an object that is that colour (e.g. 'grey' → 'cloud')
- words having a vowel in common (e.g. 'little' → 'sip') or a consonant (e.g. 'match' → 'church')
- words or phrases of formal and informal register (e.g. 'Good morning' → 'Hi', 'descend' → 'go down')

ii) If pairs swap in turn, the activity becomes more serious, but it's easier for everyone to monitor what others call out.

Tessa Woodward

1.2 One chair missing

Level
Elementary–Advanced

Materials
A class set of four to five inch rectangles of stiff paper or card

Time
10–20 minutes

Focus
Review of vocabulary in collocation

In this chair swapping warm-up, there's one chair too few for everyone in the circle.

Preparation

Choose words that you would like to review with your class and write each word on a separate strip of card (one per student). The higher the level, the more room students may need on your cards. You can make the cards three to four inches for elementary students and as long as six inches for advanced classes.

Procedure

1. Hand out the word cards. Tell everyone they can look their word up in their notes or dictionaries. They also need to find a collocation and write a complete phrase on the back of their card. Give your class an example, thus: if a student has the word 'elephant' on their card, they

can add to their card either 'large', 'grey' or 'African'. Encourage students at intermediate level to be a bit more ambitious. Give them an example like 'a herd of large, grey African elephants'. At advanced level, a good example is 'the harassed elephants stampeded'.

2. Explain that, if absolutely stuck, a student can ask you for help, but not ask another student. Start them off. Circulate, check and help out.

3. When everyone has finished, form the class into a large circle, with everyone seated except for one chairless student who stands in the middle of the circle.

4. Each student in turn around the circle reads out their phrase. The person in the middle listens hard and tries to remember as many of the phrases as possible. You might want to set four or five as a reasonable goal.

5. Once everyone has had a turn, the person repeats all the phrases she or he remembers. When finished, the person in the middle shouts 'Go!'. Everyone whose collocation was called out must move to another chair. The person in the middle joins in the rush for a seat.

6. Whoever is in the centre now has to wait and listen while those seated again read their phrases out. The phrases will now, however, be in a somewhat different order as some people will be sitting in different places.

7. Steps 5 and 6 are repeated until all or most of the phrases have been remembered by the various students who've stood in the middle.

Extension

8. Working individually, students try to recall as many of the phrases as they can and write them into sentences. Or, more ambitiously, they can try to work the phrases into a text.

Variations

i) The words you write on the cards don't need to be ones which your students know. You can, for example, use this activity to pre-teach vocabulary that occurs in a text the class is about to work with. In this case, the activity will take somewhat longer because of the additional time you'll need to allow for students to get clear about the meanings of each other's words.

ii) On the cards write verbs in different tenses/aspects. Students have to add an appropriate time word/phrase or add some other bit of vocabulary often associated with the verb form at hand. For example, 'would've washed/ + 'yesterday but'.

11

Comment

The initial in-class search for collocations followed by reading aloud and then a scramble for seats gives the activity an interestingly different sequence of paces. It's like going from first gear, to second, to third, all in a rush. Then, in Step 8, the pace slows right down again.

Acknowledgement

Written up by Tessa Woodward

Pierre Jeanrenaud

1.3   Balloon chase

Level	**Materials**
Beginner–Advanced	An inflated balloon

Time
5–10 minutes

Focus
Review

This is an excellent activity for getting students to brainstorm vocabulary at speed.

Preparation

Select a vocabulary area for review. At beginner level, for example, parts of the body or colours; at advanced level, ways of walking or snippets of colloquial English such as 'just poke your head around the corner'.

Procedure

Tell students to stand in a large circle. Explain that the aim of the activity is to keep the balloon in the air for as long as possible. It must not touch the ground. But before they can bat the balloon up again, they must first call out a word from the vocabulary area selected for revision. Let them know before you start whether repetitions are allowed.

Variations

This frame offers almost limitless possibilities for practising other areas of language, for example:

- Functions: Students must call out different ways of prefacing suggestions (e.g. 'Why don't you ABC'?, 'Maybe if you ABC', 'It might be a good idea if you ABCed', 'What I'd do is ABC', 'How about ABCing?'), paying each other compliments, and so on.
- Grammar: Write about 20 verbs on the board, in their base, or infinitive form. Students have to call out the simple past of one of them before they hit the balloon. Or, each time the balloon is hit, call out a short statement. Before anyone else can hit it they have to call out a suitable checking-question tag (e.g. T: 'You're coming.' S: 'Aren't you?').
- Pronunciation: Write a phonemic symbol on the board, /iː/, for example. Before students can hit the ball, they have to call out a word containing that phoneme. Or, write up symbols of two sounds students have difficulty discriminating, perhaps, /iː/ and /ɪ/. Student A has to call out a word with /iː/ in it before hitting the balloon, Student B a word with /ɪ/ in it, Student C one with /iː/ and so on.

Rationale

The balloon falling towards the ground creates a visual time limit. This strongly motivates students to think fast in order to keep it aloft. This is also an excellent activity to use as part of a campaign to get students used to group co-operation.

Paul Sanderson

13

1.4   I say, you do

Level
Beginner–Intermediate

Materials
Sometimes realia and props of various kinds can be useful

Time
5 minutes

Focus
Learning words and structures that can be acted out

This is for people who like to get up, move around and touch things. It's not new; primary teachers have been using it for years. If you know about the method called TPR (Total Physical Response), you'll see that the activity here is the older, informal procedure that TPR is, in part, based on. If you find that students take to it, you have, in fact, paved the way for using TPR more thoroughly if you'd like to. (See Richards and Rodgers 1986: 87–98 for background and details.)

Preparation

Think of a set of vocabulary your students would find interesting or enjoyable to work with. These words and phrases must be ones that can be embedded in commands, instructions or requests that lead to actions. Here, I'll talk about giving commands since everyone loves to do it! For example, 'Touch something green!'.

Procedure

1. Give your commands. Your students carry them out.
2. Ask a student to give instructions for the whole class to carry out. Or put students into groups or pairs so that one can give commands to the other(s).
3. Tidy up any pronunciation, spelling or meaning problems that remain after this initial demonstration and practice.

Comment

I love this type of work because it's active and you can use it to teach an amazing wealth of language. For example:

- Verbs: e.g. 'touch', 'stretch', 'bend', 'lean', 'turn', 'tap', 'pick up', 'put down', 'turn', 'drop'.
- Nouns: These can be names of things in the room or on posters or of things you can see outside the room or of things you can represent by making cut-outs, etc.
- Prepositions: e.g. 'Put the X on top of the Y in the corner of the room'.
- Adjectives: of colour, size, shape, texture, material, etc. E.g. 'Touch something red/small/round/shiny/rough/flashy/wonderful!' ('Yes, it's my nose!')
- Comparatives: e.g. 'Touch something bigger than you/more expensive than it ought to be'.
- Relative clauses: e.g. 'Pick up something (that/which) you haven't picked up before', 'Say, "hello" to someone (who) you haven't spoken to today'.
- Requests: e.g. 'Could/Can/Will you ...?' 'Would you mind ... -ing ...?' Simple conditions: e.g. 'If you hand me the x, I'll hand you the ...'
- Fun: Students can describe, draw, make cut-outs, sing, chant, intone, jump onto, hide under, lie about, give compliments.

Editor's comment

I recently taught for several months a monolingual group of teenage boys of extraordinarily low motivation. This was one of a very few activities they could all cope with and learn from. ('A proverb a day' (2.8), was another.) Once I had introduced a few phrases (e.g. 'Lean left/right/forward/back), every lesson began with one of them calling out all the commands he could remember. All the others carried out his commands. I then called out commands he had forgotten and added a new one.

Tessa Woodward

1.5   Newspaper bash!

Level	**Materials**
Elementary–Advanced	One rolled up newspaper (for each circle)

Time	**Age**
A few minutes	8–88

Focus
Practising/reviewing vocabulary in
any lexical set

This is good for practice of any lexical set: animals, furniture, clothes, countries. And it's a great way of remembering names too. Actually, the language is really incidental – the game is a great energiser and/or releaser of tension.

In response to an invitation to share ideas on a course in Hungary, Gabor said, 'I put my students in a circle and then I roll up a newspaper and hit them on the head with it. Like so ... smack!' Well, we were a little dubious about the sound of this, but asked for a demonstration and discovered a wonderful game which I have used on many occasions since then. It has always produced lots of laughter – and occasionally near hysteria. So I would like to share it with you. It's very easy to play and to demonstrate, but rather difficult to describe verbally. Here goes!

Preparation

Decide on a lexical set – 'animals', for example.

Procedure

1. Have the students sit in (a) circle(s) – on chairs or on the floor. There should be at least eight and probably no more than 16 in a circle. If you have large numbers, demonstrate with one circle and then divide the class into several circles.
2. Each student must choose an animal. Round the circle everyone says what animal they are. Go round the circle a second time as it's very important for students to remember the names of the other students' animals as best they can. It's very important for YOU to do so as well! (But you do not have to have an animal name ... yet.) Stand in the middle of the circle with your rolled up newspaper at the ready.

16

You are the newspaper basher! YOU say the name of one of the animals, e.g. 'Tiger'. The person who is 'tiger' must respond quickly with the name of another animal in the circle, e.g. 'panda!', and 'panda' must respond quickly with the name of another animal, and so it goes on.

If you have time to hit someone on the head with a newspaper before they can name another animal, that person becomes the newspaper basher. You sit in the circle (and take the name of a new animal).

It sounds easy, doesn't it? But what happens in practice is that as soon as someone hears their animal name called, they panic and go completely blank! The result is a great amount of newspaper bashing and laughter. (Amazing though it seems, people seem to really enjoy being bashed on the head with a newspaper.)

Other rules:

- If someone calls out the name of an animal which has not been chosen by anyone, they replace the newspaper basher in the middle.
- The same happens if they name the animal chosen by the person in the middle (after round one).
- If the newspaper basher hits the wrong person on the head, the circle must give them a forfeit before they carry on, still in the role of basher. The forfeit might be something like 'Sing two lines of a song' or 'Mime a washing machine!'

Acknowledgement

Many thanks to Gabor Sebők of Pecs, Hungary.

Jane Revell

1.6   Staccato start

Level
Elementary–Advanced

Materials
None

Time
5 minutes

Focus
Fun

This simple activity is very unstressful – none of the participants need say anything. Nevertheless, it gets people paying attention to each other! In a funny way, you can learn a lot about your participants (and they about each other and about you) from the way they express themselves non-verbally.

Procedure

1. Ask everyone to stand in a circle.
2. Tell them that you're going to clap something and that you want them to listen to the pattern of the clapping and then repeat it *exactly*.
3. Clap a little pattern.
4. Participants listen and repeat the pattern by clapping.
5. Invite someone else in the circle, perhaps the person next to you, to clap something. Explain that everyone should listen carefully so they can repeat it afterwards. And so it goes on round the circle.

Comment

There is a surprising need to pay close attention as people's clapping patterns can be very different.

Acknowledgement

I learnt this from Ferdinand Stefan.

Tessa Woodward

18

1.7 Singing start

Level
Elementary–Advanced

Materials
None

Time
5 minutes

Focus
Warming up people's voices

This activity works with any song simple enough to be sung as an easy round. The song mentioned below is especially cheerful and easy to learn. Although I sing myself, I never used to have the nerve to do singing warm-ups. But then a guest speaker on a course of mine led us all through one. On another course, a group participant led us through a different song. The results were wonderful.

There is usually a singer or two in a group so, if you're a bit shy, let them do the organising. Give them a bit of time to prepare, of course. If it goes well – and it will because it's so simple and pleasant – group members may well bring in other short rounds to warm the group up with.

Procedure

1. Elicit or give the words for 'Good Morning' in several languages (or for 'Good Evening', if you teach an evening class). Write four of them on the board, for example,

   Bon Giorno   Good Morning   Bona Sera   Guten Morgen

2. Ask the class to say these, twice each, to a steady rhythm, like this,

Bon Giorno	o Oo, o Oo
Good Morning	o Oo, o Oo
Bona Sera	ooOo, ooOo
Guten Morgen	ooOo, ooOo

3. Sing this to them once or twice.

19

4. All sing the same words together.
5. Divide the class into two, three or four groups. Each group starts the song a little after each other to achieve a nice, chiming morning/evening song.

Tessa Woodward

1.8   Computer talk

Level
Intermediate–Advanced

Materials
Several index cards

Time
10–30 minutes

Requirements
At least 8 students

Focus
Accuracy in speaking

This activity encourages students not only to think about word choice and syntax, but also gets them listening carefully to what others say.

Preparation

Write a single word on each of a number of index cards. Each word should encapsulate a theme. You will be asking your students to make sentences beginning with these words so begin each with a capital letter (e.g. Life ... Bosses/Teachers ... Taxes ... Men ... Women ... Parents ...).

Procedure

1. If you think your students need to, review the names for the most common punctuation marks.
2. Divide the class into groups of four to five students. Ask each group to stand in a separate semi-circle facing towards you. Tell them that each group is a computer and that each person is a component.
3. Explain that you will insert one of your theme cards into one of the computers. Add that the component which receives the card must call out the word written on the card. Then each of the other components must add a word, one by one. That is, the computer builds a sentence

by following on from the theme word one word at a time. Add that individual components can take more than one turn at adding a word if they want to make a sentence more than four or five words long. Add also that components should call out punctuation as they go along, for example:

'Life / is / very / enjoyable / if / you / have / good / luck / FULL STOP.'

4. Demonstrate the task with one computer. Then repeat with each of the other computers.
   If an error creeps into a computer's sentence, say 'Syntax error!' or 'System error!'. Or display a large card bearing the error message. The computer then has to decide where the error was and begin again from that word. Don't add any distracting explanations at this point.
5. The computers take turns asking other computers on the network 'big' questions like 'What is the meaning of life?' or 'Who will be the next prime minister?' When it receives a question, a computer must answer. All this conversation must happen with components taking turns saying words.
6. Have all the computers link up into one supercomputer. Tell them to build a sentence (or two or three) about the experience of being computer components making words. Again, each component should contribute at least one word.

Variations

i) Proceed as above but have each person repeat all the previous words (and punctuation marks) before making their contribution.
ii) Proceed as in Steps 1–6. In addition, on the board or OHP display a list of subordinate conjunctions (e.g. 'unless', 'because', 'although'), a few 'trigger words' (e.g. 'facilitate', 'cardboard' or whatever), six to twelve numbered words (e.g. 1 'maximise', 2 'premises' or whatever). Require that a group incorporate one word from each of these three lists into its sentence. Their choice from the list of numbered words is determined by a throw of the dice.

Acknowledgement

This exercise is adapted from 'Energizers: group starters' in Pfeiffer and Jones (1975, vol. 5, pp. 3–4).

Denny Packard

21

1.9 Bizarre riot

Level
Intermediate–Advanced

Materials
None

Time
5–10 minutes

Focus
Speaking; listening; fun

At the end of a workshop a few years ago a participant taught me a riotously funny little activity that's perfect for the end of term or some other moment that calls for something zany.

Procedure

1. Choose a victim. While they are steeling themselves for the dreadful ordeal which is to follow, choose three other people. One person has to prepare questions of a 'left brain' kind, ones that are analytical, logical, information-based. For example, 'How much is 2 and 17 added together?' 'What was the date of the Battle of Waterloo?' The second person has to prepare 'right brain' questions, ones that have to do with feelings, intuitions, colours, images. For example, 'How are you feeling?' 'Was John F. Kennedy like a lion or a rabbit or what?' The third person has to think of some elaborate mimes and facial expressions to do!
2. Arrange the three people around the victim so that the questioners are standing to the victim's left and right and the person miming is facing the victim.
3. The two questioners and the person miming all start questioning/ miming at once. The victim must try to answer all the questions and copy the expressions and movements of the person who is miming. All this should happen simultaneously.
4. If you have time, invite someone else to be the victim. Or, if you think all your students would enjoy it, divide people into groups of four and let everyone have a turn.

Comment

Obviously, the victim has to be fairly robust and have a good sense of humour. Try it out with some friends, maybe after a few glasses of wine, before you try it in class, with yourself as the victim first. My bet is that you'll all be in stitches in a few minutes!

Tessa Woodward

2   Warm-ups, breaks and fillers 2: Speaking

This chapter contains nine activities that make good beginnings to a lesson by allowing students to shift their thinking back into the target language more or less gradually. They provide a buffer time, before your main work begins, during which the class can absorb latecomers without getting distracted from anything vital. These activities are quieter than the ones in Chapter 1 and entail no running around.

- The first activity, 'By the way' (2.1) involves the class focusing on participants one by one. It both reminds people of each other's names and offers them glimpses into what each other notices while going about their daily life.
- 'How do you say ...?' (2.2), 'Make them say it' (2.3), 'Think of ten, five or three things' (2.6), and 'Links with music' (2.7) are designed to set up a mild buzz of talk around the room.
- 'Whatever's in my bag' (2.4) and 'A proverb a day' (2.8) involve you eliciting and presenting new language in very short bursts and also reviewing what came up the previous times you did these activities.
- 'You guess their adjectives' (2.5) is a good activity for gauging the mood of your class. You speak, your students mostly just think, listen and react.
- 'Making stress physical' (2.9) is great for enabling your students to get a feeling for the rhythms of English words and phrases. Depending on the variation you choose, it can also get students up and moving around. Like other activities in this chapter (especially 2.4 and 2.8) it is designed to be used again and again with the same class.

All the activities in this chapter are also useful when you want a change of pace between long, relatively intense study activities or when you think your students would like to wind down after a bout of intensive work – after a test perhaps.

2.1 By the way

Level	**Materials**
Elementary – Advanced	An object

Time
2–5 minutes

Focus
Warming -up

This activity helps students who are somewhat acquainted with each other to get better acquainted.

Procedure

1. Write the following on the board:
   (Name), here's a _____. By the way ...
2. Hold up your object. Tell the class that they are going to pass it from one person to another. Make sure everyone understands the route it will take around the room. (If there are more than 12 or so participants, form groups of from six to nine students.)
3. Explain that when person A hands the object on to person B, A has to follow the formula on the board. That is, A must use B's name, and then add, 'Here's a _____. By the way ...' and then follow on either with a remark that is more than just a description of the object. That is, when passing an apple a student can say:

   'By the way, I didn't have time for breakfast this morning.'
   [no connection with the object at all]

Or,

   'By the way, I eat lots of apples.'
   [about the object but about something else as well]

But they aren't allowed to say something like:

   'This is a big apple'.
   [only about the apple]

Add that if person A says something to person B that requires a response, then B must reply before turning to C. For example:

   Student A: 'Samira, here's an apple. By the way, how are you today?'
   Student B: 'Fine thank you. And thanks for the apple too.'

25

4. Start things off yourself by saying, for example, 'Tim, here's a stapler. By the way, I stayed up too late last night.'

In a spirited advanced class you can go much further, for example: 'Anna-Maria, here's a wad of paper ... because I forgot to bring along anything more interesting for this activity. By the way, on the way to school this morning I saw a sparrow mugging a large butterfly in the middle of the road. As my car bore down on the scene of the crime, the sparrow flew left and the butterfly tore off desperately to the right.'

Variations

If you vary the activity, you can use it several times with the same class.

– Use other 'topic shifters':
  'Incidentally ... '
  'This is a bit off the subject but ... '
– Review different phrase structures. For example, instead of asking students to say just 'Here's an apple', ask them to say,
  'a slightly bruised apple'
  'an apple with a big bruise'
  'an apple without a stem'
  'an apple that's been dropped on the floor'

Seth Lindstromberg

2.2   How do you say ... ?

Level
Elementary–Intermediate

Materials
None

Time
5 minutes

Requirement
A multilingual class

Focus
Asking for a translation

This is a simple but enjoyable activity for a group that has already begun to gel. It focuses on useful phrases that even advanced students often fail to get quite right. Since these phrases are ways of asking for translations, but doing so in English, they allow students to learn and practise ways of soliciting translations from other students or from you while maintaining English as the main vehicle of communication.

Procedure

1. Write one or more of the following question frames on the board:
   'How do you say X in English/German/Korean ...?' (for any item of language)
   'What do you call X in ...?' (for nouns and gerunds, keep your ears peeled for the non-standard 'How do you call ...?')
   'What's X in ...?' (for any word or phrase)
   'What's this/that in ...?' (for things you can point to – including written words – or actions you can demonstrate or mime)
2. Put students in groups of two to five.
3. Ask them to use the phrase(s) on the board to learn at least two words or phrases in each different language.

Comment

In one recent lower-intermediate class, one group of students got engrossed in ways of saying 'Hello'. There was even a bit of orchestrated drilling. My two weaker students finally got to show their colleagues they could pronounce something perfectly! In recent advanced and intermediate classes it was a near thing whether I could stop the activity at all.

Seth Lindstromberg

2.3 Make them say it

Level
Elementary–Advanced

Time
3–5 minutes. Add 5 minutes or so for the extension

Focus
Conversation; thinking about what gambits elicit what responses

Materials
A class set of slips of paper or card plus a few extra

Preparation

On each slip of paper write a single word or phrase such as:

Yesterday	No, I hate it!	Wednesday

Procedure

1. Put participants into pairs, A and B. Give a slip of paper to everyone, asking them to keep it secret and hidden from their partner.
2. A starts by asking B questions. The questions should be carefully designed to force B to say the word/phrase on A's slip. (Remember, B does not know what this word/phrase is.) Thus, if 'In December' is written on A's slip, then 'When's Christmas?' would be a good question for A to put to B because B might well respond, 'In December'.
3. Once B has come out with the *exact* words on A's slip, then A and B switch roles.

Extension

4. As pairs finish, keep swapping their slips with new ones so they have more to work on.

Variations

i) At elementary level, I call the activity 'Question practice' and give students words/phrases like these on their slips:

'No, I can't.'   'Switzerland.'   'In the evening.'
'Tomorrow.'   'Sometimes.'   'Maybe.'

This means that relatively straightforward questions get practised (e.g. 'Can you speak Russian?', 'Where do you come from?', 'When do you study?', 'When is our next class?', 'Do you do homework?', 'Are you going to go on the next excursion?')

ii) At higher levels, you can script what's on the slips to encourage practice of particular tenses, functional expressions and so on. Keep a few really difficult ones up your sleeve for the people who get absolutely terrific at the activity. Here are some samples:

'When I was a child.'   'I wish I could.'
'It depends.'   'I don't think so.'
'If I have time.'   'No, I wouldn't.'
'Yes, I would have.'   'I'm sorry, I'd rather not answer that!'

These take skill and persistence to elicit. Incidentally, it's amazing what personal questions people will actually answer before they finally say, 'I'm sorry, I'd rather not answer that'!

Notes

i) I find it helps not only to demonstrate this activity first for the class, but also to draw a little picture on the board like the one here below, in order to make it clear who should ask the questions.

ii) I also find it helps to discuss 'near misses' so that people know that their questions have to be finely tuned. An example of a near miss is 'Are you married?' – if you're trying to get your partner to say 'Single' – since typical answers to this question would be 'Yes' or 'No'. Better questions would be, 'What do you call a person who's not married?' Of course, you could get the answer 'Happy' or 'Carefree' – there is a joker in every class, thank goodness!

Acknowledgement

This activity has been around for years but deserves to be better known.

Tessa Woodward

29

2.4 Whatever's in my bag

Level
Elementary–Advanced

Materials
A handbag or briefcase

Time
5–20 minutes

Focus
Vocabulary review and extension

This activity takes off from whatever everyday object you happen to pull out of your handbag or briefcase, e.g. a box of matches, a photo, a purse, a handkerchief, a pen-knife. Whenever you have an unexpected lull in a lesson or time before the bell, you can open your bag, pull out an object and get up to 20 minutes of useful, natural vocabulary out of it without having planned it.

If, over the course of a few lessons you run out of objects, either use the bag itself or ask permission to use the contents of someone else's!

The basic idea is to use the object to review and extend vocabulary. Let's take a box of matches as an example stimulus. Here, category by category, are the kinds of lexical items you can elicit or introduce:

The object and its parts, visible features, contents
'box', 'cover', 'picture', 'slogan', 'abrasive/striking strip', 'logo', 'price', 'match-head', 'matchstick' . . .

Materials
'paper', 'card', 'wood', 'phosphorus', 'glue', 'grit', 'ink' . . .

Colours
Of the object: 'yellowish', 'beige' . . .
Of fire: 'orange', 'yellow', 'blue' . . .

Other adjectives
'small', 'light', 'rough', 'hollow', 'thin', 'cylindrical', 'box-shaped' . . .

Verbs and verb phrases
'take a match out of the box', 'hold it firmly', 'strike it (away from you!)', 'break it', 'try again', 'catch fire', 'light something', 'burn your fingers', 'blow out', 'feel the tip', 'put in the bin', 'smell smoke' . . .

Uses
The matchstick: 'to pick your teeth', 'to light the gas', 'to set fire to something', 'to clear out belt holes', 'to prop open cat doors' . . .
The box: 'to keep shells/buttons/stamps/insects in'

Crescendo
'spark', 'flare', 'flame', 'pop', 'blaze' . . .

Diminuendo
'to die down', 'fizzle', 'glow', 'go out'; 'ember' . . .

Compounds, clichés
'matchbox toys', 'a house the size of a matchbox', 'the little match girl', 'selling matches', 'legs like matchsticks' . . .

Other categories might be 'manufacturing process', 'associated people' (cooks, smokers, naughty children, arsonists . . .), 'country of origin' (especially Finland, Sweden, Canada . . .), 'objects with a similar purpose' (chest of drawers, cargo container . . .), 'objects with the same purpose' (butane cigarette lighters, car dashboard cigarette lighters . . .).

Procedure the first time you present an object

How to choose to elicit, teach, practise, review and organise the recording of the vocabulary will depend on your group and on your teaching style. Naturally, it's a good idea to involve your students as much as possible. One way of doing this is to suggest the categories and see how much vocabulary students can put in them on their own. It's almost certainly a good idea not to introduce much more than five to ten or so new words or expressions per lesson.

In following lessons

You have two basic options: (1) review and extend vocabulary associated with an object you presented in an earlier lesson and (2) introduce a new object. These options can be combined in fruitful ways. For example, you begin a lesson by reviewing vocabulary connected with an 'old' object and then go on to a new object.

Tessa Woodward

31

2.5 You guess their adjectives

Level
Elementary–Advanced

Materials
None

Time
One–two minutes

Focus
Listening; self-expression; review of
adjectives for describing feelings

Besides being brisk and interesting, this activity can give you the chance to find out how your students are feeling. If you find that everyone's tired, you might decide to do an activity from Chapter 1 before launching into your lesson plan. If everyone's hungry, you might want to scrap that lesson on ordering food in a restaurant and reach for your reserve material.

Procedure

1. Ask students to think of an adjective that describes the way they are feeling at the moment. They should not say this adjective out loud.
2. When everyone has an adjective in mind, ask the class to stand up.
3. Explain the rules: You will call out some adjectives. If someone hears you say the adjective that they have applied to themselves, they should sit down.
4. Start calling out adjectives, e.g. 'happy', 'tired', 'sad', 'energetic', 'hungry', 'thirsty', 'full', 'sleepy', etc. Allow enough time in between adjectives for people to think and, if appropriate, sit down.
5. If you keep going until everyone has heard their adjective and sat down, you've done unusually well. Normally there are still a few students left standing when you feel you've run out of adjectives.
6. Ask those left standing what their adjectives are. Then they too can sit down.

Extension

7. In a small class, ask everyone what their adjective was. Ask if anyone wants to know what one of the adjectives means.

Comment

This activity has always worked like a dream for me. The only time I ever failed to guess almost everyone's adjective was when I forgot to say 'tired'. Seven out of twelve would've sat down if I hadn't. (SL)

Acknowledgement

I learnt this from Marion Williams.

Tessa Woodward

2.6 Think of ten, five or three things

Level
Elementary–Advanced

Materials
None

Time
5–20 minutes

Focus
Conversation

This mind-opening, potentially amusing activity can begin or end a lesson. In the middle of a long lesson too (remember, some people teach for two hours at a time), you can use it to mark off the boundaries between units of study that aren't connected or just to provide a change of pace. This is an activity that encourages people to express both ordinary and strange ideas, all of which helps the participants to notice more about each other's personalities.

Procedure

1. Ask everyone to think for a moment of ten things they could do when they were one year old and to note these things down on paper. Go around and help with vocabulary.
2. In pairs, they read their ideas to each other. Ask them to make a note of especially funny or unusual ones.
3. When the pairwork is just about finished, ask people to call out any

especially unusual or funny things that people could do at the age of one. Write these on the board if you think some in the group don't understand them, but don't explain them yet.

4. After everyone has finished reporting, elicit explanations or demonstrations of what's on the board.

Variations

- If you don't have much time, ask people to think of just five or only three things.
- You can apply this activity to lots of topics, for example:

Ten things you like about a chair.
Ten things you wish you hadn't said or done.
Ten things you'd like to see in your lifetime.
Ten things that are extremely hot/cold/flat ...
Ten things that can throw a shadow.
Ten things a cat likes to eat.
etc. etc.

Tessa Woodward

2.7 Links with music

Level
Intermediate

Time
15–30 minutes; allow 5–10 minutes extra for the extension activity

Focus
Breaking the ice; diagnosing level; conversation

Materials
Optional: A sheet of poster paper or OHP transparencies

This activity is excellent for helping participants to learn about each other quickly. It will enable you to find out a lot about your students' attitudes and interests as well as about their language level. You can do it with a new class or one that you have had for a while.

Preparation

Think of links between music and yourself. These may be of various kinds. Think of:

- your favourite composer, instrument, song, singer, piece of music
- dates or occasions when you discovered a piece of music or a musician
- music you associate with important events in your life
- music/instruments played by your family or by friends

Choose five or six of these links and, on poster paper or OHP transparency write a display like the one below. Or make sure you can write the display on the board really quickly. In any case, use of different colours and various kinds of lettering seems to produce the best results. Have your class in mind when you make your choices. Ideally, some should be similar to those which people in your class might make. (If you don't know the class yet, guess on the basis of age, background, and so on.)

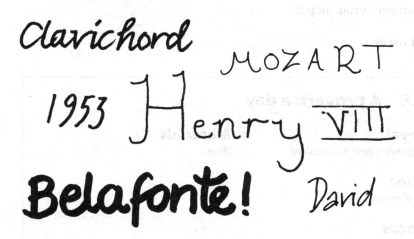

Clavichord

MOZART

1953 Henry VIII

Belafonte!   David

Procedure

1. Greet your class and suggest they ought to get acquainted with each other before starting to work or do more work. Tell them that you would like them to do this through sharing memories and feelings about music.

2. Display your transparency or poster, or quickly write it all on the board. Tell your class that these are clues about links between you and music. Invite them to try and guess what these links are by asking you 'yes'/'no' questions.
3. Begin. Qualify and elaborate your answers, e.g. 'Well, yes, but it's not really an instrument I play.' 'Well, yes, Belafonte fascinated me when I was sixteen, as he fascinated all my schoolmates. We went for … we really liked calypso and loved his red shirts without a tie.'
   This sets an example for your students' work later on.
4. When your clues have all been explained, ask your students each to prepare, on a sheet of paper, an arrangement of clues similar to yours.
5. They do the activity in pairs or small groups. The latter takes longer but spreads information around more.

Extension

6. Ask each pair or group to join up with another pair or group. Everyone says what they learned about their partner/another group member during Step 5.

Clem Laroy

2.8   A proverb a day

Level	**Materials**
Beginner–Lower-intermediate	None

Time
1–10 minutes a day

Focus
Vocabulary: pattern memorisation; pronunciation; learning proverbs as an end in itself

'A proverb a day' offers ideas for teaching proverbs one or two at a time (never in batches!) over the full length of whatever kind of course you happen to be teaching. You can use the main idea or one of the review ideas in tens or scores of different lessons. New proverbs are introduced (by you or by students) as you go along. You spend, at most, a few minutes per lesson.

Low-level students in particular like learning proverbs. For beginners, learning a proverb has extra value since learning a proverb is learning a complete text. I still recall the satisfaction of learning my first Russian proverb some 25 years ago. I also recall the proverb (*Luche pozdna chem nikagda*) and what it means ('Better late than never'). If you knew how little else I remembered from that course, that might all by itself be enough to persuade you of the value of teaching proverbs. In any case, the importance of students learning masses of prefabricated chunks of language (as opposed to rules for creating their own chunks from scratch) is once again academically respectable (see e.g. Nattinger and de Carrico 1992).

One sometimes hears it said that proverbs aren't all that commonly used anymore. That is probably true for some proverbs (e.g. 'Haste makes waste') but not for others (e.g. 'You win some, you lose some'). And even older proverbs may crop up in new guises as in these titles of newspaper articles: 'Look before you leap across the Channel' (i.e. think before you buy a house in France, *The Daily Telegraph*, 20.5.94, p. 3) and 'Silver lining for sacked binmen' (i.e. all is not bad for dismissed rubbish collectors, *The Daily Telegraph*, 9.6.94, p. 4).

Procedure

1. Make sure your students know what the word *proverb* means. If your students are beginners and you understand their language, ask what proverbs they know in their mother tongue. If they are not beginners, ask what English language proverbs they know. I say 'English language' because students sometimes offer English versions of mother tongue proverbs. Also, different English-speaking countries don't have exactly the same proverbs.
2. Choose or elicit the first 'proverb of the day'. These are your basic options:

   – Translate a student proverb into English. This sometimes yields a good result.
   – Present an English-language proverb of similar import to a mother tongue proverb suggested by a student.
   – Use an English language proverb suggested by a student.
   – Choose a proverb from the lists below – one that your class can grasp without too much explaining.
3. Make sure your students understand the proverb!

   – If necessary in low-level classes, give or elicit a literal translation. (Allow checking in bilingual dictionaries; sometimes they include proverbs and give L1 equivalents.)

- Sometimes filling in 'missing' words can help students to understand, e.g.:
  [If you sew] a stitch in time, [that often] saves [you from having to sew] nine [stitches later]!
- If possible, clarify by paraphrasing, e.g.:
  Haste   makes   waste.
  Being in a hurry   causes   wasted work and useless products!
- Suggest or elicit a situation in which someone might say the proverb.
4. Help students say it well. Pay special attention to rhythm.

   - To get the right rhythm students will need to make natural catenations. For example, words that appear to begin with a vowel may actually begin with the final consonant of the word before, e.g.: 'A stitchin time ...'
   - They will also need to weaken all naturally weakened sounds. For example, have them say /tǝbed/ not /tuːbed/ in 'Early to bed, early to rise ...'
   - They should, as well, elide (drop) sounds in a natural way, e.g.: '... wealthy an' wise ...'
   After giving initial guidance on pronunciation, encourage your students to silently chant or whisper the proverb for a half a minute or so.
5. Ask your students to copy the proverb into a special proverb section of their notebooks.
6. Move on to some other activity. Perhaps, once or twice later in the lesson ask, 'What was today's proverb?

Ways to continue in other lessons

On different days, review in different ways, for example:

- At the beginning (or in the middle or at the end) of each lesson ask a few questions like: 'What was yesterday's proverb?', 'What was the proverb before last?', 'What was our first proverb?', 'Koichi, of all our proverbs, which is your favourite?'.
- Orally quiz students (or they quiz each other) by calling out the first (or last) one or two words of different proverbs.
- Give the class (or ask students to call out) prompts such as these: 'Tell me a proverb with X words in it', 'Tell me a proverb with the word "a" in it'. (Rationale: This tends to get students mentally reviewing a number of proverbs before they finally speak.)
- Ask the class if, as a group, they can tell you all the proverbs learned so far within a set period of time (e.g. two minutes). One student

looks at the full list and ticks proverbs off as they are read. When the time limit is up, the student with the list reads the ones that weren't mentioned.
- Ask everyone to write a stipulated number (two to eight) of the proverbs introduced so far. Circulate and check as they write. Ask early finishers: 'Can you think of one more?' When most have finished, call time.
- Ask individuals to read out proverbs from their lists. When listeners hear a proverb on their list, they cross it off. Keep going until all proverbs have been read once.
  Or, ask everyone to look at the lists of a couple of other students.
- Ask someone to write a proverb on the board. Other students come up and add on other proverbs in the fashion of a crossword puzzle. A half a dozen proverbs per time is enough. It's not necessary to review all the proverbs you've done each day!
- After your students have learned ten or so proverbs, you may want to introduce a new proverb, not in every lesson but in every other lesson.
- Where proverbs are concerned, I like to avoid any activity which takes up more than five minutes, though from time to time I make exceptions if the activity includes speaking practice. Basically, except for occasional checking that students do know how to write their proverbs, the aim of the activity is oral fluency and good pronunciation. Consequently, I avoid long fill-in-the-blank, matching, find-the-mistake and other potentially time-consuming written exercises.
- For homework, after every twenty or so proverbs, ask students to group them in some way, for example:
  - proverbs that have similar or opposed imports
  - ones that have counterparts in their own language and ones that don't
  - ones they like and ones they don't

Rhyming proverbs

Haste makes	waste.
Love many, trust few;	always paddle your own canoe.
If you snooze,	you lose.
A stitch in time	saves nine.
Two in distress	makes trouble less.
Birds of a feather	flock together.
Finders keepers,	losers weepers.
A friend in need	is a friend indeed.
Early to bed, early to rise,	makes a man healthy, wealthy and wise.

Trouble	comes double.
A friend in words and not in deeds	is like a garden full of weeds.
Red sky at night, sailor's delight;	red sky in the morning to sailors a warning.
When money talks,	nobody walks.
When the cat's away,	the mice will play.
No pain,	no gain.

Alliterative proverbs

Live	and learn.
Where there's a will,	there's a way.
All that glistens	is not gold.
All roads	lead to Rome.
Look before	you leap.
A bird in the hand	is worth two in the bush.
Penny wise,	pound foolish.
Poor planning makes for	poor performance.
In for a penny,	in for a pound.
The more	the merrier.
Waste not,	want not.
What gets measured	is what gets managed.

Repetitive proverbs

First come,	first served.
You win some,	you lose some.
There's no fool	like an old fool.
A penny saved	is a penny earned.
All's well	that ends well.
What's done	is done.
The past	is past.
Don't get mad,	get even.
If it's worth doing,	it's worth doing well.
Like father,	like son.
Nothing ventured	nothing gained.
Winners never quit,	quitters never win.
Plan your work,	work your plan.

Other proverbs

There's an exception to every rule.
A leopard never changes its spots.
You can't teach an old dog new tricks.
Neither a borrower nor a lender be.

Rome wasn't built in a day.
Experience is the best teacher.
Don't count your chickens before they're hatched.
Charity begins at home.
All work and no play makes Jack a dull boy.
A new broom sweeps clean.
Clothes make the man.
Don't judge a book by its cover.
Where there's smoke there's fire.
There's more than one way to skin a cat.
A man's home is his castle.
It's the early bird that catches the worm.
If the shoe fits, wear it.
Too many cooks spoil the broth.
Two heads are better than one.
Many hands make light work.
Silence is golden.
Children should be seen and not heard.
People in glass houses shouldn't throw stones.
A rolling stone gathers no moss.
Every cloud has a silver lining.
Into every life a little rain must fall.
It's an ill wind that blows nobody good.
Don't put all your eggs in one basket.
Bad luck comes in threes.
Lightning never strikes twice in the same place.
Once bitten, twice shy.
You can't get blood from a stone.
You can't make a silk purse from a sow's ear.
It's a poor workman who blames his tools.
Money isn't everything.
You can't take it with you.
When poverty comes in the door, love flies out of the window.
Time flies when you're having a good time.
You can lead a horse to water, but you can't make it drink.
A watched pot never boils.
A change is as good as a rest.
One good turn deserves another.
Let sleeping dogs lie.
There's no place like home.
The grass is always greener on the other side of the fence.
You are what you eat.
The fruit doesn't fall far from the tree.
Honesty is the best policy.

What goes up, must come down.
The bigger they are, the harder they fall.
Never say die.
Pride comes before a fall.

Note

The definitive sourcebook on proverbs in over 60 European languages is the *Dictionary of European Proverbs* compiled by Emanuel Strauss (3 vols, 1994 Routledge).

Seth Lindstromberg

2.9 Making stress physical

Level
Any

Materials
Squares of card (for one variation)

Time
1–5 minutes, depending on the technique

Requirement
For the main procedure, you need space for everyone to stand up and walk around a bit

Focus
Pronunciation (word or phrase stress)

There are some words in English whose rhythm is hard for learners to get right. 'Vegetable' and 'comfortable' are examples. They look as if they have four syllables, but they don't. To help students to learn both how many syllables there are and how they are stressed, I often use the following techniques. They're not only fun, but bring more senses to bear on the matter of learning how to speak with natural rhythm.

Procedure

1. Ask everyone to stand up and move to a place from which they can take a few steps in one direction.
2. Explain that you are going to call out words one at a time. Each time, they 'step out the stressing' as follows. For each syllable they take a step. For a long syllable they take a long step, for each short syllable a short step. If, for example, you call out 'Comfortable!', they will

mill around the room mumbling 'COMF ta ble' and moving their feet according to your direction.

3. Before calling out a new word, ask them to suggest other words that have the same step pattern (e.g. 'furniture', 'physical', 'excellent', and so on). Tell them which suggestions fit the pattern and then ask them to do some more stepping out while mumbling a different one of these words each time.

Variations

– Students step out short phrases that have come up in a text that you have recently worked with, e.g.:
Beginner: 'PLEASED to MEET you' [O o O o]
Intermediate: 'I wouldn't've done it like THAT' [O o o o o o o O]
Note: 'wouldn't've,' is pronounced 'woodn tuv' (/wʊdəntəv/).
Advanced: 'World War THREE' [o o O]
– A student comes to the front of the class and steps out one word or phrase from a list without saying what the word or phrase is.
The others try to guess.
– Instead of standing up, students place the tips of their index and ring fingers (of the same hand!) on the top of their desk or some other surface and do the stepping out in miniature with these two fingers.
– Instead of mirroring stress in movement, mirror it with 'bubbles' as in the first variation above. Before class, prepare a list of words or short phrases your class has found troublesome, one word for each student. Write each word on a square of card. On a different card indicate the stress pattern in bubbles, e.g. on one card write 'vegetable' and on another card write 'O o o'. Mark the bubble card with the word 'top' at the top edge so that students will know which way to hold it.

In class, give everyone a word and a bubble card that don't match. Tell them that without looking at each other's cards they must each collect the right bubble card for their word card. Before you set them off, teach a few phrases like, 'Say your word again', 'That matches my bubble card', 'It doesn't match', 'See you'. If someone thinks they have found the right bubble card, they check with you before collecting it and then sitting down.

– Play 'Clap and guess'. Start by clapping out a word – one clap per syllable, a strong clap for a stressed syllable, a weak clap for an unstressed syllable. (Clap at the speed of natural speech.) Students guess what word/phrase you could be clapping (perhaps from a list you've written on the board). Once students have got the hang of this, a student can clap out a word or phrase and the others guess. Then, students do this in pairs (though now, to keep the noise level down so everyone can hear, students clap with just two fingers on the palm of the other hand, rather than with two open palms).

Rationale

Some people need non-linguistic analogies in order to grasp what rhythm is all about.

Tessa Woodward

3 Reviewing

The following nine activities each offer a way of structuring and encouraging review of past work. Some of the activities include a pronounced focus on a particular skill. To give just two examples, 'Do you know this word?' (3.2) involves the reading of short authentic texts while 'True-false student-student dictation' (3.6) includes intensive listening. All but one of the activities involve a certain amount of pair and group discussion – mostly the kind that people engage in when working on similar tasks.

The activities are grouped as follows:

Vocabulary

'Vocabulary brainshower' (3.1), 'Do you know this word?' (3.2), 'Recycling' (3.3), 'Student-produced vocabulary reviews' (3.4), 'Vocabulary on slips' (3.5)

Grammatical structures

'True-false student-student dictation' (3.6), 'Guess who grammar quiz' (3.9)

Global review

'Student-produced reference booklets' (3.7), 'Hidden shape in the puzzle' (3.8)

If you already regularly devote plenty of class time to review, you're bound to find several activities here you can add to your repertoire. If review is something you sometimes forget about, this chapter should help you mend your ways!

3.1 Vocabulary brainshower

Level
Elementary–Advanced

Materials
None

Time
10–15 minutes

Focus
Vocabulary review

I've called this activity a brain*shower* because it's more restricted than a brain*storm*. A normal vocabulary brainstorm – at least one without teacher input – tends to fill the board with words the students already know. This brainstorm begins normally enough, with students recalling well-known words (for confidence building), but it ends with more of the words on the board being ones students actually want to know. In one class, on the topic of jobs, some of the words students wanted to know were 'fisherman', 'stockbroker' and 'pimp'!

Procedure

1. Introduce the theme of the lesson, jobs, for example.
2. Ask the students to take a piece of paper each and rule into three columns. The first is headed 'words I know', the second 'words I'm not very sure about' and the third 'words I would like to know'.
3. The students write 3–5 words in each of the columns. For the last column they can write a definition in English, the word in their own language or draw it.
4. In groups of two or three they compare their lists, try to check the middle column and complete the third column, using dictionaries if necessary.
5. Fill the board with words from columns two and three.

Sheila Levy

3.2 Do you know this word?

Level
Beginner–Upper-elementary

Materials
A class set of highlighter pens and a one page advertisement

Time
30–40 minutes

Focus
Vocabulary revision; reading; spelling; confidence building

This activity encourages low-level students to begin to read foreign language magazines and newspapers and equips them with a starting strategy for getting something out of texts that are way above their level.

Preparation

Find an advertisement that includes: (1) a picture and (2) different kinds and sizes of print.

Procedure

1. Give out the copies of the advertisement and ask students to use their highlighter pens to mark every word they know. (If you don't have highlighter pens, you can ask students to use a pen or pencil to underline the words they know.)
2. Students form pairs and compare what they've marked. If they discover other words they know, they can mark them now.
3. Read out the first word and ask students if they have marked it. Proceed in this way with every word. (Sometimes after you read a word, students will mark it because they knew the word by sound but not by spelling.)
4. Ask basic comprehension questions about the text and/or ask students to tell you, in their own language, some of the ideas expressed in the text.

Rationale

The highlighting of words in bright colours encourages students to notice how many of the words in a text they already know. (If they proceed word by word, this is bound to be quite a lot.) One group of

We wouldn't expect you to expect less. Lufthansa

mind   umysł
figure   liczby, dane
[big] aircraft   [duży] samolot
expect   oczekiwać
less   mniej
demands   rządanie
becoming   staje się
improve   polepszyć
commitment   zobowiązanie
staff   załoga
survey   badanie opinii
would choose   wybraliby
backed   popierać
annual   roczny
maintaining   godne utrzymanie

Your expectations and demands are becoming higher all the time. That's why we at Lufthansa have a single-minded and uncompromising philosophy: to continuously improve our service to you. It's a commitment that's shared by all Lufthansa staff, who are constantly 'at your service' all over the world. A recent IATA survey on the North Atlantic route revealed that 92% of all our Business Class passengers would choose Lufthansa again next time. In Economy Class, the figure was as high as 94%. It's also good to know that this standard of service is backed by an annual investment of over DM 1 billion in servicing and maintaining our aircraft. And that over 11,500 highly qualified technicians feel responsible only to you. On the ground or in the air, we wouldn't expect you to expect less.
Have a good trip.

Lufthansa

children I did the activity with were overjoyed. 'We know so much English?' they asked. They could hardly believe it.

Hanna Kryszewska

3.3 Recycling

Level	**Materials**
Elementary–Advanced	Scissors; glue; sheets of stiff paper (one of each per group of 4–6 students); posters and notices remaining on the wall from previous courses

Time

30–40 minutes

Focus

Speaking; vocabulary learning/review

The idea for this activity came to me when, one day, I realised how many things I had on the classroom walls that had apparently outlived their usefulness. It's a particularly nice activity for the very beginning of a course or new school year. It generates lots of interaction and gives students glimpses of the kinds of things you cover in your courses. Also, from the moment students 'recycle' the material on the walls, the classroom becomes truly theirs.

Preparation

Place a table in the centre or at the front of the classroom.

Procedure

1. Introduce the activity by asking the students what they know about 'recycling'.
2. Instruct them to remove everything they find attached to the walls (bulletin boards, etc.), to cut out all the pictures and texts and then to place them on the table you've reserved for this purpose. (If you want to save something from recycling, you'd better take it down before class!)
3. Ask the students to form groups of four to six. Give each group a sheet of stiff paper and glue. Ask them to produce a new poster by

49

choosing cut-outs from the table and gluing them onto their sheet of stiff paper. Encourage the use of dictionaries.

While the students are working, write a list of abstract nouns on the board, e.g. 'bliss', 'fun', 'friendship', 'wisdom', 'awe', 'health', 'peace', 'love', etc.

4. As groups finish their posters, ask them each to choose two of the words on the board that are related to their poster and write them onto it somewhere.

5. Groups present their posters to the class, explaining the reasoning behind their choice of abstract nouns and dealing with any other key vocabulary.

6. Students place the posters on the walls.

Variation

Assign each group a different word category. For example, each group can concentrate on a particular part of speech or topic.

Adriana Diaz

3.4   Student-produced vocabulary reviews

Level
Intermediate–Advanced (especially exam preparation classes)

Time
60–90 minutes

Focus
Review of vocabulary in lexical sets

Materials
Available photocopier

Stage of a course
Especially the middle and end

In this activity your students select which vocabulary to review. They are encouraged to group words in lexical sets, after which they prepare exercises to pass on to their colleagues.

Procedure

1. Write on the board the names of topics that have been covered in class, for example, 'travel', 'the environment', 'the media' and so on.

2. Ask students to work in threes to sub-divide each category, for example: 'travel' – vocabulary related to hotels, different means of transport, words to describe resorts. Ask them next to brainstorm and write down all the words they can remember connected with each topic and to write them down under the sub-headings. (In general, the more sub-categories they can name, the more words they remember.)

3. Elicit familiar types of exercises for vocabulary review and write an example of each on the board, for instance:

   a) Prompted gap fill
      'In tomorrow's e_____ of the *The Guardian* there will be a special f_____ on the American presidential elections.'
      [Giving the first letter gets students to focus on the *new* word. For example, the initial 'f' for the second gap filters out 'report', which students would probably have much less need to revise than 'feature'.]

   b) Multiple choice
      'Jane went on an interesting (A) travel (B) trip (C) voyage to Madrid last weekend.'
      [Incorporating near-correct distractors serves as a memory jog to the test maker as well as to the test doer. Both need to think about why certain choices are wrong as well as about which is right.]

   c) Definition
      'This is an adjective to describe a person who usually thinks of him/herself before other people.' ('selfish')

   d) Give a near synonym (e.g. 'What is a word similar to "dirty".'), an opposite (e.g. 'What is the opposite of "spotless"?'), a super-ordinate (e.g. 'A dog is a kind of m_____.'), a hyponym (e.g. 'Give an example of a vehicle.') or a translation (e.g. 'What's the Spanish for "package tour"?').

   e) Explain the difference between two 'not quite' synonyms. 'What is the difference between "dirty" and "filthy"?'
      [(d) and (e) can be combined.]

4. Students, in the same groups of three, prepare 15 test tasks of different types. In the meantime, check tasks for errors.

5. Groups each produce a neat copy of their 15 test tasks. If computers are available, use these. Otherwise, collect the test sheets and make enough copies of each for everyone. Give each group a copy of another group's test.

6. Each (original) group works together to answer the questions they receive.

7. As groups finish, they get together with the groups who wrote tests for them and conduct a feedback discussion. Each group gets one test sheet.

8. As each group will have worked on its own test and that of one other group, the vocabulary load is more than sufficient for one lesson. Other tests can be handed out as homework or reserved as fillers for following lessons.

Rationale

Asking students to prepare these exercises has two main virtues:

- It gets them to put the words and phrases into sentences. Thus, for a verb, for example, they may need to take account of the preposition which follows it, of the grammatical structure which follows it, whether it occurs normally in the continuous form and so on – all of which they may need to know for their exam.
- It gives you free rein to monitor all the groups, checking problems with particular words and explaining pitfalls in their exercises – such as not providing a sufficiently clear context.

In short, it is an excellent way of helping them put themselves in the shoes of the test writers.

Andrew Glass

3.5 Vocabulary on slips

Level
Elementary–Advanced

Time
10–15 minutes (20–30 minutes longer with the extensions)

Focus
Vocabulary review

Materials
Lots of slips of paper; for the extension, a sheet of poster paper for each group of five

Requirement
12 or more students

With or without the extension, this is a very sociable way of conducting vocabulary review.

Procedure

1. Put your students into at least three groups of five.

2. Allocate each group a different lexical area that you want to review.
3. Ask each group to write words in their lexical area on separate slips of paper. The number of words should be the same as the number of people in the group.
4. Collect yourself, or ask a student to collect, the slips of paper. Shuffle and distribute the slips.
5. If you have space, ask the students to mill round the room saying (not showing) their words until they find other people with words in the same lexical area. Then they stand together.
6. Ask each newly formed group to read out their words.

Extension

7. People with words in the same lexical area then sit together and produce a visual poster for their set of words without using the actual words. They can use pictures (especially) and written hints about the meaning of as many of their words as possible.
8. Display the posters. Invite students to circulate, view each other's posters and complete them by adding on the words that are hinted at.

Variation

If there isn't enough space for students to stand up and mingle (Step 5), ask one student to say their word to the class. Others who think they have words in the same lexical area should then say theirs.

Sheelagh Deller

3.6   True-false student-student dictation

Level
Elementary–Advanced

Materials
None

Time
15–30 minutes

Preparation
Decide which structure you want to review

Focus
Speaking; listening; review of particular structures

Reviewing

This activity is good for recapping a particular structure (e.g. relative clauses, types of conditional, particular tenses). The content consists of recent reading.

Procedure

1. Put your students into threesomes. The total number of threesomes should be divisible by three (see Grouping 1 in the diagram below). Each threesome thinks of three true and two false (or two true and one false) statements about a text you have recently used. On the board write the structure to be reviewed, for example:

All the statements must include the structure you want them to review and each member of the threesome must make a copy. Circulate and check their sentences.

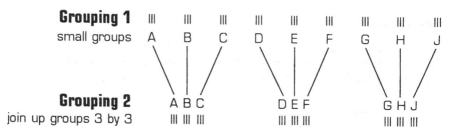

2. Combine the threesomes into larger groups consisting of three threesomes (see Grouping 2 in the diagram above). In each group of nine students, one threesome dictates their sentences to the other two threesomes. (If numbers permit, ask each student to dictate one of the sentences.) The students in the two listening threesomes write down only the statements they think are true.
3. Within each of the two listening threesomes the individual students compare dictation notes. Then these two threesomes briefly join to compare notes again.
4. They announce what they've written to the threesome that gave the dictation and this threesome tells them if they were right.
5. A different group dictates their sentences, and so on.

54

Notes

i) The dictation phase leaves each student with a written record of a number of correct student-generated sentences containing the target structure.

ii) This activity can also be used on teacher training courses to recap a previous session.

Sheelagh Deller

3.7   Student-produced reference booklets

Level
Lower-intermediate – Upper-intermediate

Time
90 minutes

Focus
Review and consolidation of knowledge about several different areas of grammar, vocabulary, and functional language

Materials
A class set of sheets of blank A4 paper plus some spares. Access to a photocopier. Optional: several grammar handbooks and/or a variety of coursebooks

---

This is a global grammar review and consolidation activity that ends with students sharing what they have (re)discovered. It's an ideal activity for the run-up to an exam. It's also an excellent means of finding out, near the beginning of a course, what a new group of students knows in key areas. If you're taking over a class from another teacher (and have a record of what students have done) this activity will give a good indication of your likely starting point.

Preparation

1. Make a list of different areas you want students to review – one area per student. Areas can include: aspects of grammar (e.g. uses of the Present Continuous, the order of adverbials), punctuation, letter format, phrases for expressing a certain speech function (e.g. ways of prefacing a request such as 'Could you ...?' 'Would you mind ... -ing ...?'), vocabulary relating to a specific topic or notion, and so on.

If the class is a new one and the students are fairly unfamiliar to you, write a list of topics that they, as lower- to upper-intermediates, ought by now to know something about. (These students will need a few basic students' grammar handbooks and miscellaneous coursebooks to refer to since they won't have relevant class notes.)

2. You need a sheet of A4 for each topic. On each sheet, write a few sub-headings or other prompts and an example or two so that students know what to add onto these sheets later on.

Suppose you have an intermediate class. You might have one sheet headed 'The Present Simple'. Down the left side, add headings like: 'Positive forms', 'Negative forms', 'Question forms', 'Situations when we use it plus example sentences and concept questions for each situation', 'Common mistakes'.

Another sheet might be headed 'Certainty and uncertainty'. Vertically, along one margin, you might draw a scale ranging from '100% certainly yes or no' at the top to 'Just above zero chance of yes or no' at the bottom. A student who gets this sheet should write, near the top of the scale, example sentences like 'It can't be true', 'It must be true'. Near the bottom should go sentences like 'It might be true but probably not' and so on.

A third sheet might be headed 'The language of presentations'. Down the left write the sub-headings 'What the presenter can say' (e.g. 'I'd like to talk about') and 'What the members of the audience can say' (e.g. 'Could you say a bit more about ...?').

Procedure

1. Hand out your sheets, a different one for each student.
2. Tell the class that everyone is going to produce a page or two of a class grammar reference booklet. Stress that each page must be easy to read, neat and interesting to look at and that the writing shouldn't be too big. Tell them as well that they will need to do some research before beginning. That is, they will need to refer to class notes, to coursebooks or to grammar handbooks.
3. Start them off. Circulate and make sure everyone knows what to do. Have extra sheets of paper handy for students whose first attempt is too disorganised as well as for those for whom one page isn't enough. As work progresses, provide editorial tips.
4. As students slow down, tell everyone to pass their sheet one place to the left.
5. Tell the class that everyone should check the sheet they've just been handed and that they should also try to add something to the sheet they've just been handed. Circulate and help out. If necessary, add

additional prompts onto sheets in order to stimulate students to delve deeper.
6. Repeat Steps 4 and 5 until the students are no longer adding much to the sheets.
7. Collect everyone's sheet.
8. After class, photocopy a class set of everyone's work. Sort the copies out to make a class set of student-produced grammar booklets for distribution to the authors during the next lesson.

Note

If you are about to be relieved by another teacher, a copy of the class reference booklet would really put them in the picture about your class.

Tessa Woodward

3.8   Hidden shape in the puzzle

Level
Beginner–Advanced

Time
Varies according to the tasks

Focus
Review of grammar; vocabulary; pronunciation

Materials
A class set of the puzzle and task sheets
(example below)

'Hidden shape in the puzzle' tells you how to combine the ideas of the crossword puzzle and the paint-by-number picture. In this type of task, creation of the right image depends on how the question clues are answered. Conversely, success or failure in creating a picture gives students valuable feedback on how well the questions have been answered. Ultimately, the picture can actually serve as a key to the exercises. This activity can be done in class or as homework.

Preparation
1. Decide on a picture or drawing of something which can be recognised by its outline alone. Trace or draw the outline onto a sheet of blank

57

paper and then draw a square, rectangle or circle around it. The outline in the example picture puzzle below is that of a clown.

2. Now enjoy yourself drawing all kinds of lines within (1) the outline and (2) the margin between it and the perimeter of the enclosing shape (see the example below). Form as many sub-divisions outside the outline as within. Try to disguise the outline of your shape. You should end up with something that looks like a black and white design for a complicated stained-glass window.

3. Write a small, neat number into each of the sub-divisions and make a note somewhere of those that are *inside* your original outline.

4. Write a list of 'double choice' tasks. For each task, the right answer should be indexed with the number of a sub-division *inside* the outline and the wrong answer with the number of a sub-division *outside* the outline. Take this double choice task for example, 'How (21)*much*/(47)*many* eggs are left?'

   The number 47 is the index number for the correct choice. On identifying this as the correct choice, the student should colour in the corresponding space which appears inside the outline on the puzzle picture. A student who makes only correct choices will colour in all and only the spaces within the outline of the clown (in this case) and thus produce a clear and coherent picture.

5. If possible, put both your sub-divided shape and your tasks on the same sheet, and then produce enough copies of this worksheet for everyone in the class.

Procedure

1. Distribute the handouts. Ask students to read the double choice tasks carefully. Check that they know what they mean.

2. Tell them that if they choose all the right alternatives, a recognisable shape will appear in the middle of the picture puzzle. If not – well, they should try again.

Variations

– Ask students each to prepare a (signed) puzzle picture. Tell them how many sub-divisions you want inside the outline of their shape. Tell them also to number all these sub-divisions before they begin numbering the ones outside it. You prepare the language tasks. Thus, if you ask students to make 17 sub-divisions within their pictures, you prepare 17 language tasks. You can either:
   i) Use all the students' pictures at once by distributing them so that no one gets their own and then give everyone the same language tasks. Or,

ii) Make a class set of each of the puzzles and use them one by one in class or for homework. Prepare a different set of language tasks for each one.
- Ask students to prepare both picture and tasks. Check the tasks as the sheets come in. When a sheet is completely ready, photocopy enough for everyone except the student who made the sheet.
- The task sentences can form a text, for example, a paragraph, a dialogue, or part of a story. If the latter, you could even tell a short story, in instalments, over a number of worksheets. At advanced level, tasks could include idioms and colloquial expressions you want to review or they could be based on a poem, say, which your class wants or needs to study in depth.
- If the tasks are based on a text, the picture could relate to the text in some, not too obvious, way.
- To review/check pronunciation, use 'X rhymes with Y/Z' sentences, e.g. '*cough* rhymes with (17) *now*/(11) *off*'.

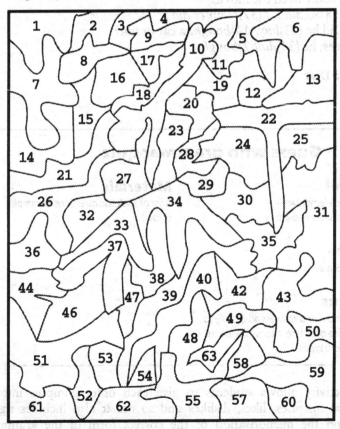

© Cambridge University Press

Reviewing

Example double choice tasks (Elementary)

a) (8)*Do*/(54)*Does* Mike (12)*has*/(23)*have* any relatives?
b) A: How (21)*much*/(47)*many* eggs are left?
   B: Only (28)*a few*/(42)*a little*.
c) These hamburgers taste (16)*well*/(10)*good*.
d) Is Mr Hammond (17)*a*/(55)*an* actor?
e) (36)*When*/(63)*Where* have you left my books?
f) She never (40)*watches*/(11)*sees* TV (59)*and*/(38)*because* she doesn't have (29)*much*/(30)*many* time.
g) She (62)*has gone* / (53)*went* to Brazil last year but she (31)*never went* / (27)*has never been* to Peru.
h) A: Is that (18)*Susan's*/(26)*Susan* jacket?
   B: Yes, that's (49)*his*/(48) *hers*.
i) There (44)*is*/(37)*are* (20)*some*/(4)*any* bananas but we don't have (7)*no*/(39)*any* apples.
j) A: I really liked the movie.
   B: (58)*So did I.* / (57)*Neither did I.*
k) A: Did he (33)*buy*/(14)*bought* a car or not?
   B: Yes, he (34)*did*/(2)*bought*.

Adriana Diaz

3.9 Guess who grammar quiz

Level
Lower-elementary–
Upper-intermediate

Materials
A list of 'skeleton questions' (examples below)

Time
20–45 minutes

Focus
Questions and answers adaptable to practice of different tenses, aspects and verb types

This activity allows students to give each other glimpses into their personal histories, likes, dislikes and so on. It also includes rigorous work on the memorisation of the correct form of the grammatical structure(s) focused on.

Preparation

1. Prepare six to eight questions, fully written out, which use the verb structure you want to focus on.
2. Reduce each of your questions to skeleton form (see examples below). You can display these on the board or OHP. If you produce photo-copied handouts, you will need one copy for every two students.
3. If you wish to participate with your students in the following activity, write your answers to the questions on a separate sheet of paper.

Procedure

1. If you think it necessary, lead the class in review of the structure(s) included in your question list.
2. Read out the questions to your students and have them write down their answers – but *not* their names – on paper. Let them decide whether to answer with only one word, with a phrase or with a complete sentence.
3. Ask your students to fold their papers with the writing inward and then to fold them once more for good measure. Then collect their papers and let the students see you conspicuously shuffling them up. Add in your own paper if you made one earlier.
4. Display the list of skeleton questions or hand out photocopies, one per pair of students.
5. Select one of the answer sheets from the shuffled pile. Tell your class that they are going to have to guess whose answers you have *and* remember the question for each answer.
6. Elicit the full form of the first question. (It won't always be necessary for students to reconstruct the precise questions you had in mind. Insist, however, that the questions they formulate are grammatically correct.)
   Then read the first answer on the paper you picked. Correct any errors and enrich the vocabulary as you read, but do nothing to indicate explicitly that you are correcting rather than simply reading what's been written.
7. Continue until the class has asked and you have answered all the questions for the mystery student. Then they try to guess the author of the answers you have just read.
8. Repeat Steps 4 to 6 with other students' answer sheets

Examples of question types   The corresponding skeletons

For beginners

| Where do you live? | – Where/live? |
| What's your favourite colour? | – favourite colour? |

Reviewing

Simple past
Where did you go on holiday
last year? — holiday/last year
What job did you dream of
getting when you were little? — job/dream/little?

Present perfect
What is the best film you have
ever seen? — film/see?
What is the most unusual food
you have ever eaten? — unusual food?

Complex sentences
If you could be famous for
something, what would you
want to be famous for? — famous for something?
What is something you
should've done last week, but
didn't do? — something/should/last week?

Phrasal verbs
What bad habit do you have the
hardest time putting up with? — bad habit/put?
What kind of boss do you find
the easiest to get along with? — boss/easiest?

Gerunds and infinitives after verbs
What common household chore
do you most dislike doing? — household chore/dislike?
What is something that your
parents always told you not
to do? — what/told/not/do?

Prepositions/idioms
Would you be in favour of electing
a president of Europe? — favour/president of Europe?
When something is bothering you
do you tend to keep it in or get
it off your chest? — bothering/keep/get/chest?

Acknowledgement

This is an extension of 'What would you do if?' in Claus-Jürgen Höper
et al. (1975, p. 130).

Denny Packard

4 Communicative pot-pourri

The eleven activities in this chapter are extremely varied in topic, class dynamics, materials used, range of skills practised, mood and so on. What they have in common is that they all get students talking, with the emphasis on fluency. Most have been timed at between 15 and 30 minutes. Activities of this length can be used as fillers. That is, they can usefully fill out a lesson when you've finished one major sequence of related activities and don't want to start another until the next lesson. Or, they can be incorporated into sequences of related activities. There are so many ways this can be done that it would be impossible to list half the possibilities. But let me give a few examples for 'The books on the shelf' (4.1) of how it could be linked to other activities.

'The books on the shelf' (timed at 30 minutes) involves discussion (with frequent use of the Present Simple) and note-taking. Thus, in an elementary level class you can use it to allow students the opportunity to become more fluent in using the Present Simple. Or, in an advanced study skills class you can use it to hone note-taking skills. Alternatively, since this activity concerns libraries and book titles, you can use it before a tour of the local bookshop or library, or before you go on to look at the life and works of a particular author.

Again, all the activities in this chapter (and indeed the book) are usable in this way to form coherent sequences of activities.

4.1 The books on the shelf

Level
Elementary–Advanced

Materials
None

Time
30 minutes

Focus
Discussing; note-taking; the Present Simple tense

Communicative pot-pourri

This versatile activity gives students an opportunity to improve both fluency and study skills. See previous page for three ideas on how to fit it into longer-term coursework.

Preparation

Make a list of 10–15 book titles. For ideas, just look along the shelves in your library or in a book shop. Or ask students to bring in titles (in the target language). In order to stimulate discussion, the titles should be ambiguous and not be well known. Copy a class set of your list (or half a class set if you need to conserve copies). Here is a list I've made for use with adults:

Breaking Rules	The City of Gold and Lead
Inside Meaning	How Life Began
Odyssey	Now Read On
Pick and Choose	Visa
Life and Death of the USSR	Connections
Sparkling Cyanide	Departures
Attitudes and Opinions	Elephants Can Remember

Procedure

1. Brainstorm the different sections where books can be kept in a library.
2. Form groups of four students and distribute your handouts.
3. Tell groups to agree on what each book is about. Ask them to take notes since they are going to report to the whole class later on. Additionally, they should agree about which section of the library each book should go in. Allow ten minutes for this step.
4. A spokesperson from each group reports on their conclusions about the first book on the list. If there are significant disagreements, encourage a whole-group discussion. If the class cannot reach a consensus about the best account of the book's story line or contents, take a vote. Proceed similarly in deciding the section the book belongs in.
5. Write the title of the book along with the section on the board.
6. Do the same with the rest of the titles.

Variations

i) After Step 3, form new groups of three such that each consists of members from three different previous groups. These new groups discuss and try to reach agreement for each title. Allow 15 minutes for this. Then, a spokesperson from each group reports.

ii) As a warm up (5–10 minutes), write one title on the board. Ask students each to note down a few thoughts about what the book is about. After a couple of minutes ask students to summarise the book.

Adriana Diaz

4.2   ETs and earthlings

Level
Elementary–Advanced

Time
About 10 minutes

Focus
Speaking; listening; asking for and
giving instructions

Materials
A number of objects or devices in everyday
use. These can be realia or in the form of
cut-out pictures

This activity incorporates a trick of the trade that's been around for a while but deserves to be better-known. Here it is applied to the functions of asking for and giving instructions. It is what I call 'linguistically low demanding' but 'creatively high demanding'.

Procedure

1. Divide the class into two large groups. Give each student in one of the groups an object in everyday use – or a cut-out picture of one. (E.g. a razor, tape recorder, bike, car, toothbrush, vacuum-cleaner, loo ...)
2. Explain that the students with the objects are beings from outer space, extra-terrestrials (ETs), who don't know anything about us earthlings. Everything here is strange for them!
3. The students pair off. The ETs introduce themselves and ask about the object they have – what it is, what it is for, generally, and exactly how to use it.

In a low-level class, provide a model exchange. For example, the model might contain a pattern we often use when saying what something is for: 'It's for ... -ing ...'. The model should also set the tone for student exchanges – that is, ETs should be as inquisitive as possible.

Variations

i) ETs can request other information, for example:

- how to make things (e.g. spaghetti)
- definitions of words
- directions around town
- clarification of a celebration they happened to witness on their arrival on earth (e.g. a wedding, carnival, Hallowe'en, graduation day, etc.)
- the shoulds and shouldn'ts of life on Earth
- what happens to earthlings as they grow older

ii) The enquirers can be amnesiacs.

Rationale

I have always found it difficult to provide motivating activities to practise asking for and giving instructions. Most seemingly realistic situations strike students as artificial and unmotivating. But then I discovered that they have nothing against being faced with motivating situations which are utterly absurd!

Adriana Diaz

4.3 Live classroom

Level
Elementary–Advanced

Materials
None

Time
15–20 minutes

Focus
Conversation

The humorous premise of this roleplay activity encourages students to feel that they can speak safely. As a result, students sometimes get deeply into their roles and when they do, they may offer an extraordinarily revealing commentary on their learning situation.

Procedure

1. Ask students each to make a list of all the inanimate objects there are in the classroom, big or small. Set a time limit.
2. Ask them to report their lists and as they do so, you write the items on the board (don't repeat items that are given more than once).
3. Form groups of four to six. Each group chooses one of the objects on the board.
4. Tell your students that every day, after the class is over, the classroom comes alive and the objects they have chosen, talk about the students and about you. Tell them that they are now the objects they have chosen and that they should discuss:
   – what each object can see from its place
   – good things about the class
   – bad things about the class
   Remind them that their point of view is now that of the object and tell them that everyone should make notes on what their objects think.
5. After five minutes, form new groups such that each new group is made up of one student from each of the former groups. The 'objects' introduce themselves and exchange the thoughts developed in Step 4. Whenever a viewpoint comes up that is shared by the majority of objects, everyone in the group should write it down.
6. Each group reports to the class about what they agreed on.
7. Ask the students:
   – how they felt about imagining they were an object
   – if what the objects said is true or not
   – if they have discovered something about the group they hadn't realised before

Variations

The objects can discuss:

– one or two other objects and the use made of them
– what you do (if you can accept some blows to your self esteem!)
– where they would rather be placed and why
– what they would like the next lesson to be about
– what they would like students to do

Adriana Diaz

4.4 The Tower of Babel

Level

Elementary–Advanced

Time

20–30 minutes

Focus

Listening; speaking

Materials

Three or four tape recorders and an equal number of recorded dialogues of as close to the same duration as possible, preferably with added background noise

---

Doing this activity is an excellent way of waking up a class who have got a bit blasé about working with recorded listenings.

Preparation

Get three or four tape recorders each ready to play an extract from a different dialogue. Place them half-hidden about the room.

All the extracts should begin at the same time. However, you may not be able to switch all the machines on at the same time (unless you have a mains switch). So, have a bit of 'dead air' before the start of the extracts on the first two or three machines you will switch on. And don't forget to note the counter settings!

The extracts should be 15 to 25 seconds long and should include language that students could understand easily if they heard it clearly. (If you are acquainted with Stephen Krashen's i +1, you should aim for i − 1 here.)

Procedure

1. Write 'Tower of Babel' on the board and ask students what they know about it. Go on to elicit/give a modern definition (e.g. *babel*: 'a scene of confusion, disorder and the noise of many voices', *Longman Dictionary of Contemporary English* 1987).
2. Form groups of four to six. Tell the groups to make a list of everyday situations that can be considered a babel. Give them a set time – two minutes, say – and then ask the groups to report to the class.
3. Tell your students that you are going to expose them to a babel. They should close their eyes and concentrate on what they will hear and try to make out (a) the setting of each conversation and (b) the age, sex and number of the speakers.

4. Play the tapes. Then ask groups to pool their thoughts on what they heard. While they are doing this, rewind the tapes. Actually, there are likely to be so many groans of 'Oh no!', 'Impossible!', 'What?!', etc. from the class that no one will hear the beginnings of the dialogues. So, be prepared to do Step 4 twice.
5. Ask students to listen again, this time with eyes closed. Ask them to listen out for (a) what the conversations are about and (b) the gist of what each of the different speakers says. Play the tapes.
6. Ask the groups to discuss. Then invite each group to report to the whole class.
7. Tell the class they can now check their first impressions. Play the dialogues one by one.
8. Write phrases on the board such as,
   'I mistook ... for ...'
   'I couldn't hear ... because (of) ...'
   Invite students to say exactly what confused them at certain points and then round off by eliciting more general comments on the 'babel effect'. For example, what are some good strategies for coping with a babel?

Variation

Use this activity with dialogues you wish to review.

Rationale

i) Once the initial shock has subsided, students listen with unusual concentration. This carries over to listening to the individual dialogues.
ii) Ultimately, this activity is a good confidence raiser. Firstly, the discussions are likely to bring out the fact that babel is difficult to cope with even in one's mother tongue. Secondly, if you've chosen tapes that are not too challenging, students will be able to glean much of the key information anyway. Thirdly, the heightened interest in the dialogues typically leads to very good comprehension of the dialogues when played individually.
iii) The activity is fun.

Acknowledgement

The idea of this activity came to me after reading John Fanselow's *Breaking Rules*.

Adriana Diaz

4.5 Two part discussion

Level
Intermediate–Advanced

Materials
Access to a word processor or typewriter; a class set of a list

Time
30–40 minutes in the first lesson;
40–90 minutes in the second

Focus
Discussion, vocabulary

I often have students who say they want to discuss serious issues. I have very rarely had classes who could keep a discussion going on their own. Here I describe a way of providing a framework for discussion, one that I've found works very well with students who want to discuss but don't know quite how.

Procedure

1 Lesson one

1. Find out from your class what issues they are interested in discussing. Perhaps suggest a few yourself.
2. Suppose, for example, that your class settles on 'mass immigration' as one recent upper-intermediate class did. Help the class to reach consensus about what this means. My class decided it meant the annual inflow of large numbers of immigrants. Thus, they decided to exclude from the discussion mass migrations across a border as a result of one-off natural disasters and individual battles. They then agreed that 'mass immigration' now referred mainly to ongoing movement of peoples from poor countries to richer ones.
3. Tell the class that they will have 15 minutes, speaking one person at a time, to say what all the pros of mass immigration are. After that, they will have a further 15 minutes to state all the cons they can think of. Tell them that now is not the time to argue with anyone's suggestion. They will be doing this in the next lesson. Say that they can, however, ask for clarification about what a given suggestion means. Allow students to use bilingual dictionaries.
4. As students speak, note down all the pros and cons that come up.
5. After the 30 minutes is up, ask if anyone has anything they'd like to add to either the pro or the con category. You may be surprised at

how many separate points come up. On the subject of mass immigration, the class I mentioned above suggested 11 pros and 14 cons, all serious and worth considering.

2 Between lessons

6. Type up the list of pros and cons. Flesh out what students have said, by here and there adding in vocabulary and turns of phrase that your class are probably not familiar with. Thus, my notes during the first phase of discussion of mass immigration began like this:

PRO
- Can make the economy go, e.g. building more houses
- We have enough to give

I reformulated this as:

PRO
- New immigrants need housing. The construction of houses and blocks of flats stimulates the economy, e.g. by creating jobs in the construction industry.
- We have plenty of resources to spare.

Here and there, add in a few pros and cons that no one suggested. These can be plausible or far-fetched.
7. Make enough copies of your list for the whole class.

3 Lesson two

8. Hand out the list. Ask your class both to read through it and underline any items which they think you might have added. Deal with any questions about vocabulary.
9. Tell the class the rules of the discussion to come:

- Anyone can make any kind of point about any item on the list.
- Anyone can respond to any point made by anyone else.
- You will intervene to control the discussion as little as possible. No one needs to raise their hand or wait to be recognised by you.
- They must speak one at a time, otherwise the discussion will not work.

In practice, students make points of several different sorts, for example:

- A given item is actually a pro rather than a con (or vice versa).
- The wording of an item should be changed.
- A given item doesn't fit the facts.
- An item fits the facts but is basically unimportant nevertheless.
- They think of things that aren't on the list.

All the while, they are justifying what they say, disagreeing, backing others up, and so on.

10. While the discussion is in progress, compose memos to the participants, e.g.:

> Olaf, Thanks for your various contributions. I found your comments on the situation in your home town particularly interesting. I think your 'delivery' was really good. That is, you made eye contact around the class when you were talking, you spoke loudly enough for all to hear, and you talked at a good speed but not too fast. One reminder about grammar – after 'avoid' use '-ing' not 'to'. E.g. 'We should avoid mak*ing* our country too crowded.' Seth

Extension

11. If the lesson period comes to an end before the discussion does, tell students to write down everything they wanted to say but didn't have time for. Say that you will read these additional thoughts out in a later class, if the contributors agree.

Seth Lindstromberg

4.6   Guess my story

Level
Lower-intermediate

Materials
None

Time
2 lessons of 30 to 40 minutes each

Focus
Listening; asking questions; note-taking; oral summarising; writing

For this activity you need to have two stories in mind, each of which you could tell your class. But you end up telling only one!

Procedure

1 First lesson

1. Tell your learners that you have prepared two stories for this lesson and that you are going to tell them only one of the two.
2. Tell them that they have to decide which of the two stories they want to hear, story A or B. Add that first they need to find out a little about each of the two stories so that it will be easier for them to decide which of the two stories they want to hear.
3. Tell the group to ask you lots of questions about each story. Do not give too much of the story away in your answers. Your answers should hook the group's interest in the story, but at the same time they should also be a little vague and fairly open.
   For example:

   S1: Is story A a fairy tale?
   T: It's not a fairy tale, but there is an element of magic in it.
   S2: Is there a magician in story A?
   T: No, all the people in the story are quite ordinary people. Erm ... apart from one person ... she's a bit ... well ... strange, you know.

4. After a while, ask your class to work in pairs. Each pair should summarise for themselves what they know about each of the two stories. Ask them to take notes.
5. Give them some more time to ask you further questions. Proceed as described in Step 3.
6. In pairs, learners decide which of the two stories they want to hear and why.
7. Get each pair to report their decision and their reasons to the whole class. Note the votes on the board as shown below:

   Story A 卌 ||||

   Story B 卌 |||| ||

8. Tell the class the story the majority wanted to hear. Ask them to keep their notes for the next lesson.

2 Second lesson

9. Get your class to work in the same pairs again. Ask them to look at their notes of the story that you have *not* told. In pairs, they write a story based on their notes.

73

10. Each pair reads their story out.
11. Tell the story.

Note

Morgan and Rinvolucri (1983) is a good source of stories which students are unlikely to have heard.

Herbert Puchta

4.7 The movies you've seen

Level
Elementary–Advanced

Materials
None

Time
30 minutes

Focus
Narrative; listening

Learners enjoy a good game. This game exploits popular culture and also builds a picture of the special character of a class. The discussion it provokes includes both narrative (film plots) and some focus on accuracy in the use of English language film titles and of such phrases as 'Have you seen ...?' and 'Five of us have seen ...?'

Procedure

1. Divide the class into pairs. Tell the pairs to think of five movies they think everyone in the class has seen. Each pair is a team. In 15 minutes each team will read out their list. (Advanced classes should need less time.) A team gets one point for each class member who has seen one of their movies. For example, if there are 20 in your group, a perfect score (20) for one movie means everyone in the class has seen it. Each team totals up their five scores and the highest total wins. Any film can be used. If there's an English-language film seen in a non-English version, students should use the original English-language title if they know it (or if you can tell them what it is). Otherwise, non-English language films keep their original titles. It

doesn't matter if different teams have some of the same movies on their lists.

2. After 15 minutes, a volunteer from each team reads out their list. Write team names, movie titles and scores on the board. Here spelling and translations can be checked. If class members cannot remember from a title whether they have seen a movie or not, it may be necessary for a team player to tell a little bit about it.

3. At the end there is a winner. In the case of a tie, each team thinks of one more film. There may be some discussion about the most popular films. (Each class is very different in what films they have seen!)

4. Ask the class now to form new pairs, in which each partner has seen a movie the other has *not* seen. They sit down and tell the stories of the movies.

Variation

Truly cinephilic groups will enjoy playing the same game in reverse, thus: 'List five films you or your partner have seen but the others have not seen'. In this case, the lowest score wins.

Rick Cooper

4.8 A radio drama

Level
Upper-elementary–Advanced

Time
60 minutes

Focus
Reading; writing; discussing;
performing playlets

Materials
Half a class set of a radio drama synopsis
(example below)

In this activity students turn written text of one type into both written and spoken text of another type. Things start out quietly but end with performances.

Procedure

1. Form groups of four. Give out your synopsis sheets (at least two sheets per group). Tell everyone that the programme has been losing listeners lately and that all the scriptwriters have been fired. They, your students, have taken over as scriptwriters.
2. Ask them to study the synopsis and write a brief outline of what's going to happen in a future episode. Remind them that they should be original if they want the programme to gain a big audience. Their new jobs depend on it! Set a time limit of not more than 10 minutes for this step so that all the groups finish at the same time.
3. A spokesperson from each group reports the outlines to the class. If there are two or more similar outlines, the groups in question have to take on board changes suggested by the class. (After all, the programme can't be the same from one episode to the next.) Keep this step to a maximum of 10 minutes.
4. Each group now writes at least two of the most important dialogues for their episode. Tell them to add in notes about sound effects and how the actors should deliver their lines. Show them how this information is given in brackets e.g.: 'JOHN [shouting]: The house is on fire!'. Allow 15 minutes for this step. Circulate and help out as necessary.
5. Ask each group to sit as far away from the others as possible and then rehearse their dialogues, with sound effects!
6. Write 'On the air!' on the board. Suggest that listeners close their eyes in order to create the effect of listening to the radio. One by one, the groups perform their dramatic readings.

Extension

7. Hold a class vote on the most interesting and best performed dialogues.

Variations

- If you think your students aren't ready for dialogue writing, stop after Step 3.
- If there isn't enough time for the dramatic readings, stage them in the next lesson. Ask students to rehearse in the meantime.

Radio drama: 'Of family bondage':

Cast of characters:
Mr Robert Wilkins and **Mrs Sandra Wilkins** They run a hotel in a well-known summer resort.

Christine Wilkins   Their youngest daughter. She helps run the hotel and stays there after the holiday season. She wants to lead her own life far from the hotel even if she has to get married to do so.

Robert Wilkins, Jr   The Wilkins' eldest son. He studies law in a nearby city. Comes to the hotel only during vacations.

Mario Scott   Good-looking tennis instructor at the hotel. Girls fall for him on sight. Ambitious.

Lesley Nolsen   Receptionist. Young and sexy. Is looking for a husband, but wants to enjoy life first.

Synopsis:

Things have not been going well between Robert and Sandra lately. She wants to divorce him but he won't accept that. Both Christine and Sandra have been meeting Mario secretly for some time, completely unaware of what the other is doing! Robert Jr is at the hotel during one of his vacations. He falls in love with the receptionist who, although attracted to him, has other fish to fry!

Adriana Diaz

4.9   **Brothers and Sisters**

Level	**Materials**
Elementary–Advanced	None

Time
20–40 minutes

Focus
Listening; comparing/contrasting two animals; writing Present Simple sentences

---

This story-telling activity also includes an element of problem solving.

Preparation

Prepare to tell the story summarised below. You will need to give free rein to your imagination, embellishing the tale and adapting it to the level and interests of your students.

Procedure

1. Tell your students you would like them to listen carefully to a story from Angola (Serauky 1986) that will require them to think. Here it is in outline:

   - 'Once upon a time there was a chicken that used to find its food on the bank of a river in Angola.' (Describe the chicken, the river-bank, the food, the river, etc.)
   - 'One day a crocodile came out of the river. It wanted to eat the chicken.' (Describe the crocodile.)
   - 'The chicken shouted, "Don't eat me, Oh Brother!" The crocodile was surprised and confused and didn't eat the chicken.' (Describe the state of mind of the chicken on seeing the crocodile.)
   - 'He kept wondering why the chicken was his brother.'
   - 'Another day, the same thing happened. Again the crocodile swam away, cursing the chicken and wondering.' (Describe the state of mind of the crocodile.)
   - 'The crocodile went to see Mbambi, the lizard, and told him about his problem.' (Describe the journey to the lizard's home, the lizard, and where it lived.)

2. In elementary classes, tell the story again with a few minor variations. In more advanced classes, ask someone to say everything the crocodile said to the lizard. (Or put students into pairs so that one person can tell their partner what the crocodile said – their partner afterwards supplying any missing details.)
   All this repetition is part of the art of the traditional storyteller.

3. Tell the class that you won't give them the lizard's answer but say that as a result of what the lizard said, the crocodile never again thought of eating the chicken.

4. Ask the class to try to discover why the crocodile and the chicken are brothers by comparing the two creatures. They do this writing lists of sentence endings. Suggest to your students that they think of physical appearance, temperament, food, habits, habitat and so on. Give them a model, for example:

The crocodile	The chicken
is ...	is ...
has ...	has ...
lives ...	lives ...
can ...	can ...
can't ...	can't ...
likes ...	likes ...
...	...

   Circulate and help with vocabulary as students write.

5. Students form pairs, compare their sentences and try to think why the crocodile and the chicken could be brothers. (In the original tale it is because they both lay eggs.)
   In a low-level class, elicit their sentences and write them in tabular form on the board. In a higher-level class, ask the pairs to say what their most interesting sentences were.
6. Tell the class that in the original tale the lizard told the crocodile about other brothers of theirs. Ask what these other animals could be. (In the original tale the lizard mentioned ducks, turtles and lizards.)

Clem Laroy

4.10   Stories that share the past

Level
Elementary–Advanced

Materials
None

Time
15–30 minutes

Focus
Listening; note-taking; speaking

The 'telling of what we did' must be one of the oldest forms of story-telling/history building/journalism. It took place after memorable hunts, raids, wars, weddings ... One of its joys is that the listeners already know what took place. But do they? This activity exploits the fact that two witnesses to an event seldom, if ever, notice exactly the same things.

Preparation

Prepare to tell your students your version of something that happened in an earlier session (of the same class), or something that happened on a group outing or at any other time when most of the group were together. Prepare to tell your version of the events accurately, from your point of view, but also to add in some things that did not actually happen.

Procedure

1. Explain to the class that you are going to tell them the story of X which happened when you were all together. Ask them to listen very carefully. (Say no more at this point.)
2. Put these headings on the board:

THINGS LEFT OUT	THINGS ADDED IN ON PURPOSE	THINGS THE TELLER RECALLED/SAW DIFFERENTLY FROM ME

   Ask the students to make notes under the three headings above (or any other headings that come to your mind). They are to work individually.
3. Cluster the students in small groups to discuss their way of hearing the story.

Variation

Learner A tells learner B what A remembers from a reading, listening, video viewing familiar also to B. B takes notes under the headings 'Things left out'. 'Things added' and 'Things seen differently'.

Acknowledgement

Thanks to Rick Cooper for the Variation.

Mario Rinvolucri

4.11   Your life in the cards

Level
Elementary–Advanced

Time
15–30 minutes in one lesson (with homework): 20–30 minutes in the next

Focus
Conversation; writing

Materials
A deck of cards for each pair of students (students can bring these in); a few spare sets of oracular statements for students who don't do their homework (see below)

Many coursebooks have a section on horoscopes. Try this instead.

Procedure

1   Lesson one

1. Teach your students vocabulary for talking about cards ('deck/pack', 'hearts', 'ace', 'shuffle', 'turn face up', etc.).
2. Begin speaking about and asking about predicting the future with cards. For instance, ask if anyone has had their future read in the cards.
3. Tell your class that in the next lesson they will tell each other's fortunes. To prepare for this everyone needs to write, at home on a sheet of paper, an oracular statement for each of however many cards you specify (e.g. each of the twelve face cards). Each statement must be written with a particular card in mind, for example: 'Queen of Hearts: you will soon change your opinion about something important.'

Your instructions on how to write the sentences will depend on what you want students to practise. For example:

– Predictions with *will* or *going to*.
– Bare infinitive commands ('Do not telephone today.' 'Write to a friend.')
– Warnings of different kinds ('There is danger around the corner.' 'Beware of . . .')
– Suggestions/justifications ('Why don't you speak to someone new today? It could change your life!')
– Comments about the past ('You have met an important man.' 'Someone broke your heart. ')
– Conditionals ('If you travel by car, you must not pick up any hitch-

81

hikers.' 'If you had asked a certain person if she loved you, she would have said "Yes".')
– Present continuous ('You are thinking of a certain man'.) And so on.

Notes

– In lower-level classes suggest that students stick to a clear model. Encourage more proficient students to write statements of a variety of types.
– Make up a few spare sets of oracular sentences for the inevitable students who will show up at the next lesson without any.

2 Lesson two

1. Set aside five minutes or so during which students who haven't finished their full complement of statements can write some more and during which you can circulate and suggest changes to those whose statements need a bit of editing.
2. Put your students into pairs. Each student needs a sheet of oracular statements and each pair needs a pack of cards.
3. Ask students to separate out the cards they will be using to tell fortunes and put them into a separate pack for use in what follows. For example, if you have asked them to write 12 statements, they make up packs consisting of the 12 face cards. If you have asked them to write 16 statements, they include also the aces. And so on.
4. Each pack is shuffled and placed in between the two partners. Student A chooses six cards without looking and then turns them face up. Student B then reads out the statements he or she has pre-pared for these cards.
5. The cards are shuffled and roles reversed.
6. As students finish, they form new pairs and repeat. Stop this phase when most people have worked with three different partners.
7. Bring the class together and ask if the statements they heard from their classmates showed any pattern. Also find out who thinks there is much truth or plausibility in the statements addressed to them. Ask how they went about matching statements to cards. Did they operate according to associations (e.g. spades with unpleasant events, hearts with matters of the heart) or not? (In a large class, this step can be done in groups of six to eight.)

Extension

If your students were making predictions, a week or so later ask if any have come true in the meantime.

Variation

In low-level classes you may need to collect the sheets during the second lesson and correct them after class. At the beginning of the third class, hand the sheets back and give students time to rewrite them. Then follows the fortune telling.

Acknowledgement

I learned this from my son Jonathan, when he was 12.

Clem Laroy

5   Working with a coursebook

The other day a colleague of mine walked into the staffroom, fresh (or rather not so fresh) from class and announced, 'All my worst lessons are based on coursebooks'. I know this feeling myself, and also what can cause it: a coursebook that suddenly veers off in a direction no one in the class wants to go, or which dwells on a negative or hackneyed topic, or which confronts you all with a dull text about bland, poorly-characterised imaginary people, and so on. Yes, some coursebooks are just right for some teachers with some classes, but often a coursebook is like the British weather – it has its good and bad points. The trick is to be clear about what its good points are and to find ways of building on them. So first of all you need to really get to know your coursebook.

One of our authors, Peter Grundy, from the University of Durham, recommends spending an hour doing the following with *each* unit.

1. Imagine you are *one* of the following:
   a) Your dentist examining your teeth – prodding, poking, scraping, using the mirror, filling, extracting, polishing.
   b) Yourself looking hard at your wardrobe. What should go (at last)? What can stay for another year? What do you need to buy – what type of clothes, what colour, to go with what?
   c) The Prime Minister of your country – which ministers should be promoted or sacked? Who should be brought in from outside politics?
   d) Yourself looking hard at your budget. What should you spend more on, what less on? What should you cut out altogether? How would you spend the money saved?
   Take this very seriously. Spend 10 to 15 minutes thinking in detail about the problem.
2. Now turn to the next unit in the coursebook you are working with and give it the same treatment. By doing so, you can provide a better quality coursebook for your students and also take the decisions you really wanted to take but until now were afraid to.

Some of the decisions Peter has in mind will be ones about what to use instead of what's in the coursebook. He and Lindsey Gallagher have suggested a way of accumulating a mass of options about this in a short time.

1. Gather together the teachers at your school who have used or who are likely to use a certain coursebook. They should all be able to set aside 45 minutes to an hour for every two units of the book that is to be considered. (Everyone would probably win this time back several-fold in reduced lesson planning in months and years to come.)
2. Ask the group to select two consecutive units to work on. If there are more than about 12 teachers, form groups of from 6 to 9. Each group tackles a different two-chapter sequence. (However, one group could work on units 1 and 2 and the second group on units 2 and 3.)
3. Everyone must imagine that the second of their chosen units has been so badly damaged in a fire that it is no longer usable. Each group must find ways:
   – to use the unburnt unit to cover (some of) what the lost unit had covered [15 minutes for this]
   – to supplement the unburnt unit so as to compensate for what was lost in the other unit [15 minutes for this too].
4. Finish off by putting ideas down in writing.
5. A possible extension is for smaller teams of teachers to make the work done in Steps 3 and 4 more concrete by putting together lists of tips and packs of supplementary materials for each unit.

Whether you decide to appraise and ponder your coursebook in any of the above ways or in some other, all the activities in this unit take it for granted that you will get to know your coursebook well before you begin to chop and add. So, here is a brief preview of what else this chapter holds:

'Judge the book by its cover (but not only …)' (5.1) tells you how to encourage your students to approach a new coursebook with a positive attitude.

'What shall I leave in?' (5.2) shares features of (5.1). It also suggests close scrutiny and rigorous selection before you embark on a new unit. It also tells you how to involve your students in decisions about what to use.

Activities 5.3–5.8 present particular ways of supplementing a coursebook – not by going outside it for material but by going beyond what the authors have suggested you do with what's there.

'Supplementing coursebooks with authentic materials' (5.3) is about what you can do if you've decided that your coursebook doesn't meet *your* students' need for interactive exposure to 'real' texts.

'Coursebook recall' (5.4) describes a simple but interesting and communicative way for students to review material covered in a coursebook.

'Personalising coursebooks' (5.5) describes a technique you can use in many or even every lesson that you base on a coursebook. As its title suggests, it uses a coursebook to get students speaking more about themselves.

'Stories in your coursebook' (5.6) sets out a highly ingenious idea for getting more out of the pictures in your coursebook.

'Reconstructing a patch on a page' (5.7) is for review and change of pace with classes of young beginner and elementary learners.

'Alternative coursebooks' (5.8) describes a long-term in and out of class project that gets students evaluating and collecting authentic texts and visuals.

5.1 Judge the book by its cover (but not only...)

Level
Elementary–Advanced

Time
45 minutes

Focus
Fluency; getting acquainted with
a new coursebook

Materials
A class set of your new coursebook; one or
more sheets of poster paper or (reversed)
wallpaper

It's important that your students develop positive feelings about their new coursebook. This activity is about how to build a nice activity around the new book in the students' hands instead of just saying, 'This is your new coursebook, open to page ...'.

Procedure

1. Ask everyone to look at the cover of the coursebook and to jot down all the words that spring to mind.
2. Hang up your sheets of poster paper (or lay them out on tables) and ask students to transfer their jottings onto them.
3. Leave the posters where everyone can see them. Ask students why they thought of the words.
4. In pairs, students describe the cover. Help with additional vocabulary if necessary.
5. Bring the class together. Ask what the title of the coursebook means.

If no one knows, explain. Ask how the title accords with their impressions of the cover.
6. Ask students to browse through their books. In the meantime, stick sheets of paper up around the room with sentence starters on, e.g.:
   'I think I'll like the book because ...'
   'I don't think I'll like the book because ...'
   'What worries me about the book is ...'
   'Why ...'
   'The illustrations are ...'
7. Students mill around writing sentence endings onto the sheets and reading what others have written.
8. Bring the class together again and see what the general feeling about the book is. (Save the comments from Step 7 for when you have finished with the book. Then hang them up again and ask students whether their first impressions were right and which, if any, they would change.)

Variation for intermediate and advanced students

They read the back cover blurb. On the basis of their first impressions, they write their own blurb in language that students might find easier to understand. As they finish, students read each other's blurbs. Save the blurbs for later use as in Step 8.

Hanna Kryszewska

5.2   What shall I leave in?

Level
Elementary–Advanced

Materials
(Optional) Multiple copies of a list (see Preparation)

Time
50–60 minutes

Focus
Involving students in decision-making; reading for gist; discussion

---

It's easy to find ourselves working through a coursebook or taking agonising decisions as to what to leave out when there is too much to get

87

through. Instead of you deciding, alone, what to leave out, this activity shows how to work with your students to decide what to leave in. Do it at the beginning of a term or course of between 30 and 50 hours.

At elementary level in a monolingual class don't worry if much of the discussion in this lesson takes place in the mother tongue. But from a low intermediate level upwards, provided the students already know some basic exponents for discussion, they should be able to cope in English.

Preparation

Look at the units in the coursebook. Draw up a list of your priorities during the coming course/term. Are there any units you could leave out completely? With what's left, be strict. Aim for a maximum of one or two activities / language items per unit. What would you like to add that's not in the coursebook? Again, be strict. Aim for only one or two activities' / language items.

Optionally, if you have more than about 12 students, make a list of the activities / language points in the units to be studied and make enough copies of your list for half the number of students in the class (since they will use the list in pairs). Leave space at the end of your list for students to write anything which doesn't appear in the coursebook but which they especially want to do.

Procedure

1. Tell your students that you would like to work with them to decide on various aspects of the course content. Explain that you would like them to look at the coursebook units they are due to cover during the term/course and decide what the priorities are (only one or two items per unit). Tell the class what you feel are priorities and how you reached your conclusions. Mention any units you want to omit completely and explain why.
2. Put your students into pairs and ask them to follow the same process that you went through. (Make sure everyone has a copy of the coursebook.) Are there any units *they* want to leave out completely? What are their one or two priorities in the remaining units? Tell them to discuss the material and try to come to an agreement as a pair. Allow 20 to 30 minutes for this, depending on how much material there is to look through.
3. If your class has fewer than 12 students, you can discuss the conclusions with them in plenary and try to come to a consensus. Note down the views your students express.
   If you have a class of more than about 12, give out the copies of your

list of what the units contain. In pairs, students vote on each item – a tick for 'high priority', a cross for 'definitely leave out', no mark for 'undecided' or 'indifferent'. Allow about five minutes for this. Then ask everyone to add at the bottom anything that does not appear in these units that they would particularly like to do in their course. Allow another five minutes for them to write these extra things down. Collect in their lists.

4. Read your notes / the students' lists and draw your conclusions. There are many ways of doing this. Clearly you need to take into account whatever your students feel strongly they want to do. To accommodate the differences in priorities, and there are almost always considerable divergences of opinion, allow a number of lessons when different individuals/pairs/groups can be working simultaneously on different things.

5. Next lesson, tell the class roughly what you intend to do during the rest of the term/course.

David Cranmer

5.3 Supplementing coursebooks with authentic materials

Level
Elementary–Advanced

Materials
A coursebook; a tape recorder and cassette; a native speaker

Time
10–20 minutes

Focus
Extending elements of your coursebook organically

The aim of this activity is to have a coursebook and authentic materials that complement each other.

Preparation

1. From your coursebook, choose an interesting picture or a dialogue which depicts an aspect of the target culture or country.

2. Find a native speaker who lives or has lived in the country under discussion.
3. Ask the native speaker to comment on the authenticity of the picture or dialogue and record what he or she says.

Now you have a comment on something in the coursebook and this comment is itself full of lots of language to work with in class. You also have a realistic, personal and informed picture of the culture supposedly represented in your coursebook.

Procedure

You can sometimes use the coursebook material first and then add your own home-made authentic materials before moving to the practice stage. (This works well with dialogues.) With a picture, you might want to work entirely with your authentic materials and use the coursebook only as a back-up.

Examples

Here are two authentic conversations with native speakers which illustrate the technique. They each show the kind of practice-rich language you can collect in a few minutes.

Dialogue 1: (compare with *Blueprint*, B Abbs and I Fairbairn, Longman, 1990, p. 9)

A: Right Julia, would you like to tell me whether this desk is like your desk or not?
B: Er, no it's not – my desk is wooden and it's much older than that desk, and it's quite scratched on top. It's got three drawers on the right-hand side like this desk – I think my desk is a bit larger
A: er huh
B: and it's certainly much more cluttered.
A: You said more cluttered: What do you mean by that?
B: Well, it's less tidy, I think – there're piles of books and papers that I never sort out so things get lost.
A: Right. Do you have a telephone on your desk?
B: No.
A: Er huh. And a lamp?
B: Yes I've got a lamp just like that one but it's on the right-hand side and it's red.
A: Er huh, OK. And what I is this, some kind of wallet or ...

B: Yeah well it looks like a men's handbag or or . . .
A: right.   D'you
   keep your handbag on your desk?
B: No.
A: Er huh, d'you keep
B: I keep
A: Sorry.
B: I keep it, well, on the floor somewhere
A: right
B: usually by the . . .
   propped up against one of the legs of the desk.
A: Um do keep a diary: I mean do you have a diary?
B: Yes.
A: An appointments diary like the one on this desk?
B: Yes, but I keep it in the drawer.
A: Right. And is yours nice 'n' empty like this or
B: [laughs]
A: are they
   about the same?
B: Well, it's nice 'n' empty for August certainly.
A: [laughs]

Ideas for exploiting dialogue 1

a) Picture dictation (i.e. students hear the dialogue and try to draw one
   or both of the desks)
b) Listing differences between the two desks
c) Comparing (i.e. listing similarities or differences and studying the
   language used in comparison)
d) Focusing on:
   - use of filler phrases and sounds
   - expressions for confirming what you hear
   - expressions that indicate tentativeness
   - 'repair' expressions (e.g. 'what I is')
e) Writing a personality profile of Julia

Dialogue 2: (compare with *Blueprint*, pp. 41–42)

A: OK, Angela, can I ask you to have a look at these pictures of,
   er, called 'the home'?
B: un hum
A: um would you like to pick any of
   those rooms, bedroom, sitting room, kitchen, bathroom, any of
   those and say whether it's like yours or not.
B: Um kitchen.

A: Kitchen, right.

B: No, the kitchen is square, ours is an L-shape, quite narrow, um the units are of a similar type although they aren't real wood

A: uh uh
and this one is real wood I suppose.

B: Yes it is, yes. We don't have a hob the same as the one shown in the picture. Hm, it's a very modern kitchen this one, although ours is fairly modern it doesn't have the amount of equipment which is shown in the diagram here

A: right

B: um we don't have a circular table, with chairs – we just have a breakfast bar, in our kitchen.

A: Right; there seems to be a book open here; is it . . .

B: A cookery book.

A: D'y, er huh, d'you keep cookery books open

B: yeah

A;   in your kitchen?

B: Yes, yes.

A: Uh huh right.

B: We don't have beams, as shown in this picture.

A: Right.

B: Storage jars, we have a similar type um and a tiled floor.

A: Can I ask you a slightly more difficult question – how does this kitchen compare with yours in terms of tidiness and cleanliness?

B: Similar.

A: Similar.

B: Yes.

A: Much tidier than ours, [laughs] much cleaner [laughs]

B: [laughs]

Ideas for exploiting dialogue 2

a) Picture dictation (both kitchens)
b) Vocabulary work
c) Estimating the cost of the two kitchens
d) Conducting interviews which enable learners to check the extent to which their coursebooks represent life as it really is
e) Redesigning the coursebook to make it more authentic

Peter Grundy

5.4   Coursebook recall

Level
Lower-intermediate–Advanced

Materials
A coursebook for each pair of students

Time
20–30 minutes

Focus
Review: fluency

This uncomplicated but ingenious activity is for students who have used at least a few units of a particular coursebook.

Procedure

1. Give the students five minutes to look through the coursebook and remember the topics, pictures and texts met so far in the course.
2. Tell them to close their books and get into pairs.
3. Student A recalls a picture, dialogue, poem or anything else in the part of the book covered to date and begins speaking about it. That is, A talks about the people involved, mentions associated grammar or vocabulary, says when the material was covered and so on. A keeps on talking until B remembers the bit of the book that A has in mind.
4. At this point, B takes over talking on the same subject – with help from A if B's memory falters – until both exhaust their recollections.
5. A and B swap roles, that is, B talks about a different bit of the book. When A knows what B is talking about, A takes over.

Allow the class to carry on in this way until you sense that they are ready to move on to something else.

Variation

You can limit the exercise to vocabulary only. Individually, students look in the coursebook for a stipulated number of different words they have learned from the book and jot them down. In pairs, students take turns reading their words out. Their partners try to remember where in the book each word was used and what the topic, context or situation was.

Hanna Kryszewska

5.5 Personalising coursebooks

Level
Intermediate–Advanced

Materials
The coursebook

Time
A few minutes in a coursebook-based lesson

Focus
This activity allows students to take control of their coursebook by stages so that eventually they are weaned off it as a result of surrounding it with their own language. The first step in this process is described below

The technique described here enables students to relate their coursebook to their own lives and experiences.

Procedure

1. Inform the students that as you are working with the coursebook, you will be pausing at 20-minute intervals and asking the class to say something very brief about the coursebook that relates it to themselves. This means that they will have to note down things they might want to tell you as they are working. Allowable contributions could include:

   – relating a picture of a place or person to a place or person they know themselves.
   – relating an experience being described to an experience in their own lives.
   – telling the class how an utterance comparable to one in the dialogue was used in a conversation they took part in or overheard, or might be useful to them in the future.
   – commenting from personal experience on the topic of any unit.
2. Pause every 20 minutes and ask for three or four short contributions before continuing with the coursebook.

Homework

Ask all those students who have not spoken to write down what they would have said if they had had the opportunity. Encourage the use of drawing, cartoon work and speech bubbles, etc. Any student who has spoken may also do this for homework.

Steve Gilbride and Peter Grundy

5.6 Stories in your coursebook

Level
Elementary–Advanced

Materials
A coursebook for every two students

Time
25–45 minutes (main activity);
60 minutes (the Variation)

Focus
Telling stories; writing (in the Variation)

My impression is that teachers ...

– typically use a coursebook illustration in the way intended by the author and in no other way.
– rarely use an illustration a second or third time for other activities.

This is an activity for getting more out of the pictures in your coursebook.

Procedure

1. Students get in pairs with one copy of the coursebook between them.
2. They open their books at the first picture and start telling a story using the characters and ideas portrayed or suggested in the picture. Then they turn to the next picture and continue the story. And so on, right to the last picture in the book.

Variation

As pairs make up their stories, they write them down, giving page references as in the example below. When finished, pairs swap their stories and read them, following the illustrations in the coursebook.

Here is part of an uncorrected example of a student story based on the pictures in *Headway Upper-Intermediate* (Soars and Soars, 1992):

'I was reading newspaper yesterday. (p. 1.) I read an article about a famous sportswoman. Her name is Maria Spiralli. In fact, I know her so I can tell you more about her. (p. 3) She is very much interested in Esperanto. (p. 5) One of the ways to practise the language is to have penfriends. One of her penfriends is Luis Gonzalez. She prefers to correspond with him in Esperanto because he makes many mistakes in English. Twenty in one letter! (p. 7) Her desk is always a mess! There are newspapers, diaries . . .'

Hanna Kryszewska

5.7 Reconstructing a patch on a page

Level
Beginner–Low intermediate
(especially young teenagers)

Time
30–40 minutes

Focus
Review

Materials
Pencils, erasers and scrap paper with one good side for everyone; several pairs of scissors; (optional) Blu-tack

---

Concentration on the layout of information can foster recall of printed information. It is said, for instance, that the best Talmudic scholars can look at one side of a page of the Talmud, stick a pin through it, and then, without looking, say which letter of which word the pin passes through on the other side. This activity does not go to that extreme but it does exercise students' memories and gives them a chance to cut up some paper!

Preparation

1. Choose a page in your coursebook that you want your class to review. It's most interesting for the class if it's a page with a mixture of graphics and text.
2. Take one of your sheets of scrap paper and make a cut-out in the

shape of an amorphous blob, starfish, violin or whatever strikes your fancy. Your blob (if that's what you've made) should be big enough, but not too big, to cover a quarter to three-quarters of your chosen page. You need to be able to position it so that it partially covers both some printed material (text, exercises, instructions ...) and some graphics (photo, drawing ...).

3. Once you've got the size and shape right trace its outline onto half a class set of sheets of scrap paper.

4. Prepare an unofficial quiz to test students' recollection of what's on your chosen page. Test recollection of the graphics and instructions (unless these are in the mother tongue) as well as of any stories, dialogues, etc. Here are some example quiz items:

    1. Write questions for the following answers:
       a) Green.   [About a picture of a woman
       b) About 25 perhaps.   of about 25 wearing a green blouse.]

    2. Which questions do you remember from the dialogue? Write them down.

    3. What is the longest word in any of the instructions on this page?

    4. Using only words that appear on this page, what is the longest sentence you can write that is true about you?

Procedure

1. Divide the class into pairs. Hand out scissors, bits of Blu-tack, and your sheets of scrap paper with the shapes traced on. A student in each pair cuts out the shape. Keep some extra sheets of paper handy in case anyone wants more.

2. Hold up a copy of the coursebook open at the page you want to review. Show them how to position their shape on the page.

3. Explain that soon each pair will, from memory, write/draw onto their blank shape (starfish, etc.) the graphics and text concealed just underneath it. If they wish, instead of drawing the graphics in detail, they can sketch them in very roughly and then add information about colour and other detail in the form of labels and captions. Tell them that, later, they'll have a short test on this.

4. Give them a minute to study the page. At the end of the minute, call time and tell them to place their shapes on the page just as you demonstrated earlier (i.e. blank side up). Tell the class they are only going to have a few minutes to write and draw onto their cut-outs what's concealed beneath. (Or perhaps they might like to do the drawing and writing on a full-sized sheet of scrap paper.)

4. Call time. Each pair gives their coursebook with the shape on it to another pair.

5. Everyone tries to add to or correct the cut-out they receive from their

neighbour. If they like, for the sake of neatness, they can cut out a new shape and start afresh.

6. As students finish, they set their sheets on their table/chair and go around looking at what other students have done.
7. Pairs take back their own coursebooks, lift off the shape and see what's really there.
8. They close their books again and you give them your quiz.

Rationale

The objective is not primarily for students to produce perfect copies of the cut-outs, but for them to become aware of what they have remembered and what they have forgotten. When they look at the pages again, they should see and remember just that little bit better.

Seth Lindstromberg

5.8 Alternative coursebooks

Level
Intermediate–Advanced

Materials
A class set of a coursebook

Time
A multi-week project

Focus
Review and extension of learning; student involvement in supplementing materials in a coursebook

'Alternative coursebooks' is a long-term project for classes set in an environment in which the students are exposed to the English of popular culture. (This includes most countries in the world.)

Procedure

1. Group the students in threes or fours. Allow each group one to two weeks to collect authentic English that reflects *their own* popular culture. Suggest sources such as recorded popular music, contemporary art and design work, cinema, posters, and in-country English

language newspapers (these exist in many non-English speaking countries).
2. When the materials have been collected, explain that each group should think about how to use some of them to teach the same things that their coursebook has taught and/or to replace illustrations. Set a date by which time you expect each group's alternative coursebook to be completed.

Lindsey Gallagher and Peter Grundy

6   Using magazines and newspapers

What can beat the popular press as a source of fresh, authentic reading? As an English teacher, you're spoiled for choice. Even outside English-speaking countries, English language magazines and newspapers are seldom wholly impossible to obtain. For one thing, you may well find that there's an English language newspaper published in the country. If so, it should provide you with articles of clear relevance to the lives of your students.

The activities in this chapter are all designed to add to your repertoire of ways in which you and your students can work with whatever magazines and newspapers are at hand. None is restricted to texts on a particular topic so you can use each one again and again. Here's a brief overview:

'Who can take notes best?' (6.1) is a full lesson activity (i.e. 60 to 90 minutes) involving medium length magazine articles and longish news-paper articles. As a study skills activity for upper-intermediate and advanced students, it is excellent for getting poor note-takers to pull their socks up. It's also an excellent reading and discussion activity for high-level general English classes.

'Meet the demand' (6.2), 'That's news to me!' (6.3), and 'Spot it!' (6.4) are three more extremely interesting full-length lessons usable in study skills or general English classes. Among other things, they all focus on improving summary writing abilities.

'Looking in from outside' (6.5) is also a full-length lesson. It aims to stimulate discussion and retelling of stories in the news.

6.1   Who can take notes best?

Level
Upper-intermediate–Advanced

Materials
Class sets of two articles (for the Variations, one or two video or cassette players plus recordings)

Time
60–90 minutes

Level
Reading; note-taking; evaluation of notes; discussion; writing

This rigorous yet interesting exercise can be a real eye-opener, especially for students whose note-taking leaves much to be desired.

Preparation

Choose two articles of about a page in length from a news magazine or ones of equivalent length from a newspaper.

Procedure

1. Remind your class that good notes should be well organised, give a good overview of all the important content, omit unimportant detail, and, above all, they should be readable. Add that, in the activity to follow, notes must be readable to others, not just to their author.
2. Divide the class into two groups, A and B. Give a copy of text A to everyone in group A and a copy of text B to everyone in group B.
3. Students read their texts and take notes individually.
4. Collect the notes into two separate piles. Keep student groups A and B separate too.
5. The groups swap piles.
6. Individually, in pairs or small groups – the students each read through all the notes in the pile they got from the other group. As they do so, they add evaluative comments (relating to the criteria in Step 1) either onto the individual sheets or onto other sheets which they attach. Ultimately, each group (A and B) must decide which set of notes in the other group's pile is the best. (Usually, students agree fairly quickly.)
7. When the best notes have been agreed on, allow students a couple of minutes to adjust or add to any comments they have written on any of the other papers. Then give the students in each group copies of

the text that the other group read so that they can compare the notes with their source.
8. The authors get their notes back. Encourage them to discuss the comments on their papers with students in the other group.
9. Hold a general discussion of note-taking. Find out if the readers followed the criteria in Step 1. Do these need refining? Were any other criteria used?

Variation

Use sound or video recordings rather than written texts. Or give one group a written text and the other group a sound or video recording.

Hanna Kryszewska

6.2 Meet the demand

Level
Upper-intermediate–Advanced

Time
90 minutes

Focus
Reading, especially skimming; summary writing; aspects of register

Materials
A class set of a scientific article 2 or 3 pages long; a selection of different kinds of newspapers and magazines

This is a marvellous activity for students who are serious about improving their reading and writing.

Preparation

Find a specialist text which has some potential for interest to lay people as well. Among articles I have had success with is one about Beethoven's deafness, from a medical journal. (Extracts below.)

Procedure

1. If your class numbers 15–20, divide it into five groups of three to four

students. If your class is larger than 20, form more groups. If your class is smaller, form fewer groups.
2. Ask students to skim the article. They then put the article aside.
3. Assign each group a type of publication or text, e.g.
   - women's magazine
   - children's magazine
   - advertisement
   - news magazine
   - tabloid or evening newspaper
4. Ask students to rummage through your pile of magazines and newspapers, pick out an example of their assigned type and then, back in their groups, to browse through this material.
5. Explain to the students that they are journalists whose editor has just given them an assignment. They have to report on the ideas in the scientific article. Remind them that what they write must fit the type of publication/text that you assigned them earlier. Add that their article should be accompanied by helpful drawings, diagrams, maps and so on which they can make themselves. Alternatively, they should draw boxes and fill them with descriptions of the necessary graphics so that the Visuals Department can draw them later.
6. As students begin writing, circulate and help with language.
7. Display the finished material. As students finish, they mill around and try to identify (in the form of notes which they add on to the articles) what type of publication the article is intended for or what type of text it is supposed to be.

Variation

If your students need experience in writing scientific papers, you can reverse the activity. That is, give out a selection of articles from newspapers and magazines (or old student work from the activity as described above). Everyone takes an article in their field. For example, a psychologist takes an article on a rapist or victim; a physicist, one about a local power station; and so on.

Hanna Kryszewska

THE DEAFNESS OF BEETHOVEN: AN AUDIOLOGIC AND MEDICAL OVERVIEW

Patricia D. Shearer, M.D., M.S.

One of the most intriguing and unfortunate ironies in all the arts is the deafness of Ludwig von Beethoven. Its precise etiology remains speculative despite the objective findings of the autopsy and the descriptive information provided by the composer in his conversation notebooks and letters to friends. Numerous physicians and historians have written on the subject; this paper constitutes the first review of the literature by a physician who is also an audiologist and singer.

Beethoven was born in Bonn, Germany in December, 1770. He was a child prodigy about whom Mozart exclaimed, "Keep your eye on that young man; someday he will give the world something to talk about." His teachers included Haydn, Salieri, Albrechtsberger, and Mozart. He was a devotee of J. S. Bach and treasured the works of Händel at his bedside during his terminal illness. He was musically quite prosperous, which he attests in a letter written on June 29, 1800 to his physician friend, Wegeler. This letter also contains the first reference to his deafness:

> Only that evil demon, my miserable health, has done me an evil turn: my hearing has grown steadily worse these last 3 years. This disability is supposed to have been caused by the condition of my stomach: I suffer from diarrhea and am extraordinarily debilitated.[1]

The intestinal malady dates to 1797, when Beethoven contracted a "terrible typhus". In contemporary parlance this was typhoid fever, although the actual translation is "typhus", which refers to fever with clouding of consciousness. Dr. Wawruch, Beethoven's last physician, called his abdominal disorder "hemorrhoidalleiden", inferring bloody diarrhea.[2] This might well have been inflammatory bowel disease.

FEATURES OF HEARING LOSS

The high frequency component of Beethoven's hearing loss became apparent early on. In 1802, at age 31, he confided that he had been unable to hear a shepherd piping merrily in the forest on a flute of lilac wood. For half an hour the composer became gloomy and quiet, though he was falsely reassured that his companions also failed to hear the notes. From a distance he could not hear the high notes of the orchestra. Poor speech discrimination with recruitment and severe tinnitus are described in another letter to Wegeler:

> Sometimes I can hardly hear people who speak softly. The sound I can hear, it is true, but not the words. And yet, if anyone shouts, I cannot bear it. My ears ring day and night.[1]

Beethoven is known to have covered his ears with cotton wool cushions during the bombardment of Vienna.

Beethoven began using his Conversation Books by his mid forties. A total of 138 remain: 264 were destroyed by Anton Schindler, Beethoven's long-time secretary and selective biographer. The notebooks date to February/March, 1818, when the composer was 47.[3] There is reference to written communication as early as age 31. In the same letter cited above[1] Beethoven wrote, "For almost 2 years I have avoided all society, because I cannot say, "I am deaf." He also pleaded with Wegeler not to break his confidence about his deafness.

The presence of a conductive component is furnished by Beethoven's use of a stick between his teeth and the keys of the piano. He continued to use this throughout his life. The fact that his speech did not deteriorate also suggests some cochlear reserve. The Conversation Books were primarily used by the other party; Beethoven answered verbally. There is no reference to vertigo.

The progression of the loss evolved from one initially only in the left ear to complete or near-complete bilateral loss by air conduction. He last played in public in 1814 at age 43 in the *Archduke Trio*. At age 52, he was asked not to conduct *Fidelio* because he could not hear the soloists. Two years later the contralto soloist, Fraulein Unger, had to turn him around to see the applause of the audience at the premier performance of the *Ninth Symphony*, at which Beethoven was serving as the honorary conductor.

TREATMENT

The stick and ear trumpets were used until the composer's death. One of the first remedies was topical almond oil, instilled by a priest. Beethoven later returned to this after the devastation of being removed from conducting *Fidelio*. The almond oil was followed by cold baths in the Danube, warm baths in the Danube, and an unknown "infusion". This was probably an enema.[4] The efficacies of the various treatment modalities are described by the composer:

> Dr. Frank wanted to restore the tone of my body with medicine and my hearing with almond oil, but, wouldn't you know it! Nothing changed. Then a medical asinus advised cold baths in the Danube. A more intelligent doctor ordered the customary warm baths. That worked miracles: my stomach improved, although my hearing problem remained or worsened.[5]

A vial of "strengthening stuff" was added to the lukewarm soaks in the river and followed unsuccessfully by the infusion. Later remedies included vesicatories, which were blistering devices made from tree bark and placed on the arms, and auditory rest. Beethoven also considered galvanism.[1]

MEDICAL HISTORY

Beethoven's medical history is pertinent not only for diarrhea and hearing loss, but for conjunctivitis, hemoptysis with epistaxis, a fungal abscess of the finger, repeated colds, and a disfiguring skin condition.[1-3, 5-7] His terminal illness was marked by increasing jaundice, *berechdurchfall* (vomiting and diarrhea) and edema that lasted 4 months. He underwent paracentesis 4 times, with 11 liters of ascitic fluid being removed on the second occasion.[7] Two days before his death Beethoven made his will. He said to the physicians in attendance. "Plaudite, amici, comedia finita est." (Applaud, friends, the play is over.) On March 26, 1827, the composer died of what is now called hepatorenal syndrome. The death scene was vividly described by Anselm Hüttenbrenner:

> At about 5:30 PM there came a flash of lightning, accompanied by a violent clap of thunder, garishly illuminating the death chamber. Beethoven opened his eyes, lifted his right hand, and with a clenched fist he seemed to say, 'Hostile powers, I defy you! God is with me!' When he let the raised hand go, his eyes closed half-way. Not another breath, not a heartbeat more.[5]

His funeral was attended by an enormous crowd. Schubert carried a torch decorated with flowers in the procession. Later in the evening the young composer raised his glass during the second toast (the first toast having been in memory of Beethoven) and said "To him who comes next." He followed Beethoven in death the next year.

DIFFERENTIAL DIAGNOSIS

The diagnosis of the hearing loss favored by most otologists is cochlear otosclerosis.[4,5,9] This would explain the progressive mixed high frequency loss with recruitment, decreased speech discrimination, and tinnitus. The age of onset in the late twenties would also be consistent with this diagnosis. However, there is no reference to stapedial fixation in Wagner's autopsy.

The case for Paget's disease rests on 3 lines of evidence: Beethoven's large, asymmetric head with massive jaws, which were not present in his youth; his ear symptoms; and the findings of the autopsy describing the thick skull vault and atrophy of the eighth nerves.[10]

Furthermore, there exists a morphologic similarity between Paget's disease and otosclerosis.[11]

However, the onset of Beethoven's hearing loss in the early years, the absence of other cranial nerve pathology (particularly the optic nerves), and the lack of reference to thickening of the axial and appendicular skeleton mitigate against Paget's disease as the most likely etiology of his deafness.

Both congenital and tertiary syphilis have been entertained based on the vascularization in the temporal bones, periods of exacerbation, bilateral involvement that began unilaterally, and progression.[12] In addition, Dr. Politzer was known to have made out prescriptions for mercury to Beethoven. However, this was the remedy of the time not only for lues, but for *Kolik*, dysentery, rheumatism, and ophthalmia. Beethoven also used a "volatile salve", said to be mercurial, but the actual translation is "liniment". He made reference to this in a letter to Countess Edody in 1818,[2] hardly a person to whom a sexually transmitted disease would be mentioned. Furthermore, a syphilitic etiology seems unlikely in the absence of vertigo, central nervous system signs, and stigmata of congenital syphilis;

McCabe is the only modern otologist who defends this etiology.[13]

The composer himself thought that typhoid fever was the cause of all his maladies. *Salmonella typhi* can cause both sensorineural hearing loss and middle ear effusions; the autopsy did not demonstrate the latter. Chronic liver disease could certainly explain the systemic findings at autopsy, including the petechiae and edema. Pancreatitis is also a possibility. Finally, both vascular insufficiency[5] and collagen vascular disease must be included in the differential diagnosis.[2-6]

MUSIC AND DEAFNESS

In correlating Beethoven's music with the deafness, the hearing loss became obvious only at the end of his first period of composition, i.e., after the *First Symphony*, the first two piano concerti, and the sonatas through the "Pathetique". It progressed during the second period, during which the *Third* through the *Sixth* symphonies and the *Appassionata* and *Moonlight* sonatas were written. Most of his popular pieces were written while he was still hearing reasonably well. The most notable exceptions are the *Missa Solemnis* and the *Ninth Symphony*.

It is through the latter colossal work that the irony between the psyche of the composer and the impact of his music is made manifest. Psychologically devastated by the compromise of his interpersonal relationships that was the inevitable result of his hearing loss, Beethoven wrote to Wegeler in 1801, "My weak hearing haunts me everywhere like a specter, making myself appear a misanthrope. Oh, I would embrace the entire world if it were not for this miserable disease!"[3] He also stated that he would have committed suicide if it were not for his art. (In fact, Bezold's original patient with cochlear otosclerosis did commit suicide.) Toward the end of his life Beethoven wrote, "Oh that Heaven would grant me but one day of pure joy! Oh, but that would be too much!"[5]

That joy was not received, but, rather, bequeathed to posterity. His sentiment bore full expression in Schiller's "Ode to Joy" used as the text for the choral setting of the last movement of the *Ninth Symphony*.

Ode to Joy

Joy, thou source of light immortal,
Daughter of Elysium
Touched with fire, to the portal
Of thy radiant shrine we come.
Thy pure magic frees all others
Held in custom's rigid rings;
Men throughout the world are brothers
In the haven of thy wings.

He who knows the pride and pleasure
Of a friendship firm and strong
He who has a wife to treasure,
Let him swell our mighty song!
If there is a single being
Who can call a heart his own
And denies it–then, unseeing,
Let him go and weep alone.[14]

REFERENCES

1. Wegeler G, Ries F: Beethoven remembered. Arlington, VA: Great Ocean Publishers. 1987.
2. Cooper M: Beethoven: the last decade. New York: Oxford University Press. 1985.
3. Thayer AW: Life of Beethoven. Princeton, NJ: Princeton University Press. 1973.
4. Nager G: Personal communication.
5. Stevens K, Hemenway W: Beethoven's deafness. JAMA 1970;213:434–437.
6. Larkin E: Beethoven's illness: a likely diagnosis. Proc R Soc Med 1971;64:493–496.
7. London SJ: Beethoven: case report of a Titan's last crisis. Arch Intern Med 1964;113:442–448.
8. Seyfried: Beethoven: studies, translated by Henry Pierson (Liepzig, 1953). In: Thayer AW, ed. Life of Beethoven. Princeton: Princeton University Press. 1973.
9. Sorsby M: Beethoven's deafness. J Laryngol Otol 1930;45:528–544.
10. Naiken VS: Beethoven's deafness. JAMA 1971;215:1671.
11. Nager G: Paget's disease of the temporal bone. Ann Otol Rhinol Laryngol (Suppl 22) 1975;84:1–32.
12. Grove G: Dictionary of music and musicians. London: McMillan and Co., 1879.
13. McCAbe BF: Beethoven's deafness. Ann Otol 1958;67:192–206.
14. Schiller A: An die Freude. Thalia 1786. Zentes Heft (Part II):1–5.

The author wishes to acknowledge Drs. George Nager, Ira Papel, Hiroshi Shimizu, Brigid Leventhal, and Carl Leventhal for their assistance in the preparation of this manuscript.

(*The American Journal of Otology* Volume 11, Number 5, September 1990, pp. 371–5. The article has been abridged.)

6.3 That's news to me!

Level
Intermediate–Advanced

Time
60 minutes

Focus
Reading; note-taking; summary writing

Materials
Old magazines (*New Scientist* and *National Geographic* are especially good) and newspapers

This is a well-disguised summary writing exercise with a difference. Namely, students concentrate on new information rather than main points.

Procedure

1. Put a pile of magazines and newspapers in the middle of the classroom. Ask each student to find and cut out or mark an interesting article (300–600 words) that appears to contain something new to them.
2. Everyone takes notes on all the information they find in their article that does turn out to be new to them. Note that they do not write a complete summary.
3. Collect the articles. Then ask students to exchange notes.
4. On the basis of a set of notes received from someone else, everyone writes a short article for a mass appeal newspaper beginning perhaps, 'Did you know that ...?' Ask everyone to leave an extremely wide margin on one side of their paper. Circulate and help students polish their language.
5. As student articles are finished, display them around the room.
6. Put all the articles in one pile. Tell everyone to take someone else's article and look for the corresponding summary. When they find it, they compare the original with the student summary of the new information. Then, in the form of margin notes, they add onto the student article any information new to them which the student author did not mention. Finally, the reader displays the source article beside the student article so that others can read, compare, and add comments.

Variations

i) If you wish to concentrate on a particular language point or topic or if you wish to avoid students choosing articles that are too easy or too difficult for them, present students with a set of articles and let them choose from those. This also saves time since it shortens the browsing phase.

ii) Source articles can be in students' mother tongue(s). This speeds the activity up even more.

Hanna Kryszewska

6.4 Spot it!

Level
Lower-intermediate–Advanced

Materials
A class set of a text of at least 350 words

Time
30 minutes plus a 30-minute extension

Focus
Scanning; reading aloud; summary writing

This is another reading/speaking/study skills activity. Step 2 describes an extremely versatile task which you can also apply to longish texts in your coursebook. It involves short, alternating bursts of reading aloud. Don't worry. This is about to come back into fashion!

Procedure

1. Form students into pairs and give everyone a copy of the text.
2. One student (A) reads one or two sentences at random. Student B tries to find the passage in the text. When B has succeeded, A and B swap roles and keep on swapping roles for about ten minutes. If the text is longer than one page, suggest that students work through it page by page. Before setting students off give an example of what each partner might say and do. Write a few prompts on the board, e.g.
(It's in) column 1, paragraph 2, line 3.
It goes from line 4 to line 6.

It's near the beginning (end) / in the middle of paragraph 5.
It starts 6 lines up from the bottom.
3. Collect the text sheets.
4. Ask students to write a summary of the text.
5. Display students' work around the room so that they can mill around, read and compare.
6. Hand out the text sheets again. Students re-read to confirm exactly what the text is about.

Extension

7. In pairs, students choose one fragment of the text and prepare a cloze test for their colleagues with a maximum of 20 blanks. They also prepare a key for their cloze passage. Tell them that they can alter the original passage by, for example, re-ordering words or phrases, by paraphrasing, and so on. They should not, however, alter the meaning of the passage substantially.
8. As students finish, they show you their texts and keys and, if these are OK, they swap them for a set produced by another pair.
9. Rather than fill in the blanks in the cloze passage they have received, each pair adds to the key other words which they think will fit in the blanks. They have to check with you, though, before adding a new word to the key.

Variations

i) Summary writing is a task some students don't like much, perhaps because they've had to do a lot of mechanical summary writing in other classes, perhaps because of the relatively uncreative nature of the task. If you see that some of your students feel this way, suggest that they write a criticism of the task rather than a summary of the text you've handed out. These criticisms can then be displayed along with the summaries in Step 5. They can also be used in the making of the cloze tests.
ii) If there are a lot of new words in the text, divide it and allocate a different passage to each pair. Instead of producing a cloze test, pairs prepare a glossary of the new words and patterns in their fragment. As students finish, they pass around their passages and glossaries.

Hanna Kryszewska

6.5 Looking in from outside

Level
Intermediate–Advanced (adults)

Materials
One English language newspaper per student

Time
60–90 minutes

Focus
Talking; reading; retelling

This activity tackles the issues of cultural awareness and openness to the target language culture head-on. The final step invariably generates very interesting exchanges.

Procedure

1. Make about eight groups of students. Tell them that they are going to spend three months working in a very foreign culture that they have some idea about. (The idea of working among Japanese goes down well with Europeans, since they know something about Japanese culture, but the idea of working among Patagonian Indians does not.)
2. Introduce the idea of being permeable to a foreign culture, of being open to it and accepting of it. Ask students to work individually and rank the other seven students in their groups, and themselves, in order of cultural permeability and openness.
3. In fours, the students compare the rankings they have produced.
4. Now ask the whole class to organise themselves in a single line across the space available, with people who feel themselves very close to 'Englishness' (or whatever your target culture is) at one end of the line and people who feel that 'Englishness' is alien to them at the other end of the line.
5. Ask them to justify the position they have chosen in the line, talking to the people on either side of them.
6. Give each student a newspaper and ask them to scan through and pick an article that they feel is particularly English, either because of its content, or its approach to the topic, its style, its prejudices or whatever. (This involves them in comparing the paper with ones in their own country/ies.)
7. Students work in threes and explain to each other what is in their article and why they think it's particularly English.

111

8. (Optional) Bring the class together. In turn ask the different groups to say a little about the highlights of their discussion in threes.

Variation

The idea also applies to English language newspapers published in such countries as Nigeria and India and to the notions of 'Nigerianness' or 'Indianness'.

Mario Rinvolucri

7 Theme texts, affective texts, stories

Like the activities in Chapter 6, the nine recipes in this chapter all involve the use of one or more reading texts to stimulate and structure some sort of classroom work that goes beyond reading. Where many activities in Chapter 6 can be used with different types of reading text, the activities in this chapter can only be used with certain types of text. Consequently each one is accompanied by one or more example texts to get you started. But don't let our choices of example distract you from noticing that each activity in this chapter can be done with texts you find (or write) yourself. Another difference from Chapter 6 is that most of the activities here presuppose that learning proceeds best in an environment that permits occasional consideration of emotive topics.

In this chapter, you will find the following activities: 'Stories with opposite messages' (7.1) involves the use of two texts on the same theme. The aim is to prompt your students to tell stories on this theme which have a message, moral or outcome that is as different as possible from the ones you present.

'Flip the frame' (7.2) works most straightforwardly when you begin with one or more texts which exemplify some sort of cultural stereotype. I won't tell you how this works here, but the results tend to be very interesting for all concerned.

'Milk bottles and dustbins' (7.3) exemplifies a way of using texts to generate discussion on an emotive topic.

'Creative criminality' (7.4) and 'Are you a worthy owner?' (7.5) demonstrate ingenious ways of using texts to prompt and structure out-of-class writing. The latter suggests, additionally, a way of getting students reading each other's homework.

'Inseparable' (7.6) shows how you can introduce a longish reading text with a problem-solving exercise.

'Correcting the teller' (7.7) is about a way of structuring student-to-student storytelling in pairs or small groups. The material used is a story and a cartoon depiction of key events in that story. Every teacher knows stories they could use in this way. You are hereby challenged to draw the cartoons!

'Comparing texts – a person-related way' (7.8) describes a demanding and highly rewarding exercise based on the use of autobiographical articles.

'Discussion from key words' (7.9) offers a simple but very effective way of stimulating student discussion of any recently read short story.

7.1 Stories with opposite messages

Level
Elementary–Intermediate

Materials
Two brief stories on one theme (examples below); you need a few copies of one of them

Time
20–30 minutes

Focus
Telling stories

Stories are a pithy, natural way of explaining cultural differences. The stories given below touch on friendship, authority and rule systems. Of course, you can use this antithetical stories technique for explaining many other areas.

Procedure

1. Tell the class the first of your two anecdotes. It's better to tell than to read. Your grip on students' minds will be stronger.
2. Once the students have had time to react to the story, ask them to produce a story of their own about a policeman and a person the policeman knows as different as possible to the story you told. Tell the students to write their stories in exactly five sentences, neither more nor less. Go round and help with language during the writing phase.
3. Ask students to pass their stories round, reading as many as they can. While this is going on, hand six students copies of your second story, the one in five sentences.

Variation

Divide the class in two and send half of them out of the room for two minutes. Tell the first story to the students in the classroom and ask them to write five-sentence antithetical stories. Go outside and tell the other half of the class the second story. They write stories antithetical to this one. In the exchange phase, the students tell each other the stories they have written and the stories they were originally told.

Story one (for oral telling)

Policeman and friend playing golf.
Both went to bar.
Friend drank two pints of beer.
Friend drove off.
Policeman followed him.
Stopped him and breathalysed him.
Over limit by a point or two.
Policeman charged him.
No more golf – policeman did not understand why.
[Note: This story is given here in skeleton form; elaborate it to suit the level of your class.]

Story two

Abdul's taxi ignored the red light and a police car immediately gave chase. Abdul drove as fast as possible to the house of a friend, who happened to be a police captain. As he rang the doorbell a patrolman rushed up the path to arrest him. The captain opened the door of the house and slapped the patrolman in the face. 'What are you doing trying to arrest my guest on my doorstep?'

Note

Expand/Embellish these two story skeletons to suit the level of your group.

Acknowledgement

I owe the first two stories to Jim Brims. For more storytelling techniques see Morgan and Rinvolucri (1983) and Lindstromberg (1990).

Mario Rinvolucri

7.2   Flip the frame

Level
Elementary–Advanced (depending on
the text)

Materials
For the main activity, two versions of a text,
half a class set of each

Time
15–30 minutes

Focus
Reading/listening to narrative;
cultural awareness

Often, when we read, we bring our pre-formed certainties and prejudices
to the task. This exercise gives students a chance to notice how a 'flipped
frame' can change the way they understand a text. Creating a flipped
frame involves choosing a text and then doctoring or retyping it so that
everything is the same except the protagonists. Often, when these
change, the stereotypes we operate with leap out at us.

1. Find a brief text and make a 'flipped' version of it, as in the examples
   below.
2. Make half a class set of each version.

Procedure

1. Give Text A out to half your students and Text B to the other half. If
   you have equal numbers of males and females in the class, you could
   give the Master story to the women/girls and the Mistress story to the
   men/boys, or the other way round!
2. They read their stories without talking to people who have the other
   story.
3. Pair Text A and Text B people. They tell their stories orally and then
   compare the written texts.

Text A: The Master

A man was married to a shrew who ordered him around the livelong
day. Once, when she had several women friends calling on her, she
wanted to show off before them what absolute control she had over her
husband:

'Francis!' she ordered, 'get under the table!' Without a word the man
climbed under the table. 'Now, Francis, come out!' she again com-

manded. 'I won't, I won't!' he defied her angrily. 'I'll show you that I'm still master in this house!'

Text B: The Mistress

A woman was married to a bully who ordered her around the livelong day. Once, when he had several of his friends calling on him, he wanted to show off before them what absolute control he had over his wife:

'Frances!' he ordered, 'get under the table!' Without a word the woman crawled under the table. 'Now, Frances, come out!' he again commanded. 'I won't, I won't!' she defied him angrily. 'I'll show you that I'm still mistress in this house!'

Alternative text

HUSBAND/DOG LOST

From: Addenbrookes Hospital

When: Thursday 8 August

White, rough-coated husband/dog with one tan ear. Wearing a leather/dog collar.

Have you seen him/her wandering around or perhaps even befriended him/her? If so, please make his/her return possible by phoning C.8428189 or 3566475 anytime.

This is a much loved companion of some years, any information would be very welcome.

REWARD OFFERED

Variation 1

1. Record this story onto a portable cassette machine. (Expand the skeleton into a fluent text; in so doing you can make the language easier or harder):

    Bear in Canadian wilds. Loves travelling. Sees brochures offering bear holidays in Frankfurt Zoo. Takes plane to Frankfurt – zoo people put him in a cage. Bear paces up and down, 'One, two, three, four, five, six, one, two, three ...' Looks sad. Frankfurt people don't like him. Zoo people ship him back to Canadian wilds. Bear paces backwards and forwards, 'One, two, three, four, five, six, one, two, three ...' After a week of this the bear suddenly paces, 'One, two, three, four, five, six, seven, eight, nine, ten ...'

2. Give the recording to half your class to listen to outside class in a corridor or open space while you tell the second version of the story to everyone else. But, in the second version the keepers from Frankfurt Zoo go to the Canadian wilds with a tranquilliser gun and capture the bear. In this version he does not read travel brochures!

Variation 2

1. Tell the class this story. Adjust the language to present your class with a reasonable challenge. Describe the two men as being of whatever nationality is the normal butt of jokes in the country you are in:

   Two men saved up to buy a car. They scraped and pinched till they had enough money to buy a Mercedes. There it stood, gleaming black. They went out for a trial run. Onto a motorway – faster and faster. The driver sees a blue flashing light in the mirror. Police pull them over, order them out of the car. A police sergeant draws a chalk circle on the ground. He orders the two men to stand inside the circle. He tells them they will be arrested if they step beyond the chalk line. The police then smash up the Mercedes. They kick in the doors, throw a brick through the windscreen and slash the tyres. The two men laugh and laugh. The sergeant asks why. One of the men says: 'While you were smashing the car, we were jumping in and out of the circle!'

2. Three or four weeks later, tell the same story but describe the two men as Germans or as being of some other country people may resent or envy because of its past or present power. The story may well take on a quite different meaning from the first time you told it.

Acknowledgements

'The Master' is taken from Brown (1979). I learned the second version of the bear story from Hans Jörg Betz and both versions of the car story from Rick Shepherd.

Mario Rinvolucri

7.3 Milk bottles and dustbins

Level
Elementary–Advanced

Time
50 minutes

Focus
Discussion; very concentrated reading

Materials
Enough chalk or board pens and board space for as many as 15 people to work at the board at the same time. A class set of readings on an emotive topic

---

This activity describes a way of dealing with any emotive topic. The procedure described here relates to the example texts below.

Procedure

1. Ask up to 15 people to come to the board and be ready to draw whatever comes into their heads when you give them a key word. Ask them to draw all at once and not to wait to see what others are drawing. Give them the key word *racism*.
2. Go to the back of the room and ask people about the meaning of what they have drawn. There is often a complex meaning behind apparently clear drawings.
3. With their permission, clear the board and divide it into two sections:

QUESTIONS   COMMENTS

4. Hand out the 'Milk bottles' and 'Dustbins' readings and ask the class to go through these silently. If they have any questions about language or content, they should come up and put them up on the board, leaving a space below for someone else to answer. If they have thoughts or comments, they should write these up on the other side of the board, leaving space for comments on their comments.
   In the right class atmosphere a silent dialogue will build up on the board.
5. Encourage discussion. The silence may have been thought provoking and, to some extent, frustrating. Speech is the way out of such frustration.

119

Theme texts, affective texts, stories

Acknowledgement

I learnt this silent dialogue technique from an Australian colleague on a training course in Canterbury in 1978.

Milk bottles
'Kusim's milk bottles have been emptied, the contents seeping in dirty-white streams over the muddied concrete at her front door. It has happened every morning for a week. She gets up specially early to bring in the milk, before the children are awake. Her slim body shivers in the November cold as she pulls on her dressing gown and hurries downstairs. She undoes the bolts, top and bottom, and opens the door. The rain drips in the dark from the gutter above her head. The street is silent – there is no one about.

But she is not early enough. Whoever it is has been there before her. The bottles have been emptied; the step will have to be scrubbed again.

Now she has cancelled her order with the milkman, and will walk each morning to the corner shop instead.'

(Marion Molteno, *A Language in Common*, The Women's Press 1987, p. 50.)

Dustbins
'With Tejinder, it's her dustbin. She puts it out on Monday evening, to be emptied Tuesday morning early. A dog knocks it over, every week, before the dustmen get there. At least that's what the neighbour said, when she came back from shopping to watch Tejinder bending her large, heavy body to pick up the mess and shove it back into the overflowing bin; to wait for next week's collection. 'Must have been the dogs', the neighbour said, and stood and watched for a few minutes. Friendlily. 'Dogs.'

'Maybe dogs', says Tejinder. 'But not *every* week dogs. And these dogs are clever, only *my* bin are they wanting. All other people's bin in this street they are leaving.'

'Dogs *are* clever', says Jaya. 'In East Africa our dogs were barking at African people passing. Never barking at Indians. Dogs do it for people, people smile quietly, clean hands.'

(Ibid., p. 51.)

Mario Rinvolucri

120

7.4 Creative criminality

Level
Intermediate–Advanced

Materials
A class set of crime readings; access to a photocopier

Time
30 minutes in the first class;
15 minutes in the third

Focus
Reading; writing; asking questions

This activity describes an excellent way of getting students to produce interesting homework. It also suggests how to use the homework in a later class in order to establish that virtuous cycle wherein interested readers encourage writers to put more into their writing which makes readers more interested in reading which ... and so it goes on. The procedure described here relates to the example texts below.

Procedure

In the first class

1. Write the following words on the board: 'BIRD' 'POLICE' 'HOME'. Tell the students that the words are key ones in a story you have in your head. They ask you yes/no questions to find the story:

   'In Taiwan Province of China thieves tow your car away and leave a homing pigeon where your car was. Attached to one of the pigeon's legs is a message which tells you to put 1,000 dollars in the container on the other leg and then to release the bird. You are then, at a given time, to go to a designated place to pick your car up.'

2. Hand out the crime readings and ask the students to read through them for homework. Point out how inventive criminals have become in the last 20 years. Ask them to write you accounts of new, inventive forms of crime they have recently heard of and encourage them to ask around for information.

In the second class

3. Take in their crime homework. Do whatever you normally do with homework and then make a class set of photocopies of the best papers.

121

In the third class

4. Hand out the copies for everyone to read. (If the homework is worth doing, then it's worth someone other than the teacher reading it.)

Crime readings

A. A group of thieves in Germany realised that certain ticket machines identified bank notes by minute focus on the corner of the left eye of the note. The criminals cut corners of left eyes out of banknotes and glued them to similar sized bits of paper. This way they milked ticket machines. The banknotes they took the bit of eye from mostly passed unnoticed. They must have enjoyed beating the system because they couldn't make that much money.

B.

Beware of the fakes: Sophisticated forgeries circulating, warn police

MOST counterfeit banknotes can be spotted by vigilant retailers, but police warn that some increasingly sophisticated forgeries are circulating. Counterfeit notes produced on a quality photostat machine with special paper look genuine enough, but will not pass careful scrutiny or a check under ultraviolet light.

The counterfeits which police are most concerned about are printed by plate, a very skilful process, and are likely to fool even the most careful bartender or shop owner.

People deliberately passing forgeries will typically try to buy an item of small value with a fake note of reasonably large denomination to get the maximum amount of change in good money.

There are reports that they operate in small gangs, targeting retail areas. When one is able to pass a counterfeit to a bartender or shopkeeper, two or three others will then visit the same place. Obvious clues to watch for are a missing watermark, the vertical silver thread not appearing as an uninterrupted line when held up to the light, and the quality of the paper.

Cambridge police crime prevention officer, Sgt. Ted Easy, said even the best notes produced on photocopy machines have a sheen which is obvious under a small ultraviolet light machine. But the most sophisticated notes printed by plate will often pass a check under a conventional ultraviolet light machine.

Cranfield Laboratories in Bedfordshire have developed a new machine, utilising a combination of lighting techniques, which they claim will detect even the most state-of-the-art counterfeits.

The developers of the machine, called 'counter fit', are so sure that they are ahead of the fraudsters that they guarantee to reimburse any fake notes which get through. Counterfeiters, however, pay little attention to guarantees and their ever-growing expertise suggests they will eventually outsmart the new machine.

(*Cambridge Town Crier* 12.9.92, p. 9)

Mario Rinvolucri

7.5 Are you a worthy owner?

Level
Intermediate–Advanced

Materials
A class set of readings about ownership
(examples below); access to a photocopier

Time
In class 1: 5 minutes
In class 2: 3 minutes
In class 3: 30 minutes

Focus
All four main skills

Isn't it bizarre that most homework is read only by the teacher? Here is an alternative you can apply to any interesting student-written work.

Procedure

Class 1

1. Give out the readings and ask the students to write a page (as homework) about any similar experiences they have had or know of. Add that other students may eventually read what they write.

Class 2

2. Take in the homework.
3. Choose the ten most interesting pages. Correct any major errors, working within students' wording as much as possible.
4. Photocopy a class set of each of these ten sheets.

Class 3

5. Give out the copies of students' writing and allow time for reading and reaction.

Acknowledgement

To a class at the Cambridge Academy in summer '92 that made me realise how powerful the Ishiguro reading is, and especially to Susana and Martine.

The readings

1.

I have heard tell
that in Lithuania when a
man buys a horse he is asked
to get underneath it and lift it
an inch or two off the ground. If
he fails the test, he is not man
enough to purchase the
horse and the deal falls
through.

2.

'It is of the first importance to us', she went on, 'that the house our father built should pass to one he would have approved of and deemed worthy of it. Of course, circumstances oblige us to consider the financial aspect, but this is strictly secondary. We have therefore set a price.'

At this point, the younger sister, who had barely spoken, presented me with an envelope, and they watched me sternly as I opened it. Inside was a single sheet of paper, blank but for a figure written elegantly with an ink brush. I was about to express my astonishment at the low price, but then saw from the faces before me that further discussion of finances would be considered distasteful. The elder sister said simply: 'It will not be in the interests of any of you to try to outbid one another. We are not interested in receiving anything beyond the quoted price. What we mean to do from here on is to conduct an auction of prestige.'

They had come in person, she explained, to ask formally on behalf of the Sugimura family that I submit myself – along, of course, with the other three applicants – to a closer investigation of my background and credentials. A suitable buyer could thus be chosen.

It was an eccentric procedure, but I saw nothing objectionable about it; it was, after all, much the same as being involved in a marriage negotiation. Indeed, I felt somewhat flattered to be considered by this old and hidebound family as a worthy candidate. When I gave my consent to the investigation, and expressed my gratitude to them, the younger sister addressed me for the first time, saying: 'Our father was a cultured man, Mr Ono. He had much respect for artists. Indeed, he knew of your work.'

(from *An Artist of the Floating World*, Kazuo Ishiguro, Faber, 1986, pp. 8–9)

3.

'I was around seven years old then. I was
growing up very fast so my clothes were soon
becoming too small. One day, a gypsy woman
knocked on our door, asking for money, food or
clothes. My mother, without saying anything to
me, gave her all the clothes that didn't fit me
anymore. Among them, there was a dark blue
dress which I liked very much. Some days later
I was shopping in the city centre when I saw a
little gypsy girl wearing 'my' blue dress. She
was begging from passers-by, holding a baby in
her arms. The first feeling I had, as I recall,
was anger. I couldn't understand how she had
managed to get 'my' dress. Then I guessed that
she must have been given it by my mother, or
perhaps she had picked it up from a dustbin.
Anyway, I felt rather disappointed to see that
such a poor human being was wearing my
favourite dress without my permission. The
feeling lasted only one minute, I can remember, but was deeply experienced. I soon
realised that it was a stupid and fairly mean
thought.'

(Susana Irigaray)

4.

'When we moved in and I started to meet
neighbours, I was surprised and upset to hear people
referring to our home with the former owners' name.
'So, you live at the Verhaerens'?', they would say.
And I began to realise the house and the firm were
part of the village history.

'Later on, little by little, we got to learn a few
things about the people who had lived there. They
were Catholics. The father had died some 18 months
before we moved in and had been ill for some time. A
room had been specially decorated for an old widow
who had come to look after him. The mother had died
long before when the children were still teenagers.
The family had told us she had had a nervous
breakdown and had committed suicide. We later heard
that she might have been murdered and that her son
had been suspected. Anyway, the children grew up
alone. And there were - and are still - many clues
as to how they spent their time, for example, they
used to organise parties for their friends in the
warehouse and this was not always in the taste of
the local community.

'Anyway, for many older people many of these
memories are still alive and unconsciously they
believe that we must be the same sort of people.

'That's why I would suggest that, if anyone wants to
buy a house, they should try and get as much
information as they can about the former occupants
and then decide if they can accept the image that
will be imposed on them by the local community.'

(Martine Virgo-Dubois)

Mario Rinvolucri

7.6   Inseparable

Level
Intermediate–Advanced

Time
30 to 40 minutes

Focus
Discussion; reading

Materials
A class set of a text on a controversial topic (example below)

'Inseparable' demonstrates a way of rounding off work on a controversial topic by handing out a text for students to read at home. The planning process, though, might well reverse this order. That is, you may begin with a text which not only suggests the topic but also a brain teaser with which to get the ball rolling. As you will see.

The procedure described here relates to the example text below

Procedure

1. Dictate this story:
   'A woman shot and killed a person. She was arrested and brought to trial. The jury returned a verdict of guilty. The judge had no idea how to sentence her.'
2. Tell your students you have the solution to this mystery story. (The murderess was a Siamese twin.) They are to ask you yes/no questions to discover it. As they question you, they may grope for legal words. Help them with these and write the new vocabulary up on the board as the questioning proceeds.
3. Tell them that while the story above is fiction, winter 1991 saw Siamese twins born in Poland. This is what one of the doctors said about the twins soon after their birth:
   'We have three choices: to separate them straight down the middle with a leg each, to give one both legs and lose the other baby or leave them as they are.'
   Group the students in threes to discuss what the doctors should do.
4. Now ask students to read the text in class or at home.

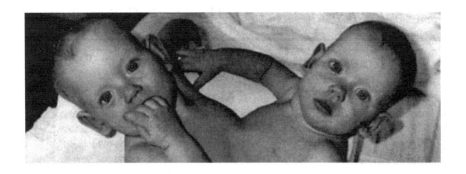

Krakow's babies

'We had three choices' says anaesthetist Chris Kobywiz, who was present at the birth. 'To separate them straight down the middle with a leg each, to give one both legs and lose the other baby, or leave them as they are. I'm just glad I don't have to decide.'

He explained how, soon after they were born, one of the girls fell very ill. The doctors secretly hoped she would die, leaving them with no choice but to save the other. But little Julia (who is on the right) slowly gained strength and is as strong as her sister.

The question of whether or how they should be separated has divided doctors at the Polish-American children's hospital in Krakow, both morally and professionally. Some have complained about being forced to play God by going against nature.

According to one young pediatrician, Peter Wojechowski, the girls have an equal chance of survival if left to grow as they are. 'I think any attempt to divide them will end in failure. They will both die from the trauma of surgery. The rate of survival for this kind of operation is very low and in some countries they only do primary surgery to make their lives more comfortable. I would simply treat the one bad leg and leave well alone.

But other doctors fear the girls would end up as sideshow freaks – like Chang and Eng – the original Siamese twins, who earned a fortune as international touring attractions. They lived for 60 years, married normal women and fathered 21 children between them. Dr Adam Bysiek says he would not like to be the one to make the final decision, but favours separation: 'I know the risk is that one might die, maybe even both, but we must try to do what we can.'

The hospital has separated three other Siamese twins over the past 10 years. One pair died and one each of the remaining sets survive. Another pair of twins – who were not divided because their parents refused to give their consent – died after a few weeks. Several other Siamese children have been successfully separated in the West.

Debra and Julia have not seen their parents since they were born. The couple, who have other children, returned to their home in Gdansk after giving the hospital permission to decide the children's fate. Since then doctors have been testing to find out which organs belong to whom. They have determined that each child has a leg, but share a bladder, an intestinal tract and a gut.

They have tentatively agreed on a 50:50 split, which according to Dr Bysiek, is the only viable option. 'We are trying to save both by giving each a leg and doing reconstruction surgery to make them whole. They will never be completely normal, but we shall try our best to give both a chance of survival.'

(*Weekend Guardian*, 31.8.91, p. 7.)

Mario Rinvolucri

7.7 Correcting the teller

Level
Intermediate

Time
20 minutes

Focus
Storytelling; reading out loud; listening and commenting

Materials
Photocopies of a story for half the class; photocopies of an uncaptioned cartoon version of the story for the other half of the class (examples below)

This activity practises interactive storytelling. That is, some students tell, the others correct and guide.

Procedure

1. On the board, write a few stock expressions that might be used by a listener to correct another person's telling of a story which the listener knows better. For example:
   'It's not quite like that.'
   'She didn't ... She ... -ed ... '
   'No, she did something else.'
   'No. What she did was ... '
   Then give your students the chance to practise the correction phrases. Tell (with glaring errors) a bit of some story all or most of them are likely to know well – 'Hansel and Gretel', perhaps. Elicit corrections. Now say that they are going to do something similar.
2. Form pairs (A and B). Give copies of the story to all the As and copies of the cartoon strip to all the Bs. The As read their story silently while the Bs, who have got the cartoon strip, decide what the story is. Circulate and help out with vocabulary.
3. The Bs then tell their stories to their partners. The As' task is to listen, to correct whenever necessary, and to help with verbal prompts if their partners get stuck or start to wander far off track.
4. When the Bs have finished telling their versions of the story the As read out the text.

Note

This activity works best if your cartoons are a bit less than 100 per cent clear about the story. This means almost anyone can draw their own cartoon strips. So, if you find, or hear, a nice little story, get out your drawing pen ...

The dog and the rabbit

One afternoon Mrs Stone decided to visit her friend Mary King, who lived in a nice house with a large garden in the suburbs. Mrs Stone took her dog with her. While the women were having coffee on the porch, the dog was running around in the garden. The two friends were, however, very shocked when the dog appeared after some time with a dead rabbit in his mouth. Mary King was appalled since she knew that her neighbour kept rabbits in a hutch in his garden. As the dog and the rabbit were muddy, the women thought that the dog had killed the rabbit and had then tried to bury it. The two women took the rabbit and carefully cleaned it in the bathroom. When it got dark, they sneaked through the hedge into their neighbour's garden and quietly put the rabbit into an empty hutch.

The following afternoon, Mary's neighbour, the one with the rabbits, spotted her in the garden and beckoned her over. She went to the hedge feeling very guilty. 'You know what?', her neighbour said, 'Yesterday morning I found one of my rabbits dead in its hutch. So I buried it in the garden. And this morning,' he started to whisper, 'it came back from its grave. It's back in its hutch! So this time I'm going to take it to a proper pet cemetery.'

Günter Gerngross and Herbert Puchta

7.8 Comparing texts – a person-related way

Level
Intermediate – Advanced

Time
Around 2 hours, preferably in a single whole morning or whole afternoon session

Focus
Aspects of vocabulary: difficulty, affect, imitability, covetability,

Materials
Two texts containing information which can be compared and a class set of an instruction handout (examples below)

There are two special features of this series of interrelated exercises: At Step 1 the unknown vocabulary is accepted as unknown rather than laboriously explained. And at Step 4, the students cross out all those parts of the text that don't satisfy a particular criterion. Giving the learners the power to sidestep understanding unknown vocabulary and to cross out substantial parts of a target language text are rare but important confidence-building opportunities.

This sequence of exercises builds up from vocabulary exercises such as those advocated by Morgan and Rinvolucri (as in Morgan and Rinvolucri 1986) to an original reading exercise (Step 4) which is virtually a writing exercise, although only crossing out and no original writing is required. It works well for me on first term English for Academic Purposes courses where the groups tend to be large, drawn from various subject departments and thus consist of students with few academic interests/specialisms in common. Our work at this stage has to (a) relate aspects of the new culture our students have recently arrived in, (b) rehearse study skills that have general application, and (c) raise awareness of real, contemporary language usage. The texts below are suitable for our context – any comparable texts are equally suitable.

Preparation

Prepare the instruction handout according to the content of the texts. Make a double class set of each of your chosen two texts. (Everyone will get two of each.) If possible, arrange the desks higgledy-piggledy around the classroom.

Procedure

Distribute handouts and one copy of the texts to each student. From now onwards your role is to make sure that the students understand the instructions and are working productively. Only offer assistance or comments if invited.

The procedure described here relates to the example texts below.

Instruction handout

1. Working individually, choose *either* Sara Parkin's *or* Clive Sinclair's Decade and make a list of all the words in it that,
   – you don't understand and,
   – you don't use in your own writing but would like to.
   When you've done this, find a partner who's made a list for the same text as you and together divide all your words into three categories. You must choose the appropriate categories together. When you've done this, leave your partner and sit by yourself.
2. Take the text you didn't work with before. Make a list of all the phrases you admire.
   When you've done this, find a new partner who's made a list for the same text and together classify each phrase as *male* or *female*. When you've done this, find another new partner and sit together.
3. Arrange each of Sara Parkin's ten paragraphs on a scale from most to least like Clive Sinclair's in terms of the views she expresses. Then do the same for Clive Sinclair's nine paragraphs.
   When you've done this, leave your partner and sit by yourself.
4. Take a new copy of both articles. Cross out every sentence written by Clive Sinclair that Sara Parkin could not have written and every sentence written by Sara Parkin that Clive Sinclair could not have written.
   When you've done this, find another new partner who's reached the same stage as you and compare your results.

Extension

5. This step can be done in class or set as voluntary homework:
   – Either:
   Write two to three paragraphs explaining which of the two people you would rather be.
   – Or:
   Write two to three paragraphs comparing their careers to date and the future prospects of each of the two.
   When you've done this, either in class or as homework, find two other people who've reached the same stage and in a team of three discuss the ways in which each of your pieces of writing could be improved. Write any critical comments you have on each piece.

My Decade

Sara Parkin, 43, is set to become an important political voice in the Nineties. As international liaison secretary for the Green Party in the UK and one of four co-secretaries for the Greens in Europe, she is emerging as popular, if unofficial, leader of the party. She lives outside Lyons with her husband Max, and her two sons, Colin, 15, and Douglas, 13. She talked to MARK COOPER.

SARA PARKIN

1980 Joins the Green Party's national council as representative for Yorkshire and Humberside.

1981 Moves to Lyons with husband Max Parkin, who works for the World Health Organisation.

1983 Becomes international liaison secretary for the British Green Party.

1985 Becomes one of four co-secretaries for the European Greens.

1987 The Green Party contests 134 seats at the general election in Britain and wins 1.4 per cent of the vote.

1989 Publishes the *International Guide to Green Parties*. Greens win 15 per cent of the vote in June's European elections. *Spitting Image* prepares a puppet of her.

It was in 1979 that I started to learn about politics. I had moved down from Scotland to Leeds, which was the most northerly outpost of the Ecology Party, and went to the local meetings, and the more I got to know about it, the more I suspected that putting pressure on from outside was not enough. I went to see Keith Joseph, who was my MP, on behalf of the Conversation Society.

He had produced a little booklet called the *Right Approach to the Economy*, which we felt was not an awful lot of good to the environment. So I did my homework and turned up stiff with facts at his constituency surgery. I remember, he opened the door, a swing door, and called me in and let it swing back in my face, and he sat at a desk so he was much higher than I was, and when he realised that I wanted to talk about economic policy and not holes in the pavement, he got rather cross. I found myself standing up and saying, 'In that case, I'm going to stand against you in the next election, if that's what it takes to get my views over.' He sprang to his feet, became very charming, and held the door open for me on the way out.

I think politicians lead a very artificial life. When I have posed questions to senior politicians, they have asked me what I would do in a certain situation. They are often astonished, because what I come up with is something that would never have entered their minds but yet would be quite reasonable to think of if you were leading an ordinary life.

Fortunately, I've had a wide range of experience. I've always been very curious. Nothing, even the bad experiences I may have had, has gone to waste. I've worked as a nurse and seen road accidents. I've worked in family planning and seen people at their most intimate time. I've been to India with my husband, who was working on a small-pox epidemic.

When my husband's work took us to France in 1981, I began working with the growing parties in other countries. I started off with just a couple of files, and now I have them wall to ceiling.

I've been married for 20 years. He's a superb man. Marriage should be a place from which you do things, not a constraint. Max feels one politician in the family is enough. He is more pessimistic about the future than I am. I don't neglect what is really important at home. Women are always guilty. While I'm sitting here, I think I should be with the kids, but women cannot be ruled by their guilt. If I was looking after the children all the time, I'd feel guilty about not doing this.

I actually believe that the green movement represents the greatest shift in human thinking since the Enlightenment. Francis Bacon said we must torture nature's secrets from her. Now we're seeing that we cannot be supreme. Our economy is totally dependent on our environment and we've distanced everything we do from that reality. The Greens are different because in politics you are traditionally negotiating the interests of one group against another, whereas we have put the future of the species on the negotiating table.

Green consumerism? *The Green Consumer Guide* gives you everything from shampoo to champagne, but there's nothing there about arms or about consuming less. Women in the Third World put pots on their heads and walk 20 miles to get water from the river. We get in our cars and drive 20 miles to buy it in plastic bottles in the supermarket. So what is progress, what is civilisation?

People are beginning to make these connections in their everyday life, so when we got 15 per cent of the vote in June, a lot of organisations commissioned more detailed polls to see if it was a flash in the pan. They discovered a big shift of values, and women are especially concerned because historically they have had responsibility for continuity. It was us who went and collected the berries, looked after the children. It didn't really matter whether the men came back or not, as long as a few did.

Businessmen may actually be the last to become green, but they will eventually have to go because we have no choice. We're all going to have to green our lifestyles in order to survive. Is it going to be forced on us by external, maybe unpleasant circumstances, or are we going to do it in an orderly way, by choice? That is the question of the Nineties.

THE SUNDAY CORRESPONDENT, 5 NOVEMBER 1989

My Decade

Sir Clive Sinclair, 49, is Britain's best known inventor. His success as a businessman has been erratic – the Sinclair C5 electric trike was one of the most publicised flops of the Eighties. The chairman of British MENSA, he lives alone in Mayfair and has three children by his ex-wife Ann.

CLIVE SINCLAIR

1980 Launched Sinclair Z-80 home computer, the first available for less than £100.

1982 Launched ZX Spectrum computer amid controversy over delivery delays.

1983 Microvision mini-television launched. Customers complain of waiting up to a year for it. Sinclair is knighted and made Young Businessman of the Year.

1984 QL Computer launched; many did not work. Sinclair divorced.

1985 The Sinclair C5 goes into liquidation within months of launch with £8.6 million losses.

1986 His rival, Amstrad's Alan Sugar, buys Sinclair Research.

1988-9 Work begins on plans for a cheap portable telephone and revolutionary lightweight bicycle.

I don't think of myself as having failed in any way in the Eighties. I don't think of the C5 as a success or a failure. An explorer has to explore blind alleyways to find the right way. People say, oh, you got the C5 wrong, but the C5 was a stepping-stone to the electric car. The products are totally radical, so you'll have trouble with all of them. I'm only disappointed because it set the electric car back.

There have been depressing moments, however, like when Sinclair Electronics got into cash-flow problems. We had to sell out to Alan Sugar. But I didn't find that painful. I also went through a sad period after I was divorced by my wife, an in some ways I am lonelier now than I was. On the other hand, I have adjusted, and I like my life.

If I had to characterise the Eighties, I would mention the extension of freedom, · the concentration on the individual, the breaking down of international barriers, and the loss of American world dominance. Ecology got into Western politics – about time too – and that will have colossal implications.

The Eighties started in 1979 with the coming of the Conservative government. I feel very proud and lucky to live at the same time as someone with Thatcher's extraordinary ability and courage. But it has had a downside. The weak have gone to the wall. I

went to Newcastle recently and people are ill-fed. Long-term unemployment grinds you down. But it's an absolutely necessary evil. It was always there – the Government simply exposed it. Society has changed. Morality has declined – the rise of the lager lout is in evidence. Perhaps that is the price we pay for a free society.

In technology, it has been a quiet decade. The main innovation has been the personal computer, which is simply a convenient mental tool; it hasn't changed the way people live. But I think its significance will be seen in retrospect as the beginning of something immensely important: the rise of artificial intelligence. The creation of machines as intelligent as human beings is not far off – reproductive machines that can design themselves. This is the way to wealth: to replace men with machines. Machines can work as doctors, dentists, teachers; every old person could be looked after. It is frightening in some ways, because it raises a lot of difficult religious questions about the nature of existence. But these are questions we have to confront.

I recognise that the Eighties, like the Sixties, have seen the rise of a sort of technophobia. And certainly technology can have its dark side – look at the atomic bomb. The green movement is basically rational, where the Sixties movement was irrational, but I disagree with the greens fundamentally about where we should look for progress. We need economic growth – it has turned London from a squalid, smog-ridden mess into somewhere pleasant to live. Technology is the way to solve ecological problems, not politics. You cannot solve the carbon dioxide problem by saying to people, 'Don't drive your car' – you do it by developing an electric car. People say technology is the cause of pollution, but it's the cure.

Another obvious trend has been the globalisation of business. Countries are beginning to lose their nationality. As this develops, businesses will not feel restricted by nations, and national governments will begin to lose control. The companies will then be a danger to national sovereignty. So governments are going to have to get together to control it. I think that global government will be a tendency in the Nineties. It is probably a good thing, in my opinion, but it will make the world a more boring place.

Britain in the Nineties could be the richest country in Europe. Simultaneously, there may be a revival of the hippie ethic; they'll be able to get away with it because there will be an abundance of jobs instead of a shortage. And I expect a shift to the Left. These things do seem to go in 14-year cycles.

I have not undergone any major changes in the way I look at life. My lack of belief in God is as intense as ever. The biggest change for me has been the move from Cambridge to London. I like the anonymity here. I am a lot richer than I was at the beginning of the Eighties, but not as rich as I was in the middle.

THE SUNDAY CORRESPONDENT, 1 OCTOBER 1989

Acknowledgements

The word categorisation ideas in Steps 1 and 2 are to be found in Morgan and Rinvolucri (1986, pp. 108–11) who acknowledge earlier sources themselves.

Peter Grundy

7.9 Discussion from key words

Level
Intermediate–Advanced

Time
20–30 minutes for Procedure 1
20–45 minutes for Procedure 2

Focus
Discussion of a short story or novella

Materials
Optional: two posters bearing lists of key words

I had often wondered how to get students to talk about short stories and novellas after they have read them, then I (re?)discovered this simple idea. It has always worked well, provided most of the class has completed the reading!

Procedure 1

1. Pick out fifteen to twenty key words or short phrases from the reading and write them on the board in the order they first come up. For example, for early chapters of L. P. Hartley's *The Go-Between* I recently wrote a list beginning: 'box', 'magnet', 'spoiled my life', 'zodiac', 'vanquished', 'three curses', 'spells'.
2. Tell the class that the words on the list will be discussed one by one and that, going around the class in a predetermined order (e.g. left to right), everyone will have at least one turn to make a short comment. (Sometimes it helps to say that no one's comment can be longer than 20 words or so.) Add that anyone who doesn't have anything to say when their turn comes can say something like: 'Someone's already said what I was going to say', 'I can't think of anything to add', 'Can I have more time to think?', 'I'm afraid I'll have to pass'. (The first time or two you do this activity it helps to write a couple of these sentences on the board.)
3. Say as little as possible while students are speaking. I generally do nothing but circle the word being discussed and occasionally point to whoever's turn it is just to maintain the pace of the rota. After going around the class once with one word, ask, 'Does anyone have anything else to add, in brief or at length?' When comments have dried up, cross the word out and go on to the next.
   After you've led this activity once yourself, try having a student take over your role.

Variations

- When dealing with important events, situations and characters, have one round of factual comments and a second of opinions.
- If you have a class of more than 18 students, after you do the activity in plenary with the first word, divide the class into two groups. In each group, one student takes your role. For this variation you might need to have two posters with your list of words on, one poster for each 'teacher'.

Rationale

Writing up words or short phrases instead of sentences leaves more for students to say. Following a set rota gives everyone a turn. Stipulating that comments must be short encourages responses from less talkative students in two ways. Firstly, even shy students can generally manage to say something like, 'There was a diary in the box' which, though short, is a vital piece of information. Secondly, talkative students can't blurt out everything there is to say about one word on one turn.

Procedure 2

After you have tried Procedure 1 with a class, try Procedure 2, which gets you talking even less and students even more.
1. Form groups of three or four. (If you have a few students who haven't done the reading, either spread them around different groups or send them off somewhere to catch up with the reading.) Each group makes a list of ten key words or short phrases from the reading. Perhaps suggest they avoid writing down names. It could just be my imagination but it seems to me that students say more if the key is something like 'sister' or 'friend's sister' rather than, say, 'Marian'. Add that everyone in a group should be clear about how every item on their list fits into the story. Discussion arises in the groups quite naturally about what their key words should be and why.
2. One student from each group writes their key words on the board.
3. Working in the same groups, students now try to agree about the significance of each item in the other groups' lists.

Seth Lindstromberg

139

8   Writing

The eleven activities in this chapter are by no means the only ones in this book which exercise the writing skill. But they do stand out as focusing most especially on writing as opposed to some other area of performance or knowledge. Most of these activities include a step where students get feedback on their writing. All of them are based on the premise that a meagre and woolly task frame tends to produce meagre and/or woolly writing. On the other hand, a well-fleshed out and fully contextualised brief to the writer is much more likely to result in writing that can be really worth reading – writing that students can take pride in having done and which can boost their confidence immensely. Because these activities have this aim of generating interesting writing, they fit well with the policy of encouraging students to let other students read or hear what they've produced. Such an approach, incidentally, seems a good way of motivating students not only to write with extra interest but also to reflect more on content and wording and to pay more attention to legibility. (Student-to-student sharing of writing can take place before or after editorial input from you, as you think appropriate to the level of your learners and the nature of what's written.)

The first two activities, 'Be my scribe' (8.1) and 'Lyrical letters' (8.2), share the feature of encouraging writers to reflect on who they're writing for. Both have other highly interesting and effective features too which I'll now leave you to discover on your own.

'From novelists to publishers' (8.3) is a particularly good example of how you can promote better writing by simulating a communicative context that is at once realistic and endowed with an aura of excitement.

'From doodling to writing' (8.4) begins with a story to which you ask learners *not* to pay attention. This is just one of the tricks it involves which allow you both to guide writing and leave plenty of room for creativity.

'Squalid things' (8.5) is about a way of stimulating students to write short pieces (on an unusual subject) which they compare in a following class.

'L1 poem to English prose' (8.6) is about how to put into effect the idea of using a mother tongue poem to prompt and structure writing in English.

'As if a wild animal' (8.7) is for helping students first to notice features of relatively academic language and then to use them when writing about themselves as if they were wild animals.

'Letters to literary characters' (8.8) begins with a session of letter writing and ends with group discussion of characters in a literary work.

'Sentences about countries' (8.9) involves students in mixed nationality classes writing lists of sentences about their own and their classmates' countries. It ends with oral sharing of what everyone has written.

'Creative plagiarism: manipulating a text' (8.10) describes how to take further the familiar technique of providing students with a model text before they write. It also borrows a feature of the dictogloss (or 'dictocomposition'); however, there is no dictation!

One idea behind 'End of course certificates' (8.11) is to avoid ending a course with the bureaucratic gesture of handing out official reports of certificates. Instead, students make their own.

8.1   Be my scribe

Level
Intermediate–Upper-intermediate

Materials
None

Time
20–40 minutes

Focus
Writing; speaking

For any piece of writing to be meaningful, and therefore motivating, to its writer, it needs a reader. If the writer has a particular reader in mind, then what s/he writes is likely to have more force and clarity. In this exercise, the actual recipient of the letter is absent, but a 'real reader' is supplied by asking the student to write on behalf of someone present, who will thus be acting as a highly motivated, and therefore motivating reader. This, I think, is more effective than, say, asking students to roleplay recipients of letters.

Procedure

1. Ask the students to think of a person, especially someone in a position of responsibility or trust (e.g. lawyer, policeman, sales

assistant, teacher), who on a specific occasion cheated, disappointed, annoyed or offended them. Ask the students to think carefully and try to recall in detail the occasion in question.

2. Ask the students to form pairs.
3. Tell the students that the first member of each pair should talk for up to a minute to their partner, as if their partner were the person they were thinking of in Step 1. They should say clearly what happened and how they felt about it. Meanwhile, the partner should listen attentively, but not attempt to respond or interrupt.
4. When the first member has finished, the second member may ask any questions to clarify the situation, and should then, as carefully and objectively as possible, restate what they have understood. There can then be a further stage of questioning and clarification.
5. Repeat Steps 3 and 4, with the second member of each pair as 'protagonist' and the first member as listener.
6. Ask the students to think for a moment about the situation they have described, and to decide for themselves precisely what they would like the person involved (see Step 1) to do in order to put the matter right or to make amends, for example, apologise, pay money, resign from their job or whatever.
7. Each student should tell their partner what they decided in Step 6.
8. Each student, as 'scribe', now drafts a letter (80–150 words) for their partner to sign and send to the person who aggrieved them, incorporating any necessary references to facts, and stating clearly the expected outcome.
9. The pairs discuss each letter in turn, and decide on final versions. The last word on each letter will, of course, be that of the person who is to sign it.

Rationale

i) We are accustomed to asking students to work collaboratively or co-operatively in small groups, but often ignore the negative aspects of collaboration. One of these, which arises frequently when students are asked to produce a joint effort, is that the final product arises out of compromise, to the extent that none of the participants is fully satisfied with it. In this activity, although the work is definitely collaborative, the final product must, by definition, satisfy *one* only of the pair – it is the protagonist, not the scribe, who must be satisfied. The task can thus be seen as an act of service by one member to the other.

ii) An important part of writing is the process of drafting and revision. This can be, at least psychologically, a difficult thing for many writers to accept. They wish, for example, to plunge directly from raw ideas to finished, perfect copy. Others may simply dislike intensely either the labour involved in revision, or the sight of a draft copy covered with deletions and insertions. In this activity the process of drafting and revision is built in, naturally, at these points:

- the oral restatement of one's partner's account
- the first written draft, which incorporates what has been established in Step 1, and
- the commenting on and approval/revision of the scribe's letter by the protagonist/signatory.

John Morgan

8.2 Lyrical letters

Level
Lower-intermediate–Advanced

Time
60–90 minutes

Focus
Reading and letter layout; speaking; listening

Materials
Gapped song lyrics presented in the form of a letter (example below); a recording of the song; optional, a questionnaire (example below)

This activity begins by recasting song lyrics in the form of a letter, one which calls for a fairly emotional response. Often, students working individually will feel somewhat insecure about this. I've found that making the letter writing a group task (as in Step 3) reduces this insecurity considerably and generally speeds things up. It also makes it possible for you to help students more in the writing phase.

Preparation

Write out the lyrics of your song in letter form. Below is an example. For best effect, it needs an address, the addressee's name and a recent date. It should, as well, be handwritten and not typed. If you decide to use a questionnaire at Steps 6 and 7, produce one of those. Photocopy enough questionnaires for each group of 3–4 students.

Writing

Procedure

1. Ask students to read through the gapped 'song as a letter'. (But don't let them know it's a song!) Suggest that they note any vocabulary they don't understand.
2. Teach/elicit the meaning of each noted vocabulary item.
3. Put your students into small groups and ask them to consider the following questions:
   - What is the relationship between the people mentioned in the letter?
   - At what stage is the relationship?
   - What is the writer trying to say in the letter?
   - What is the mood of the letter?
   - How do you think the recipient would feel after reading the letter?
4. Bring the class together. Elicit the different groups' answers and lead a discussion of them. Keep a record on the board of useful new language for describing relationships. This may come in handy later.
5. Either in groups or in plenary, students offer guesses about which words could fill the gaps. In reacting to guesses try to clarify differences in intensity or connotation of apparently similar words and relate these differences to what has already been decided about the mood of the letter.
6. Working collaboratively, groups of students now draft an appropriate reply. They should have enough vocabulary from the original letter and from the board to create quite an emotional piece of writing!
   Circulate and help keep the language accurate.
7. Groups exchange letters and read them. The groups can either award points (1–10, perhaps) or add comments about suitability of message, originality, intensity of emotion, poetic quality, accuracy of language or whatever you decide to ask them to look for.
   An alternative is for students to complete a questionnaire (which is then given to the authors of the letter being read) about their reactions as readers.

Example questionnaire
   - Are all questions and other key thoughts responded to?
   - Is the reply encouraging or not?
   - Is the reply more or less passionate than the first letter? Why do you think this is so?
   - Will the recipient think the writer took a lot of care not to hurt his/her feelings? Draw a wavy line under any bit that seems to you especially gentle or considerate.
   - Put a solid line under any other bits you especially like. Say why you like them.

- Do you think the writer has a poetic nature? Why?
- A split personality? Why?
- What do you think of the handwriting? Romantic? Hasty?
- Do you think the letter is well-constructed? Or is it more like a collection of unrelated points?
- How do you think the author feels about Phil?

Incidentally, if you decide to use questionnaires, it might be a good idea to hand these out at Step 6 in order to provide the letter writers with additional guidance and motivation.
8. Explain that the letter is actually the lyrics to a song. Now, play it and get students to listen for what actually occurs in the blanks. This is a nice way to wind down from a period of fairly concentrated language work. The fact that students have been working with the song for a long time beforehand means that comprehension of the lyrics when sung is a lot easier than would have been the case if you had just played it 'cold'.

Variation

An alternative to presenting the lyrics in gapped form is to give students a complete letter but change the wording here and there. In this way you can make a well-known song completely unrecognisable. This can add to surprise and interest at the listening stage. A listening task can be: 'Tick the words that are different'.

Note

This song is called 'Something happened on the way to heaven' by Phil Collins from his album *But Seriously* (Copyright 1989, Philip Collins Ltd, Hit and Run Music Ltd). A lot of his lyrics work well in this activity.

The original love letter (see opposite)

Key

In order, the missing words are:

lose   now   wrong   answers   run   problems   someone   heaven   here

Tuesday 11th September 1990

8 Vernon Place
Canterbury, Kent

Dear Rachel,

We had a life, we had a love, but you don't know what you've got till you _____ it. Well, that was then and this is _____, and I want you back. How many times can I say I'm sorry?

How can something so good go so bad? How can something so right go so _____? Well, I don't know, I don't have all the _____. I want you back. How many times can I say I'm sorry?

Well, you know, you can _____ and you can hide, but I'm not leaving unless you come with me. We had our _____ but I'm on your side. You're all I need, please believe in me.

I only wanted _____ to love, but something happened on the way to _____. It got hold of me and wouldn't let go. I want you back. How many times can I say I'm sorry?

They say you can't take it with you when you go—and I believe it. But taking what I've got or being _____ with you, you know, I'd rather leave it.

With all my love,

Phil

Many genres of popular song offer usable lyrics, especially standard ballads from the 30s and 40s (e.g. 'Smoke gets in your eyes') and deep soul ballads from the early and mid-60s (e.g. 'I've been good to you'). Elvis Presley's 'It's now or never' works exceptionally well. Refrains and other repetitions, of course, can be edited out.

Acknowledgement

This activity is related to one demonstrated by Gerry Kenny at a Pilgrims Staff Development seminar.

Joe Buckhurst

8.3   From novelists to publishers

Level
Elementary–Upper-intermediate

Time
60–120 minutes

Focus
Discussion

Materials
Invented novel titles on slips of paper (1 per group); one novel per group; a few pairs of scissors; dictionaries

---

Students love handling foreign novels. And this provides an opportunity for classroom dictionary work that they don't find dull. Even if students are unable to read novels yet, they feel very satisfied at being able to know what a real novel is about. They enjoy taking the roles of authors and publishers. For one thing, this gives them a reason for creative writing that they can identify with.

Preparation

For each group of four to six students, prepare a slip of paper with an invented novel title on it, or perhaps the title of a novel you think your students may never have heard of. Also, bring in at least one best-seller or thriller for each group.

Procedure

1. Form an even number of groups with four to six students each. Give each group a novel (or let them select one from a pile). Give the groups time to look the novels over and then elicit a report from each group on what kind of novel they think they have. Ask them how they arrived at their conclusions. For example, did they read the back cover blurb?

2. Elicit from the students the route a novel travels from the time the writer gets the idea until it is published. Outline the (simplified) steps on the board, e.g.

   idea → plot → writing → rewriting → editing → production of proofs → proof-reading → cover design → production → finished book

3. Instruct students to study the front and back covers and the author's biographical details carefully. They should make notes of the elements they find there. Encourage them to include a wide range of things, for example – illustrations (Technically interesting? Colour? What style? What subject matter? What appeal?), different kinds of print, reviews (Who by? What's their gist? Any interesting language?), the outline of the plot (What kind of book does the style lead them to expect? Any interesting language? Does it perhaps give too much away? If not, what does it make them want to find out?), etc. At elementary level, encourage students not to concentrate too much on language but instead look also for visual clues.

4. Groups report their findings.

5. Hand one slip bearing an invented novel title to each group. Tell them they are novelists and that they should write an outline of the plot in not more than ten lines. Remind them that the plot is 'what happens'. Ask them to write this outline using Present tense verb forms. Ask them to invent a name for the author too.

   Set a strict time limit for this phase before you start the students working (15 to 20 minutes). Make them aware of how time is passing so they can avoid long discussions and finish at about the same time.

6. Groups exchange papers. Now each group is a group of publishers. Tell them to read, discuss and design the front and back cover and write the biographical details. (As the students still have their novels, they can use them as models.)

7. The groups exchange papers again, this time to a third group of proof-readers, whose job it is to spot mistakes.

8. When proof-read, the papers are handed back to the 'authors' who now produce the final copy as well as mock-ups of the covers. Suggest that the groups divide the labour so that no one sits around

doing nothing. If one student finishes a job earlier, they should help another student, perhaps by proof-reading.

9. Circulate the finished products from group to group. If you wish, ask the groups to vote on the best-produced book, the book they'd most like to read, the most interesting author and so on.

Variation

The novelists and publishers meet to discuss the book before Step 8. This could take place in two phases, with each group having one meeting as authors and another as publishers.

Adriana Diaz

8.4   From doodling to writing

Level	**Materials**
Intermediate–Advanced	Background music; a story that can be read aloud in about 3 minutes
Time	
35–45 minutes	
Focus	
Speaking; listening	

This is a writing activity triggered by 'not listening'.

Procedure

1. Ask students for the meaning of 'doodle'. If no one knows, ask them to use their dictionaries.
2. Form students into groups of 4 to 6. In each group students find out who doodles, when, and what sort of doodles they make. A group secretary takes notes.
3. The secretaries report the groups' findings to the whole class.
4. Make sure everyone has paper that is approximately A4 in size. Then, say that you're going to read a story aloud and that, for once, they shouldn't pay attention to you but rather doodle as they listen. However, there is a rule: The 'doodles' should be words. Like

149

picture doodles the word doodles will probably be different from what they hear although they can be suggested by what they hear.

5. Start playing your background music (if you haven't started it before) and read the story. Speak as quietly as you can without being inaudible. (Typically, it takes students about half a minute to begin doodling.)

6. When you have finished reading, tell students to draw a single boundary line around the area of their paper covered in doodles. When they have done this, ask them to go on working individually and write – on the blank part of their sheets – words or phrases connected with the story you have just read to them.

7. Ask students whether they have more words inside their doodle area or outside it – in other words, were they doodling more when they were listening or when they were not?

8. Re-form the original groups. Ask everyone to get out a blank sheet of paper and draw a vertical line down the middle of it. On one side they write 'doodles' and on the other 'story'.

9. Explain that the students in each group should pool all their words in each category and that each student should keep a complete record.

10. Bring the class together. Someone from each group reads out each of the word lists. Students in other groups can add what they hear to their own lists.

11. Form pairs of students from different groups. Pairs each write a collaborative 20- to 30-line story including all the words they have in both columns. Tell them that they can try to adapt the story they heard or write one that's completely different. Add that at some point they must give their story a title and sign it.
Circulate and help with language.

Extension

If forewarned, students generally appreciate having their stories 'published'. Some of the options here include:

– As students finish, they exchange stories, read them, exchange these for new stories and so on.

– Hang the stories on the walls or lay them on tables so that everyone can circulate and read them.

– If students have been using word processors in class, they circulate and look at each other's screens.

– Hand out the finished stories. Students read them and then pass them on along a predetermined (perhaps circular) path. (In a large class, students circulate stories within groups.)

'Publication' is especially appreciated if you have emphasised accuracy and perhaps asked your students to re-write their stories in line with 'editorial' comment from you or other students.

Variation

Step 10 can be omitted if students all have a good number of words in both columns.

Comment

Being told not to pay attention comes as a surprise to students; and the unfamiliarity of this instruction accounts for the usual delay in beginning to 'doodle'. However, they soon begin to enjoy the lack of strain in the activity so much so that no matter how many times you do it, it's one of those activities that never loses its welcome.

Adriana Diaz

8.5   Squalid things

Level	**Materials**
Intermediate–Advanced	Lists (below)

Time
5 minutes in the first class; 20 in the second

Focus
Creative writing; relative clauses; possibly also 'possessive *with*'

If you like to get back to really interesting homework, try this activity.

Procedure

In the first class:

1. Give out the lists below and explain that they were written by a lady-in-waiting at the Japanese court in the ninth century.

151

Writing

2. Ask the students to:
   - read both lists for homework
   - make their own list either of 'squalid things' or of 'things that have lost their power'
   - write a text using their list as a starting point. (Some students, following the models, write tersely; others really write profusely and creatively.)

In the second class:

1. Divide the students into groups of four to six. Don't mix students who have written about squalid things with students who have chosen the second topic. Students tell/show each other what they've written.
2. Pair 'squalid' students with 'power loss' ones. They compare their texts.

Squalid things
- The back of a piece of embroidery
- The inside of a cat's ear
- A swarm of mice, who still have no fur, when they come wriggling out of their nest
- Darkness in a place that does not give the impression of being very clean
- A rather unattractive woman who looks after a large brood of children
- A woman who falls ill and remains unwell for a long time. In the mind of her lover, who is not particularly devoted to her, she must appear rather squalid.

Things that have lost their power
- A large boat which is high and dry in a creek at ebb-tide
- A woman who has taken off her false locks to comb the short hair that remains
- A large tree that has been blown down in a gale and lies on its side with its roots in the air
- The retreating figure of a defeated Sumo wrestler
- A man of no importance reprimanding an attendant
- A woman who is angry with her husband about some trifling matter, leaves home and goes somewhere to hide. She is certain he will rush about looking for her; but he does nothing of the kind and shows the most infuriating indifference. Since she cannot stay away forever, she swallows her pride and returns.

(*The Pillow Book of Sei Shonagon*, Oxford University Press, 1967)

Comment

The Pillow Book of Sei Shonagon is full of short readings that are ideal starters for creative writing. Here are the titles of some of her jottings:

A lover's visit
Things that cannot be compared
Nothing can be worse
On one occasion a man . . .
To feel that one is disliked by others
Men have really strange emotions

Mario Rinvolucri

8.6   L1 poem to English prose

Level
Any, depending on the poem

Time
45–60 minutes

Focus
Dictionary skills; interpreting a poem; writing a narrative and (in the extension) poetry

Materials
Copies of a short poem, monolingual and bilingual dictionaries, L2 thesaurus or the *Longman Language Activator* (1993)

This activity is designed for monolingual groups. I first used it in teaching translators, but it's just as successful with a general language group. You need to choose a poem in your students' mother tongue which they can understand and identify with in some way. Working with a group of upper-intermediate Spanish young adults, I chose a 30-line narrative poem in which the Peruvian poet, Cesar Vallejo, recalls an evening from his childhood.

Preparation

Prepare your own prose translation of the poem before class.

153

Procedure

1. Hand out copies of the poem and read it aloud. Give any information about the author, the poem's setting or its content which you think might be interesting or useful to know.
2. Ask students to read the poem to themselves. Answer any questions that may come up but try not to guide the way in which students interpret the poem. The interpretation should always be their own.
3. Ask them to write a prose translation of the poem. Make it clear that they should concentrate on following its story-line, and that this will certainly mean changing the order or presentation, sentence structure, and many other aspects of the original.
4. Once they have completed their narratives, they exchange texts with others in order to compare the many varied ways in which they have interpreted the poem. Much of the ensuing discussion will spring from their surprise at the different ways in which they have read it.

Extension

5. Have them write their own L2 poem, based on their prose translation but reflecting one or more aspects of the original. Depending on the poem they started from, you might like them to try to follow the same or a similar verse structure, or even rhyme scheme.

Variation

Begin with an English rather than an L2 poem. Suitable examples are William Carlos Williams' *This is just to say* or Roger McGough's *40-Love*.

Bryan Robinson

8.7   As if a wild animal

Level
Intermediate–Advanced

Materials
Multiple copies of a few short texts about
animals

Time
60 minutes

Focus
Aspects of formal writing; vocabulary
about animals and their habits

'As if a wild animal' describes an amusing and memorable way of learning how formal language can differ from colloquial language. It is also an excellent activity for helping students to get better acquainted with each other.

Preparation

1. Cut out from a nature magazine or copy from an encyclopedia one or more texts about animals that include a common name (e.g. 'Hedgehog'), a scientific name (e.g. 'Erinaceus europaeus'), and phrases such as 'Commonly found. .... Its habitat is. .... It prefers. .... It builds its nest. .... is nocturnal ... '
2. Make enough copies for your class.

Procedure

1. Work through the text(s) with your students, making sure that they understand key phrases. Explain that these phrases are special to biology.
2. Describe yourself using similar terms. (Explain that -*a* is for females and -*us* for males.)

'Tessa' (Professoria Hilderstona)
Commonly found in the North East of Kent although occasionally found in other parts of the British Isles and abroad. Its habitat is a small leafy village but by day it is to be found in small coastal cities. Its diet consists of fruit, vegetables, berries and nuts. By day ...

3. Students write similar descriptions of themselves. You will probably have to go around and help, especially with the scientific name. For

155

example, ask students what they especially like doing or what their habits are and suggest mock Latin translations. In a recent class some scientific names were: 'Discosius guyus', 'Studenta non seriosa', 'Studentus everydayus laytus' and 'Studenta gymnastica'.

4. Once people have written their texts and they have been checked, ask them to read them out loud to each other. Students will soon start laughing as they hear others describing themselves as 'seldom found outside in winter', 'active at night in local discos', and 'it mates for life'.

Extensions

- Students scan more texts on animals for phrases that they can apply to themselves or to other people.
- Discuss the Latin origin of many formal and scientific words. Teach common prefixes (e.g. 'inter') and roots (e.g. '-act', '-spect', '-tract').
- Students 'translate' phrases, sentences and short texts from scientific/ formal English to informal English, or vice versa. For example, 'An omnivorous creature' → 'An animal that eats anything'.

Tessa Woodward

8.8   Letters to literary characters

Level
Intermediate–Advanced

Materials
None

Time
50–80 minutes

Focus
Getting under the skin of literary characters; writing informal letters

Writing essays about or discussing characters can be a very dull activity and tends to focus on the characters' overt behaviour. This activity probes more deeply into what motivates their behaviour.

Preparation

Your students need to have read or heard a story – a short story, tale or novel.

Procedure

1. Tell your students to choose a character from the story they have recently read or heard that they would like to think more about – one they specially liked or didn't like or found difficult to understand. (You, as teacher, may have reasons for wanting to choose the character or there may be more to be gained from diversity.)
2. Tell them to write a letter to the character asking them to describe the kind of person they are and why they behave as they do. They should choose particular incidents to ask about. According to the level of your students and the time you have available, allow 10 to 20 minutes for this.
3. Collect the letters and redistribute them to other members of the class. It works best if the recipient is sitting well away from the writer. Ask the recipients to write an answer to the letter as the character, answering questions and explaining their behaviour and motives. Allow 20 to 40 minutes for this.
4. Collect the answers and give them to the student they are addressed to. The original letters remain with the 'character', as in real life.
5. Divide the class into groups of four and ask them to discuss the letters they have received. The simplest way is for each member of the group to tell the others roughly what they wrote in their letter, read out the answer and suggest what insights this exchange of correspondence has given them into their character's behaviour.

Comment

a) This activity works particularly well with characters who behave badly but who the author makes the reader in some way sympathise with – Jane Austen's Emma, Emily Brontë's Heathcliff – but it can also give students a greater understanding of the motivation of really nasty characters and clarify others that seem difficult to understand.
b) As a way of bringing the letter-writing time limit to life you can put it in terms of a mail collection time. Put a collection box on the teacher's desk or some other suitable place. You, or one of your students, are the postman who collects the mail at collection time and distributes the letters.

David Cranmer

8.9 Sentences about countries

Level
Elementary–Advanced

Materials
None

Time
15–30 minutes

Focus
Writing; speaking; listening

This activity is for classes that consist of students from at least two countries.

Procedure

1. Write these sentence beginnings on the board, or dictate them:
   'My country is . . .'
   'My country has . . .'
   'Country X is . . .'
   'Country X has . . .'
2. Tell everyone they must write at least four (or so) sentences that begin with each of the first two beginnings and, additionally, that they must write three (or so) sentences that begin with the name of every other country represented in the class. So – if a class consists of Thais, Japanese and Spaniards – everyone should write 20 sentences – eight about their own country, and six about each of the other two countries. If you have lots of different nationalities, decrease the number of sentences everyone has to write about each country. The more proficient your students, the more sentences you should encourage them to write; the less proficient, the fewer sentences they write. In lower-level classes circulate and provide editorial tips.
3. Name one of the countries. Ask each student who comes from that country to read out their sentences. (Or, in higher level classes, only the sentences they like best.) Then ask those who don't come from it to read out their sentences. Encourage comments. Move on to the next country.

Variation

In higher level classes add one or two other sentence 'seeds', e.g.
'My country . . .' / '. . . my country.'

Rationale

One is unusually attentive when others are talking about one's country. Such is the power of patriotism that students often seem to take more care in writing about their countries than they do when writing about themselves.

Seth Lindstromberg

8.10 Creative plagiarism: manipulating a text

Level
Lower–Upper-intermediate

Materials
A short text

Time
60–90 minutes

Focus
Academic writing

Students at university not only have to write creatively and energetically in order to express their own ideas in an original way, they also have to cope with reading and reporting on the literature of their subject. This is a very difficult area both to teach and to master. How does a language learner learn to use complex texts and assimilate them successfully into a report or essay, without copying directly in a plagiaristic fashion, or without adding huge chunks of quotation?

The following exercise is designed not only to teach new vocabulary and structural variations, but also to give practice in manipulating and changing texts in the way that native speakers do. When one reads in an undergraduate essay, '*Hamlet* is chiefly remarkable for its astonishing orchestration of theme', one does not presume that the formula for that sentence is entirely original. The chances are that the student has come across a similar sentence in another context – something on *Middlemarch* or Mozart, perhaps – and applied it, changing and adapting it to a new purpose. The student has imitated and learnt from the reading. The two processes are inseparable. That, to some extent, is how we learn

159

both language and academic conventions. EAP learners need practice in this type of manipulation of academic texts.

Preparation

On the board or OHP display a text that illustrates the type of language your students have to deal with. I feel, for example, that it is vital for EAP students to develop the argumentative, discursive and analytical elements that are so characteristic of academic writing. So, I would choose a text that is interesting in terms of content, and powerfully written, with a strong argumentative, even controversial line. If you cannot find one, write one. Something like this will do:

Nationalisation

The great concept behind nationalisation was that it would provide the solution to the problems of capitalism. It was supposed to make it easier to plan the economy and to harness wealth for the good of society, rather than the profit of the rich. Moreover, the employees would be both cared for and caring, and this would be greater than the thrust of private enterprise.

However, in reality, the nationalised industries have proved to be difficult to manage, inefficient and uncaring of customers and employees alike. It seems that the state is too abstract a concept to hold people's enthusiasm and maintain an essential competitive edge.

Procedure

1. Underline words and phrases in the text that you feel are significant, either because you want to concentrate on vocabulary, on linking words, discourse markers, structural variations, or a mixture of these. Ask students, individually or in pairs, to think of at least one alternative to each phrase or word underlined.
2. Call the class together. Go through the text adding on the board or OHP transparency all the acceptable alternatives. Some contributions will not be acceptable but that provides a useful opportunity to clarify points of structure and meaning.
3. Go through the text again erasing all the alternatives (including the originals) and leaving blanks in their place.
4. Ask students to read quietly through the text on the board and see how many of the alternatives they can remember. If they like, they can pool their recollections with a neighbour's.
5. To get all the alternatives back on the board, the class dictates all the alternatives they recall to you or to another student.
6. Erase the text and ask students to write a paragraph summing up the argument against nationalisation.

Extension

7. As students finish, ask them to swap and read other students' texts, and/or collect the texts and read some or all of them out loud, unobtrusively correcting any mistakes as you go.
8. For homework, students write a similar argument on another subject such as the results of the rush in the '70s to give loans to Third World countries or the spread around the world of Western farming technology.

Rationale

The summaries will probably all follow a similar pattern, but students will have used different alternatives, so the texts will differ from each other as well as from the original. The students have learned to repeat an argument but have also learned to make changes an important step away from text dependence towards creativity. I believe that the native speaking undergraduate who writes 'astonishing orchestration' has gone through a similar process during their O- and A-level and early university years. 'Creative plagiarism' allows non-native speakers to experience the same process in a more guided and intense way.

James Banner

8.11   End of course certificates

Level
Elementary–Lower-intermediate

Time
30 minutes

Focus
For students: copying and altering text
For you: gaining feedback

Materials
A double class set of sheets of quality paper or card

Age range
Children

This activity not only leaves students with certificates they understand but also creates a satisfying sense of ceremony on finishing a course.

Procedure

1. Tell the students that they will get certificates today. Show them your blank sheets of paper (or card).
2. Ask the class what should be written on them. As students suggest sentences, write them on the board, e.g.
   '... is a nice boy/girl.'
   '... she/he can ...'
3. Organise the layout together with the students. Leave gaps for name and (if appropriate) grade.
4. Give out the paper for the certificates. Students copy the wording and add decoration.
5. As they finish, they come up to you and read what they have written. You fill in the blanks and sign the certificates.
6. Hand out more sheets. Using the same text as a basis (they can alter it as they wish) your students each prepare a certificate for you.
7. Formal presentation of all the certificates.

Variations

i) At Step 6, collect the finished certificate forms, jumble them and fill them out so that no one gets the one they made. However, children may wish to get back their own certificates. Find out what they prefer.
ii) More proficient learners can individually produce their own certificate wording.

Hanna Kryszewska

9   Language through literature

The focus in this chapter is on using the basic appeal and seductiveness of literary forms to encourage imaginative and uninhibited language use. Students react to the stimulus of a literary text by a mixture of respectful mimicry and creativity which is in fact similar to the way original artists simultaneously assimilate influences and create something new. By 'literary forms' I mean both specific texts which you offer the students (e.g. the C. Day-Lewis poem 'Sheepdog trials in Hyde Park') and specific structures (e.g. a haiku, a fairy tale) which you ask them to use in their own way.

This chapter could also be called 'literature through language' since the exercises also offer a method of teaching literature which is less likely to intimidate or alienate students than many other methods. Basically, the distinction between teaching language and teaching literature is deliberately blurred in these activities.

The activities I have included here were first invented and practised in workshops run by the DUET (Development of University English Teaching) project. The activities contributed by John Morgan, David Cranmer and Andy Rouse share the underlying philosophy of DUET. (See Evans 1993.)

Colin Evans

The activities in this chapter can be grouped as follows:

1. Most of the activities in this chapter take one or more poems as a starting point for creative work of some kind. 'Dialogue from a poem' (9.1) begins when you present one or more poems which your students use to compose dialogues. 'Copycats' (9.2) begins with one or more poems and ends up with poems that have been altered. 'Identifying with characters' (9.7) follows the reading of a poem or short story with a sequence of activities designed to get students to exchange reactions and interpretations. 'Enactment' (9.10) is about letting advanced students decide for themselves how to do an in-class dramatic reading of a poem.
2. Two activities outline ways of structuring the writing of poetry, 'This is how it ends!' (9.3) and 'A walk through the seasons' (9.5).

163

3. 'Completion' (9.8) falls halfway between these first two groups of activities in that students begin with a large part of a poem and write the rest.
4. Two activities, (9.3) and 'Façade' (9.6), aim to promote an awareness of rhyme and rhythm.
5. Two activities concern other forms of literature than poetry. 'Signing as a character' (9.4) describes a way of encouraging your students to reflect on the personality of a character in a short story, novel or play. 'Collective fairy tale' (9.9) describes a way of organising the writing and telling of fairy tales in class.

9.1 Dialogue from a poem

Level
Elementary–Upper-intermediate

Time
15–30 minutes

Focus
Listening; writing and performing dialogues

Materials
A class set of copies of a poem or the poem displayed on a poster (example poems below)

This activity begins with students hearing a poem. As they recall the vocabulary of the poem, they will also recall associations, personal memories, other texts they have read or heard, and so on. These recollections form the basis of dialogues they then construct.

Preparation

Choose a short poem with a theme related to human relationships. It should be suitable for reading aloud, fairly rich in vocabulary and slightly above the group's average language ability. Open, allusive poems may be more successful than closed, detailed ones.

Procedure

1. Read the poem once. Afterwards, students write down any words they remember.

2. Students look at each other's word lists. If they see a word they recall hearing but didn't write, they add it to their list now.
3. Repeat Steps 1 and 2. Then repeat Step 1 again.
4. Form groups of three or so. Ask the students to produce a single sheet on which the words they heard are put either under the heading 'he' or under the heading 'she'.
5. Using only words and phrases from these two pools, each group composes a 'he' ⟷ 'she' dialogue that expresses what they understood of mood, feelings and relationship. Each group member makes a copy. Circulate and help with language.
6. Form pairs and swap papers around so that, either:
   - each pair has two copies of a dialogue they had no part in composing, or:
   - each member of each pair has a copy of the dialogue by their earlier group. (They decide whether to practise just one dialogue or both.)
   The pairs rehearse reading their dialogues aloud. Circulate and coach.
7. Pairs perform before the whole class or, in large classes, before halves or quarters of the class.

Variations

- If you have only short poems, read more than one.
- At higher levels, allow students to add articles, prepositions and auxiliaries into their dialogues but not verbs, nouns, adverbs or adjectives.
- Depending on the poem you have chosen and on the class, the categories 'he'/'she' may be replaced by any other pair of categories such as 'senior'/'junior', 'town dweller'/'country dweller', 'driver'/'passenger', 'teacher'/'student', 'victim'/'criminal'.

Rationale

Restricting choice of words to those contained in a poem makes the composition move along more quickly and, as well, tends to discourage production of the rather silly and pointless dialogues students will tend to produce if they are given too free a rein. An additional reason for the restriction is that it fosters use and, therefore, retention of new words and phrases occurring in the poem.

Language through literature

Poems for elementary students:

The visa	What else?	I wonder if you remember.
Life	The sea	You
is	and	and I,
great.	the sky.	the heath
Great love.	A sailing boat	and the sky.
Great hopes.	and a star.	An afternoon
Great Britain.	What else	in September.
Have you got	do you need	The wind
the visa	in life?	in the trees.
already?	A little	I wonder
	more	if you remember.
	courage	
	perhaps.	

A full moon	Quite unnecessary	A merry-go-round
A full moon	You are	The world
again.	gentle	is
Again	and	a sphere.
without you.	thoughtful	We will travel
Must I	and	together,
accept it?	kind.	you and I
What else	So careful	on a merry-go-round.
can I do?	not to hurt	
	that I dare not	
	tell you	
	That it's all	
	quite	
	unnecessary.	

Poems by Leon Szkutnik. Lyrics in English for Comprehension and Interpretation 1989 Wiedza Powszechna (Panstwowe Wydawnictwo, Warsaw). Page nos. 'The visa' p. 7, 'What else?' p. 9, 'I wonder if you remember' p. 11, 'A full moon' p. 8, 'Quite unnecessary' p. 12, 'A merry-go-round' p. 10.

John Morgan

9.2 Copycats

Level
Near beginners–Advanced

Time
15–30 minutes

Focus
Noticing and reflecting on wording; conversing; reading aloud

Materials
Short to medium-length poems or excerpts from prose passages and longer poems. For near beginners, each text needs to be accompanied by a translation (probably fairly literal)

In this activity, students begin by reading a short or shortish literary text. They then either copy it word for word or alter it a little or a lot. Next comes reading out loud and a guessing game!

Preparation

Prepare sets of short literary texts possibly but not necessarily on a common theme. You will need a set for each group of four to eight members.

Procedure

1. Give out the texts – one set to each group, one text per student.
2. Students have five minutes (this is a deliberately short time) to copy out and think about their extract and, if they wish, to rewrite all or part of it as they do so. Students may use dictionaries. They may also ask questions of you only (in order to preserve secrecy).
3. In each group, the students read out their copied (not the original) texts.
4. For each text that is read out, group members decide whether it has been modified, totally rewritten, or left unaltered – at first without reference to the original, later, perhaps, with.

Variation for near beginners

You can use this activity in near beginner monolingual classes if you (1) add glosses to the texts and (2) let students use their mother tongue in Step 4. Szkutnik poems such as those at the end of 9.1 are suitable for students just learning how to form letters and words in the Roman alphabet. Somewhat longer poems like Eleanor Farjeon's 'Cats' suit near beginners.

John Morgan

9.3   This is how it ends!

Level
Lower-elementary–Upper-intermediate

Materials
Prepared 'ends of lines' (examples below)

Time
10–30 minutes (depending on level of learners and length of poem)

Focus
Awareness of rhythm and rhyme; freedom of word order in poetry; creative writing; grammatical accuracy; reading aloud

---

This activity combines creative writing with an emphasis on accuracy in grammatical expression as well as on all aspects of pronunciation, rhythm especially. Although students compose rhyming poems, no particular poetic talent is necessary. Almost everyone finishes with a feeling of success – provided your poem frame is right for your class. (You can adjust the number and length of lines or choose vocabulary that is more or less common.)

Preparation

Devise a poem frame along the lines of the examples given below. Or, if you like, use (some of) the end words of an existing poem. Keep a few additional line ends in reserve for students who finish early and need a bit of extra work.

Procedure

1. Tell your students they are going to write group poems. Tell them the rhythm will be: 'tee-TUM' 'tee-TUM' 'tee-TUM' 'tee-TUM'. Write this on the board (The 'TUM's' are stressed.)

Explain also that the rhyme scheme will be AA BB CC DD. That is, that lines one and two will rhyme, lines three and four will rhyme, and so on.

By now your class may be looking at you with some alarm.

2. Provide the good news ... 'To help you, here are the ends of the lines of the poem you are each going to write'. Write the ends of the lines on the board.

3. Form groups of three or four. Tell groups how much time they have. For example, 15 minutes for an eight-line poem with intermediate students. Double-check that everyone understands the task; in particular, remind them of the rhyme scheme. Point out that it takes time and thought to make a good poem – the poem written fastest is not necessarily going to be the best. Tell the class that each group member should make a copy of the group poem.

4. While the students are writing, go from group to group assisting as necessary. When you spot a line that doesn't fit the stipulated rhythm, read it out in a way that highlights the mistake. (Often students will get the number of syllables right but forget to think about stress.) For example, if a group has written, 'He WAS a NICE beauTIful MAN' (where the words in capital letters are stressed), read this aloud (perhaps overstressing the 'ti' in 'beautiful'). If the group is still unclear about what's wrong or about how to remedy it, you might suggest they remove 'nice', bring 'beautiful' forward, and then insert an appropriate one-syllable adjective after it (e.g. 'old') – 'He was a beautiful old man'.

5. As groups complete their poems, check them a last time. If a group has finished early give them some additional line ends and ask them to extend their poem.

6. Allow each group a few minutes to rehearse reading their poem out loud. Circulate and coach.

7. Either,
   – bring the groups together and have students read out their poems before the whole class,
   or
   – form new groups made up of students from each of the earlier groups. Students read out their poems in groups.

Extension

8. Collect the poems. After class, type them up for posting on the classroom wall or elsewhere in the school. You can also include them in a school/class newspaper or poetry anthology.

9. Ask the students to punctuate their poems. (This could be a useful bridge to a punctuation lesson.)

Variations

i) Here and there you can give students a choice of end word. For example, in the elementary text, line 4 could end with 'see' or 'sea'.

ii) Allow students to substitute for any end word any other word that rhymes with it.

iii) Poems can be written individually.

Rationale

Collaborative writing has two advantages. Firstly, it generates discussion. Secondly, it seems to make it clearer to students that the aim is not that of writing a poem of the highest possible order. That is, they should not rack their brains in order to maintain a theme all the way through, but rather that they should attend mainly to rhythm and pronunciation and have some fun as well.

Example poem frames

Elementary	Intermediate	Advanced
.... go	.... sent	.... rave
.... know	.... went	.... slave
.... me	.... ran	.... rich
.... see/sea	.... began	.... which
.... coat	.... start	.... before
.... boat	.... part	.... deplore
.... say	.... men	.... lied
.... day	.... again	.... defied
	.... lied	.... head
	.... died	.... had said
		.... gains
		.... chains

Note

- You can also take the ends of the lines of existing poems. Whether you do this or work from scratch, you should not have a poem in mind and expect students to recreate it. Their work will, and should, be unpredictable.

- Avoid choosing end of line words for elementary learners that encourage 'enjambement' (i.e. the carrying over of the last part of a clause onto the next line) as below in lines 1 and 2:

I ran so fast I could not catch
My breath, but not a man could match

My speed. I ran so very fine
That I was first across the line.

Here is an example of a poem written by a group of teenagers. It was written with no assistance from me – indeed, as I walked around the room they hid it from me until it was finished.

In spite of all
In spite of all the love I gave
She wanted me to be her slave
She was not young, not nice, not rich
But still she saw a man with which
She never had made love before
And this is why I do deplore
The way she treated me and lied
I made her leave but she defied
So what I want now is her head
Alive or dead but he had said
That notwithstanding all the gains
I'd still be locked in golden chains.

Ilse, Matthias, Erik (14 mins)

Note

Rather than correcting the two instances of unusual usage in this poem, I let them stand but did say what I thought they meant in the context of the poem's message, as I saw it. For example, 'I especially like your clever use of *which* instead of *whom*. It depersonalises both the man and the woman who has cheated the poet.'

Andy Rouse

9.4 Signing as a character

Level
Intermediate–Advanced

Materials
None

Time
15 minutes +

Focus
Understanding characters in novels

This activity presupposes that you and your students have been working on a novel or play and have finished it. The procedure depends in detail on the number of main characters in the work. Here it is for one main character. The variation shows what to do if there are several.

Procedure

1. Ask your students to take a blank piece of paper and to have their pen ready on the desk. Ask them to close their eyes. Say something like this: 'I want you to try and imagine you are (name of character). What is his/her hair like? Imagine yours like that. What colour are his/her eyes? Imagine your eyes that colour. How would he/she sit? Sit like that. You are now (name of character). You are going to write a letter to (name of another character). What is the letter about? Imagine yourself writing it ... (pause briefly) ... Now you're coming to the end of the letter and you're going to sign it. As (name of main character) what is your signature like? Open your eyes and write that signature.
2. Ask them to write a sentence or two below, explaining why the signature takes the form it does.
3. Put the class into groups of about four to show each other their signatures and why they take the form they do.
4. Ask the class what aspects of the character's personality arose in relation to the signatures in their group.

Variation

1. If there are two or more main characters, divide the class into groups – the same number of groups as there are main characters. Assign a character to each group. Then proceed as in Steps 1 to 3 above. When it comes to the letter they imagine they are writing in Step 1,

the different characters will probably be writing to different other characters and you need to decide which.

2. After Step 3 you may want to regroup the class into groups containing one representative of each character. They then discuss their own character signatures and the signatures of their partners in Step 3. This gives a good idea of the insights each original group gained into their respective character. Step 4 is then optional.

Acknowledgement

I first applied this idea to the character Holden Caulfield in J. D. Salinger's *The Catcher in the Rye* with a class of about 30 sixteen- and seventeen-year olds. They loved it. I first wrote about it in the Portuguese *Newsletter* (Vol. IX No. 3, June 1988).

David Cranmer

9.5   A walk through the seasons

Level
Intermediate–Advanced

Materials
None

Time
45 minutes

Focus
Evocative vocabulary; writing poetry

This activity has a very good effect on the group dynamic of a class which is familiar with a four season, temperate zone climate.

Procedure

1. Pre-teach any vocabulary you plan to use that you think your class may not know.
2. Do a short physical warm-up exercise just to loosen your students up.
3. Tell your students that you're going to take them for a walk through the seasons. Form an inward-facing circle consisting of all the class and yourself. Ask everyone to turn to the right, put their hands on the

shoulders of the person in front, close their eyes and begin to walk gently forward. (If the furniture won't permit this, you can do the walk by everyone standing beside their desk and walking on the spot.)

4. As you walk, talk everyone through the scenes you pass. Talk slowly and gently, pausing briefly after each word or phrase, so that everyone can imagine what you are describing. It might go something like this: 'It's a spring morning – bright, crisp, you're in a meadow beside a river, birds singing, frogs croaking, blossom, fresh colours; now moving to the sea and beach in summer early in the afternoon – heat, bright sun, glittering light, warm water, sand, relaxation; moving on to a wood in late afternoon – the many-coloured leaves of the trees, toadstools, woodpeckers, mellow warmth, gentle yet strong light, beyond the trees a field with corn, ripening grapes; moving into the darkness and cold of winter – snow, night, twinkling stars, snug coat and gloves, red nose, a cottage in the distance, a light, the wooden door, opening it, the coal fire, sitting beside it, hot chocolate; end of walk.' Ask everyone to picture the classroom, open their eyes gently and return to the here and now.

5. Ask your students to reflect on their walk and decide which season they most enjoyed going through. Divide them into groups according to the season they chose – don't worry about the groups being of different sizes – and subdivide each group into pairs. If, as occasionally happens, only one student has chosen a particular season, make up the pair by joining in yourself.

6. Ask each pair to write down 12 adjectives, eight nouns and six verbs ending in '-ing' that they associate with their chosen season. They can be words from your narrative or others.

7. Tell them they are now going to write a poem. Don't be put off by any groans and reassure them, if necessary, that they will all be able to write good poems. Tell them they are to use all the words they have written down and no others except articles, prepositions, 'and', 'or', 'but', 'yes' and 'no'. I occasionally allow other words so long as they are not nouns, adjectives and verbs. Be reasonable but firm. I allow them to repeat a word if it is for rhetorical effect. They usually find the first few lines easy but it is the last few that challenge their imaginations and are therefore more fun.

Note

It is important to make autumn and winter especially evocative so that not everyone chooses spring and summer. This is especially true with teenagers.

Here are two uncorrected poems written by fifteen- and sixteen-year-old state-school students at Torres Novas, Portugal. They wrote them in difficult conditions – as it was a demonstration session, they had never met me before, we had no desks or chairs and had to work on the floor and fifty teachers were watching us.

Summer

Happy days
Blue and shiny sky
Sunny summer
Flying birds

Swimming in the water
In a cold beach
Hot sand
Shiny sun

Big ice-creams
In holidays
Fishing, loving
In a yellow boat
Lovely drinking

Sheila & Teresa

Winter

Walking on the cold, white, freezing snow
Drinking good hot chocolate, sitting besides the big warming fire
Coming in the little dark house
Seeing the beautiful mountain, trees, hills, the rainy foggy sky

Elizabete & Carlos

Acknowledgements

This activity owes its inspiration to a similar walk I experienced with Bernard Dufeu of Mainz University and to the computer program *Wordplay* by Anita Skraker. I first wrote about it in the Portuguese *Newsletter* (Vol. IX No. 3, June 1988).

David Cranmer

9.6 Façade: exploring rhythm and rhyme in nonsense poetry

Level
Intermediate–Advanced

Time
50–60 minutes

Focus
Rhythm and rhyme in English

Materials
A class set of a poem text (example below); for the optional extension Walton's *Façade* (music)

Walton wrote the music for *Façade* to be played while Edith Sitwell's nonsense poems are recited. The two combine to form an 'entertainment' in words and music. I am taking the poem *En famille* to exemplify the technique.

Procedure

1. Explain to your students that there is a tradition of 'nonsense verse' in English. Poems of this kind have very little real meaning but they contain a certain 'logic' based on sound, metre, rhyme and associations between words. If you have one handy, read one of Edward Lear's nonsense-rhymes or one of Lewis Carroll's nonsensical poems, by way of example. Here is one of Lear's limericks:

   There was an Old Man of Cape Horn,
   Who wished he had never been born,
   So he sat on a chair, till he died of despair,
   That dolorous Man of Cape Horn.

   Tell your class you are going to work with them on a nonsense-poem to help raise their awareness of the sound and rhythm of English.

2. Divide the class into four and subdivide each quarter into pairs. Tell the class you are going to give each group three words and you want them to work with their partner to think of other words in English that rhyme with these three. Tell them that they can use proper nouns (names of people and places) if they want to. Allocate the words as follows:

Group 1	Group 2	Group 3	Group 4
tea	notion	swell	finer
slam	sliding	set	trees
call	nation	thin	proper

If your students are worried about the meaning of any of these words, explain it.

3. Put all the pairs in group one together to compare their lists of rhyming words. Do the same with groups two, three and four.
4. Give out the poem and tell the students to see whether they included in their list any words that the writer uses as a rhyme in the poem.
5. Copy the first four lines onto the board and explain how the rhythm of the poem works in these lines – there are stressed and unstressed syllables. Underline the stressed syllables (four per line) and read these lines aloud so that the students hear clearly where the stresses fall. Ask the students to go quickly through the rest of the poem and underline the stressed syllables (four per line). Tell them they have ten minutes to do this. (Give an extra five minutes if this proves to be necessary.)
6. Ask the class to comment on the kinds of words they find are typically unstressed – articles, monosyllabic prepositions, subject pronouns, possessive adjectives, auxiliary verbs, words such as 'and'/'or'/'as'/'that'/'than'.

Extension

7. Tell your students that the English composer Walton wrote some music, to be played while this poem is recited. You are going to play a recording of it. Ask them as they listen to check whether they chose the right syllables as being stressed.
8. Play the poem/music.
9. Ask your students what they feel the music contributed to the words. Also ask them whether after all this work on the text it makes any kind of sense to them.

En famille

In the early spring-time, after their tea,
Through the young fields of the springing Bohea,
Jemima, Jocasta, Dinah, and Deb
Walked with their father Sir Joshua Jebb –
An admiral red, whose only notion,
(A butterfly poised on a pigtailed ocean)
Is of the peruked sea whose swell
Breaks on the flowerless rocks of Hell.

177

Under the thin trees, Deb and Dinah,
Jemima, Jocasta, walked, and finer
Their black hair seemed (flat-sleek to see)
Than the young leaves of the springing Bohea;
Their cheeks were like nutmeg-flowers when swells
The rain into foolish silver bells.
They said, 'If the door you would only slam.
Or if, Papa, you would once say "Damn" –
Instead of merely roaring "Avast"
Or boldly invoking the nautical Blast –
We should now stand in the street of Hell
Watching siesta shutters that fell
With a noise like amber softly sliding;
Our moon-like glances through these gliding
Would see at her table preened and set
Myrrhina sitting at her toilette
With eyelids closed as soft as the breeze
That flows from gold flowers on the incense-trees.'
. . .
The Admiral said, 'You could never call –
I assure you it would not do at all!
She gets down from table without saying "Please",
Forgets her prayers and to cross her T's.
In short, her scandalous reputation
Has shocked the whole of the Hellish nation;
And every turbaned Chinoiserie,
With whom we should sip our black Bohea,
Would stretch out her simian fingers thin
To scratch you, my dears, like a mandoline;
For Hell is just as properly proper
As Greenwich, or as Bath, or Joppa!'

(Edith Sitwell, from *Collected Poems*)

Note

Many of the poems in *Façade* and *Façade 2* can be used in this way.

David Cranmer

9.7   Identifying with characters

Level
Intermediate–Advanced

Time
90 minutes

Focus
Listening; reading; oral question and answer among students

Materials
Class set of a poem (examples below) and one 8 × 5 card or sticky label per student; several large sheets of paper and markers

This is a good activity for getting students to share viewpoints about a medium-length or longish poem that refers to a number of characters, places or objects.

Procedure

1. Distribute the poem. Give each student a card too.
2. Read the poem aloud, have it read or play a recording of it being read.
3. Ask the students individually to put a ring around all the characters in the poem. They should interpret 'character' widely – so, for example, in the poem 'Sheepdog Trials in Hyde Park' (see below), this would include vocabulary like 'viable space', 'time' as well as 'sheepdog' and 'shepherd'.
4. Ask the students to put the 'characters' in three sub-groups by making columns, each with a heading. An obvious grouping is 'human', 'animal', 'abstract' but there are others.
5. Ask them to highlight the three 'characters' they *most* identify with and the three they *least* identify with. They should write the name of the one they *most* identify with on the card (or on the sticky label).
6. Now ask them to move around the room displaying their card (or with the sticky label stuck on their forehead). They should try to form sub-groups of students who have identified with the same 'character'. So, for example, there may be a sub-group of 'shepherds' or 'sheep' or students who identify with the 'I'. If they find no one has the same identification as them, they should go down their list and join the group closest to their choice.
7. Each sub-group gets a large sheet of paper and writes on it its name (i.e. the character its members identify with) so that other sub-

groups can see it. Each student tells the others in the sub-group why they chose the way they did and what the choice signifies, that is, what they *represent*. The sub-group works out what they represent compared with the other sub-groups.

8. Each sub-group chooses a messenger or a pair of messengers to go to the other sub-groups one by one and say what they represent. It's best if A goes to B and B goes to C rather than A and B exchanging messengers (as in the illustration on the next page). By the end of this step, every sub-group will have received a message from all the others.
9. On the basis of the messages, the sub-groups discuss the difference between them and the other sub-groups.
10. Students pin up the cards and the sheets of paper. Working with the whole class, try to bring the various parts together by organising a group-reading with different individuals or groups reading different parts.

Variations

- Hand out the poem the day before the class if you like so the students can look up any words they don't know. On the other hand, you lose the spontaneity and surprise you get if they are seeing it for the first time.
- Use a short story. If you do, handing it out in an earlier lesson is essential unless it's very brief. Also, if you use a short story, reading aloud will probably be too time-consuming.

Note

This exercise can be used with any suitable poem, for example, Frost's 'Mending Wall' and D. H. Lawrence's 'Song of a man who has come through'.

Sheepdog Trials in Hyde Park

A shepherd stands at one end of the arena.
Five sheep are unpenned at the other. His dog runs out
In a curve to behind them, fetches them straight to the shepherd,
Then drives the flock round a triangular course
Through a couple of gates and back to his master; two
Must be sorted there from the flock, then all five penned.
Gathering, driving away, shedding and penning
Are the plan words for the miraculous game.

1

Messenger
from A to B

A   **B**

C

Messenger
from C to A

Messenger
from B to C

2

Messenger from
C with sub-group A

Messenger from
A with sub-group B

Messenger from
B with sub-group C

3

Messenger from
C now goes to B

A   **B**

C

Messenger from
B now goes to A

Messenger from
A now goes to C

Etc., till each messenger returns to own group

An abstract game. What can the sheepdog make of such
Simplified terrain? – no hills, dales, bogs, walls, tracks,
Only a quarter-mile plain of grass, dumb crowds
Like crowds on hoardings around it, and behind them
Traffic or mounds of lovers and children playing.
Well, the dog is no landscape-fancier; his whole concern
Is with his master's whistle, and of course
With the flock – sheep are sheep anywhere for him.

The sheep are the chanciest element. Why, for instance,
Go through this gate when there's on either side of it
No wall or hedge but huge and viable space?
Why not eat the grass instead of being pushed around it?
Like blobs of quicksilver on a tilting board
The flock erratically runs, dithers, breaks up,
Is reassembled: their ruling idea is the dog;
And behind the dog, though they know it not yet, is a shepherd.

The shepherd knows that time is of the essence
But haste calamitous. Between dog and sheep
There is always an ideal distance, a perfect angle;
But these are constantly varying, so the man
Should anticipate each move through the dog, his medium.
The shepherd is the brain behind the dog's brain,
But his control of dog, like dog's of sheep,
Is never absolute – that's the beauty of it.

For beautiful it is. The guided missiles,
The black-and-white angels follow each quirk and jink of
The evasive sheep, play grandmother's steps behind them,
Freeze to the ground, or leap to head off a straggler
Almost before it knows that it wants to stray,
As if radar-controlled. But they are not machines –
You can feel them feeling mastery, doubt, chagrin:
Machines don't frolic when their job is done.

What's needfully done in the solitude of sheep-runs –
Those tough, real tasks – becomes this stylized game,
A demonstration of intuitive wit
Kept natural by the saving grace of error.
To lift, to fetch, to drive, to shed, to pen
Are acts I recognize, with all they mean
Of shepherding the unruly, for a kind of
Controlled woolgathering is my work too.

(C. Day-Lewis, from *The Oxford Book of Twentieth Century English Verse*, 1973,
Philip Larkin ed., pp. 355–6)

Song of a man who has come through

Not I, not I, but the wind that blows through me!
A fine wind is blowing the new direction of Time.
If only I let it bear me, carry me, if only it carry me!
If only I am sensitive, subtle, oh, delicate, a winged gift!
If only, most lovely of all, I yield myself and am borrowed
By the fine, fine wind that takes its course through the
    chaos of the world
Like a fine, an exquisite chisel, a wedge-blade inserted;
If only I am keen and hard like the sheer tip of a wedge
Driven by invisible blows,
The rock will split, we shall come at the wonder, we shall
    find the Hesperides.

Oh, for the wonder that bubbles into my soul,
I would be a good fountain, a good well-head,
Would blur no whisper, spoil no expression.

What is the knocking?
What is the knocking at the door in the night?
It is somebody wants to do us harm.

No, no, it is the three strange angels.
Admit them, admit them.

(D. H. Lawrence, from *The Oxford Book of Twentieth Century English Verse*,
1973, Philip Larkin ed., p. 187)

Colin Evans

9.8 Completion

Level
Intermediate–Advanced

Time
60 minutes

Focus
Developing a sense of rhythm and stress; encouraging creative use of language

Materials
A class set of a specially prepared poem; several large sheets of paper; (optional) a copy of the original version of the poem

---

Here is an activity designed to show students that poetry is not so lofty and out of reach that they cannot turn their hands to it.

Preparation

Remove certain words from a poem, leaving blanks all of the same length. (If you give the number of letters, the activity turns into a guessing game, which is not the point.)

Procedure

1. Form three or four sub-groups each with a large sheet of paper and copies of the gapped poem.
2. Students complete the poem (by filling in the blanks on the large sheet) and write it on their sheet of paper. Stress that the task is *not* to guess what the original was. If they can't think of a real word with the right rhythm/rhyme, they can make one up.
3. Each group reads out its version.
4. Decide whether it's appropriate to show the original. (You probably won't get away with not showing it. But stress that it does not show that their versions are wrong.)

Example 'prepared' poem:

Why have such **** of ****, **** girls
  Married **** men?
**** **** may be ruled out
  And **** **** nine times out of ****
Repeat **** men: not merely ****,
  **** or ****

(**** **** chosen to show the world
  How well women behave, and always have behaved).

**** men: ****, ****,
  ****, ****, ****,
For whose **** even in **** ****
  Excuses must be made to **** passers-by.

Has ****'s supply of **** husbands
  **** in fact so ****
Or do I always over-value ****
  at the expense of ****?
            Do I?
                 It might be so?

A Slice of Wedding Cake

Why have such scores of lovely, gifted girls
  Married impossible men?
Simple self-sacrifice may be ruled out,
  And missionary endeavour, nine times out of ten.

Repeat 'impossible men': not merely rustic,
  Foul-tempered or depraved
(Dramatic foils chosen to show the world
  How well women behave, and always have behaved).

Impossible men: idle, illiterate,
  Self-pitying, dirty, sly,
For whose appearance even in City parks
  Excuses must be made to casual passers-by.

Has God's supply of tolerable husbands
  Fallen, in fact, so low?
Or do I always over-value woman
  At the expense of man?
            Do I?
                 It might be so.

(Robert Graves, from *The Oxford Book of Twentieth Century English Verse*, 1973,
Philip Larkin ed., pp. 299–300)

Colin Evans

9.9   Collective fairy tale

Level
Elementary–Advanced

Time
60–90 minutes

Focus
Writing sentences; forming past tense narratives; reading aloud

Materials
Sheets of A4 paper; 10 × 5 cards; coloured sticky dots

Requirements
For this activity you need a class of at least five people. If the class numbers more than ten, divide people into groups of from five to ten members. If your class is so large that you end up with several groups, there is an extension (see Step 9).

Procedure

1. Collect the names of fairy-tale characters from the students – The Giant, The Seventh Son, The Fairy Princess, The Witch – and write them on the board.
2. Give out enough A4 paper and cards for everyone. Each student takes a card and writes the name of one of the characters written on the board. On the paper they write 'Once upon a time ...' and complete the sentence using their character. For example: 'Once upon a time a prince fell into a deep lake.'
   Remind them to write clearly because someone else will have to read what they have written.
3. Everyone passes their card to the *left* and their paper to the *right*.
4. Each student now has the first line of a story and a character to incorporate into the story. For example: a student receives a card saying 'The Frog' and a story beginning with the sentence given in Step 2. The student could continue the story by writing: 'He sank like a stone because he was wearing all his armour but as he sank he saw a Frog.'
5. And so on. When students get their original sentences back, the round is over and the storytelling can begin.
6. Rearrange the seating so that one chair faces all the others.
7. One by one, the students sit in the storyteller's seat and read their stories.
8. Pin the stories to the wall. Each student gets six dots to stick on the stories to indicate which he or she thinks the best. (All six on one story or one on six different stories or whatever.)

186

Extension

9. Where several groups have operated simultaneously, the best stories from each group can be compared in a further dot-sticking exercise.

Note

This activity links well with the reading of contemporary fairy tales. Two recent collections are Angela Carter, *Second Virago Book of Fairy Tales* (Virago 1992) and Caroline Heaton and Christine Park *Caught in a Story, Contemporary Fairytales and Fables* (Vintage 1992).

Colin Evans

9.10 Enactment

Level
Advanced

Materials
A class set of a poem (example below)

Time
30–60 minutes

Focus
Speaking in unison; developing a sense of the language; negotiation in groups; (extension) writing narrative

---

The literary angle of this activity is obvious. But there is something else to it as well. Advanced students not infrequently express a desire to measure up to the highest standards of pronunciation. This is a super activity for motivating and structuring work on every facet of articulation and delivery.

Procedure

1. Give out the poem. Students read it silently. Answer any questions.
2. Create groups of between eight and twelve students.
3. Announce that each group is going to produce a dramatised reading aloud of the poem for the rest of the class. They should discuss how best to do this and rehearse their production before giving it.

4. As groups prepare their performances, you can be available to answer questions they have, or circulate to monitor and coach where necessary.

Extension

5. In writing, students complete the story contained in the poem.
6. In groups of three or four they read their versions to each other and then combine them into *one* ending.

Note

This activity also works with Edward Morgan's 'Mercury men', an excerpt from John Betjeman's 'Beside the seaside' (the one reproduced in Larkin, pp. 372–73) and Wallace Stevens' 'Domination of black' (in his book *Harmonium* 1923 and also in his *Selected Poems* 1953 Faber, p. 13). Philip Larkin's 'Night mail' (in Larkin p. 411) is excellent for the reading but less good for the extension.

Welsh Incident

'But that was nothing to what things came out
From the sea-caves of Criccieth yonder.'
'What were they? Mermaids? dragons? ghosts?'
'Nothing at all of any things like that.'
'What were they, then?'
                    'All sorts of queer things,
Things never seen or heard or written about,
Very strange, un-Welsh, utterly peculiar
Things. Oh, solid enough they seemed to touch,
Had anyone dared it. Marvellous creation,
All various shapes and sizes, and no sizes,
All new, each perfectly unlike his neighbour,
Though all came moving slowly out together.'
'Describe just one of them.'
                    'I am unable.'
'What were their colours?'
                    'Mostly nameless colours.
Colours you'd like to see; but one was puce
Or perhaps more like crimson, but not purplish.
Some had no colour.'
                    'Tell me, had they legs?'
'Not a leg nor foot among them that I saw.'
'But did these things come out in any order?

188

What o'clock was it? What was the day of the week?
Who else was present? How was the weather?'
'I was coming to that. It was half-past three
On Easter Tuesday last. The sun was shining.
The Harlech Silver Band played *Marchog Jesu*
On thirty-seven shimmering instruments,
Collecting for Caernarvon's (Fever) Hospital Fund.
The populations of Pwllheli, Criccieth,
Portmadoc, Borth, Tremadoc, Penrhyndeudraeth,
Were all assembled. Criccieth's mayor addressed them
First in good Welsh and then in fluent English,
Twisting his fingers in his chain of office,
Welcoming the things. They came out on the sand,
Not keeping time to the band, moving seaward
Silently at a snail's pace. But at last
The most odd, indescribable thing of all,
Which hardly one man there could see for wonder,
Did something recognizably a something.'
'Well, what?'
                         'It made a noise.'
                                    'A frightening noise?'
'No, no.'
                    'A musical noise? A noise of scuffling?'
'No, but a very loud, respectable noise –
Like a groaning to oneself on Sunday morning
In Chapel, close before the second psalm.'
'What did the mayor do?'
                                  'I was coming to that.'

(Robert Graves, from *The Oxford Book of Twentieth Century English Verse*, 1973,
Philip Larkin ed., pp. 296–7)

Colin Evans

10 Music and imagination

Clem Laroy, who contributed most of the activities in this chapter, sent me the following quote: 'All art constantly aspires to the condition of music' (Walter Pater). Clem adds that his activities all 'encourage students to establish a link between music and personal experience. Some, as well, evoke links between music and different kinds of art. This appeal to different senses often yields a deeper and better understanding of art as a welcome result.'

Elsewhere Clem has written, 'Music has sometimes been described metaphorically as a language without words ... For many centuries musicians have tried to convey sounds and images from the real world ... in the 19th century [this] developed into what is known as "programme music", where composers tried to portray characters, scenes, storms, journeys, stories and so on ... Such music can easily induce visualisation, whatever the cultural background of the listener. So we could produce a variation on the old joke, "Put on your glasses, you'll hear better" and say "Listen to the music and tell me what you see".'

'For musicians it has always been a problem that the images the composer was trying to convey were often heard quite differently by the listener ... For teachers though, this very failure is most interesting: everyone is bound to have some personal perception, and something unique to say. We are a long way [here] from the traditional information gap where one person knows the time of departure of the [imaginary] train while the other does not. With music, the learner is far more deeply involved. David Cranmer [the other contributor to this chapter] has aptly coined the expression 'curiosity gap' to describe 'a powerful double phenomenon: the students on the one hand have an enormous desire to tell one another what they have heard and, on the other hand, they have a great curiosity to find out what the others have heard'. (Laroy 1993)

This introduction from Clem captures the essence of each and every activity in this chapter. The thing to do now is read on and get acquainted with them one by one.

10.1 Story in the music

Level
Intermediate–Advanced

Materials
Instrumental music (see below)

Time
20–40 minutes

Focus
Oral and written narrative

A number of composers have written music that explicitly aims to tell a story. This activity exploits the narrative quality of this music and the different ways listeners perceive it.

Procedure

1. Tell your class that in a few moments you are going to play them a piece of music which tells a story. As they listen, they should make notes about the story they hear, so that they can tell it afterwards.
2. Play the music.
3. Put your students into groups of six to eight to tell the story they heard. Help with vocabulary as needed and correct more serious errors.
4. Ask your students to write a paragraph telling the story they heard.

Suggested music

- Dukas: *The Sorcerer's Apprentice*
- Mussorgsky: *Night on a Bare Mountain*
- Saint-Saëns: *Danse Macabre*
- Stravinsky: *The Rite of Spring* (final section, 'Danse Sacrale')

Variation

With students who know about 'Carnival' (Shrove Tuesday), first discuss Carnival, then elicit vocabulary like 'processions', 'masks', 'fireworks', etc. then play Berlioz's *Carnival Romain*. Then proceed as in Steps 3 and 4. (A full version of this variation has appeared in *The Journal for Teachers of English in the Portuguese-speaking world*, no. 1, May 1992.)

David Cranmer

10.2 Silent film mimes

Level
Elementary–Advanced

Time
15–20 minutes

Focus
Telling stories; discussion; action; fun

Materials
Silent film music (see suggestions below);
(optional) a short excerpt from a silent film

This activity is a good lead-in to the two following activities (10.3 and 10.4). By itself it's a wonderful energiser.

Preparation

Choose an excerpt from a silent film. These are obtainable from video shops and libraries and usually have a musical sound track. Or, if you can't show a film for one reason or another, see below for the alternative procedure.

Procedure

1. Either:
   show a short scene from a silent film with musical background. Preferably, the scene should not have too many people in it, perhaps just two.
   Or:
   play suitable music and act out a scene yourself, adding voice-over explanation. (It can be fun if you play two different characters.)
2. Ask students about silent film music. What are its main characteristics? (Instrumental; relatively few instruments, perhaps just a piano or organ; etc.) How does it reflect the action in the film?
3. Explain to your students that they are going to mime as if they were actors in a silent film. Ask them for any tips on what to do.
4. Get a couple of students to mime the scene viewed in Step 1.
5. Lead a whole class feedback on the performance just seen. Is there anything silent film actors particularly need to remember to do or not do?
6. Encourage other groups to mime the same scene. Elicit feedback on the relative merits of each rendering. Emphasise what the different actors were particularly good at.

Suggested films

Films with Chaplin, Laurel and Hardy, Buster Keaton, and Harold Lloyd are accompanied by interesting music. The minor (and shorter) films Chaplin made at the beginning of his career provide better material than his classics.

Suggested music

From Chaplin's *Modern Times*: the theme from 'Titine'; *City Lights*: 'Two little shoes'; *A dog's life*: theme; from *A King in New York*: 'Loving mandolins' and 'Love song'; *The Pilgrim*: theme; *Shoulder Arms*: theme.

   Rags, by Scott Joplin or James P. Johnson, for example. Records with silent film music are available commercially, for example, *Musique pour films muets* (Ivory Sam and his piano, Vogue, VT 403 500746).

Clem Laroy

10.3 Silent film sequels

Level
Elementary–Advanced

Time
20–30 minutes

Focus
Discussion; writing; telling stories;
action; fun

Materials
A short excerpt from a silent film; (optional)
a piece of silent film music

This activity can be done on its own but works especially nicely if preceded by activity 10.2.

Preparation

Choose an excerpt from a silent film; you will need suitable background music too (see the suggestions at the end of 10.2).

193

Procedure

1. Play the beginning of your excerpt.
2. Stop the video and tell your students to imagine that they are film scriptwriters and that they are going to work in small groups to write scripts for the rest of the scene. Add that they will be acting out their silent films later, miming actions and emotions implied by the musical background.
3. Play the music three or four times while your students work on their scripts. (Turn the TV set around for this or hide the screen.) Help with language as needed.
4. Each group acts out the scene in front of the class to the accompaniment of the music and without dialogue. After each performance, members of the audience comment and ask questions about what was going on. (Spectating groups often carry on distracting last minute discussions about staging while another group is performing. You can cut down on this if, before the first performance, you request that all groups break up and sit scattered around the audience.)
5. Show the rest of the silent film scene and invite comparisons with their own performances.

Clem Laroy

10.4 Silent film scripts

Level
Elementary–Advanced

Time
30–70 minutes

Focus
Writing; telling stories; action; fun

Materials
A piece of silent film music; (optional) props such as false moustaches; (optional) a video camera

This activity is a continuation of 10.2 and 10.3.

Preparation

Choose a piece of suitable music (see the suggestions at the end of 10.2).

Procedure

1. Start off by telling your students that they are going to write a script for a scene in a silent film.
2. Dictate a series of prompts, for example:
   'The action takes place in ...'
   'It's ... o'clock.'
   'There are two characters, a ... and a ...'
   'The first one is ...' [Describe him or her]
   'The second one is ...' [Describe him or her]
   'They know/don't know each other.' [If they know each other explain how they met]
   'In the film, they meet as a result of ...'
   'What happens at this meeting is that ...'
   If you think it necessary, write some script beginnings on the board, for example:
   a) At a fashionable seaside resort an attractive young woman is on her way to go swimming ...
   b) In an old castle in the Alps Dr Silverstein is trying to change pebbles into gold. It is a stormy night ...
   c) Joe Pane is cleaning the shop window when Sir Arthur passes and is struck on the nose by a drop of water ...
   d) The police are trying to catch Mack the Knife ...
3. Form groups of four. Make available any props you have collected and brought in. (These greatly help students to overcome their inhibitions. Masks and other facial disguises are especially effective in this regard.) Play your silent film music as they work.
4. When the scripts are finished, get each group to act out their sketch as the music is playing. The spectators take notes (so they can tell the story being acted out.)
5. Pair students from different groups. Ask students in each pair to tell each other how they understood their partner's group's performance. (For a more vivid telling, students should use the Present tense.)

Extension

6. In small groups, students decide who to nominate for Silent Film Oscars. They must think of categories for their Oscars (e.g. 'An Oscar for the best script', 'A special laughter Oscar') and reasons for awarding them (e.g. 'for having made us all shake with laughter for two whole minutes').
7. Voting followed by Oscar presentations and short acceptance speeches.

In subsequent lessons

- Once students have done this a couple of times, video-record the performances for showing to another class. This other class gives the awards.
- Students bring in their own soundtrack music, operate the video camera and organise the showings to other classes. In this case there should be an Oscar for best music.

Clem Laroy

10.5 Musical constructions

Level
Intermediate–Advanced

Time
30–60 minutes

Focus
Speaking about architecture, shapes, the location of things

Materials
Music as suggested below; photos of different buildings (or slides of buildings plus projector and screen)

This activity has produced all kinds of 'works of art', from the hilarious to the truly impressive. Usually, plenty of discussion results and everyone gets to listen to some nice music.

Procedure

1. Prepare your students by revising or studying the names of three-dimensional forms in English – 'cube/block', 'rectangular block', 'cylinder', 'sphere/globe/ball'. Add a few useful qualifiers such as 'slightly squashed', 'truncated' and specifically architectural terms like 'cupola', 'dome', 'column', 'obelisk', 'buttress', 'steeple', 'spire'.
2. Show your photos or slides and ask your students to identify the shapes and parts they recognise in the buildings.
3. Display or read out the sentence 'Architecture is music made solid'. Add that there is truth in the converse too – some musical constructions are architectural.

4. Tell them that they are going to hear 'architectural' music. Explain that they should allow the music to build architectural shapes in their minds, but for this to work well they will need to listen with their eyes closed.
5. Play the music.
6. Ask your students to quickly draw the outline of the buildings they have seen.
7. Individually, students prepare to describe their drawings in words. Help with vocabulary and encourage students to use any bilingual dictionaries that are handy.
8. Form pairs. Partners describe their pictures to each other. The person listening draws what they hear described. Those describing should not look at drawings in progress!
9. Partners show each other their drawings and discuss.
10. Wind up with a whole class discussion of what people saw.

Suggested music

- Mussorgsky orchestrated by Ravel: *Pictures from an Exhibition: The Great Gate of Kiev* or Mussorgsky: *Boris Godunov: Coronation Scene (Prologue scene 2)*. These tend to evoke images of Byzantine or Russian cupolas and domes.
- Ligeti: 'Monument' from *Three pieces for two pianos* or *Volumina I & II*. These pieces tend to suggest modern architecture.
- J. S. Bach: *Toccata in F major*.
- Tchaikovsky: *1812 Overture*, the final section with bells.
- Brahms: *Symphony no. 1 in C minor, op. 68*, the main theme of the 'Finale' (especially the repetition). This often evokes a grand, stately home in large gardens.

Clem Laroy

10.6 My home

Level
Intermediate–Advanced

Time
30 minutes

Focus
Speculating about someone's home;
speaking about one's own home

Materials
One or more musical excerpts; (optional) a
photograph of where you live

This is an excellent activity for deepening all participants' acquaintance with each other. It's one you can do repeatedly with different presenters each time.

Preparation

Choose one or a couple of pieces of music that you associate with your house or flat. A photo can be useful too.

Procedure

1. If you have brought a photo of your home, show it around the class.
2. Tell your students that you are going to play some music you associate with your home.
3. Play your music.
4. Ask them to make guesses about what your home is like. Perhaps write some sentence starters on the board first, e.g.
   'Your home must be ... '
   'The music suggests that ... '
   'The music makes me think of ... '
5. After the guesses have stopped flowing, tell the students which you feel were right.

Extensions

a) Ask your students each to bring, one by one on different days, a piece of music they associate with their home or a dwelling (of any kind) that has been important in their lives. In class, their classmates ask ten yes/no questions to learn about the place and the reasons for associating it with their piece of music.

b) The main activity and the extension above prepare the ground well
for writings (especially poems) that relate homes to music, for
example, 'My house/flat and music', 'My ideal house is like ...'.

Variations

- Play three quite different musical excerpts, only one of which
expresses your impressions of where you live. Play them and then ask
students to guess which of the three you had in mind, and why. Finish
by showing them your photo.
- One by one, on different days, your students bring in three different
excerpts of music and a photo, elicit guesses, then explain and show.
- Do the main activity or a variation with your parents' house or any
other house or building or place (e.g. a workplace) that has played a
part in your life.

Clem Laroy

10.7 Paintings and music

Level
Intermediate–Advanced

Time
15–20 minutes (more with 'Variation i')

Focus
Describing paintings and music of
different styles; artistic awareness

Materials
Three reproductions of paintings (or slides,
projector and screen); a piece of music
(see below)

'Music has this over painting – it can bring together all manner of
variations of colour and light.' (Debussy, Feb. 25, 1906)

Clem writes, 'This activity can be adapted to suit different audiences
from the artistically unsophisticated to students of art.' I'll add that it's a
great opportunity for both teachers and students to learn. It has
encouraged me to read about art history, a most pleasurable experience
in itself. If you think, as I do, that you're not teaching enough if you're
not teaching more than just language, this is the activity for you. SL

Preparation

Choose your colour reproductions or slides and your music. If your reproductions are too small to show from the front of the class, you will need enough of each for students to look at in pairs or small groups. (Use of photographs of paintings or of reproductions is also a possibility.)

Procedure

1. Start a conversation about links between music and painting. Ask your students what they see as common to both music and painting. Start your students thinking by giving them the following quotations from Berlioz:

    'Colour is a metaphor of music.'

    'Instrumentation is, in music, the exact equivalent of colour in painting.'

    Perhaps add that Gauguin spoke of 'symphonies and harmonies of colours' and that he also said that his paintings 'should provoke thoughts as music provokes thoughts, without the help of ideas or images, simply through the mysterious relationships which exist between our brains and these arrangements of lines and colours.'

2. Tell your students that they are going to see three reproductions of paintings and hear a piece of music. Explain that you would like them to associate one of the paintings with the music.

3. Play the music.

4. Ask your students to rank the three paintings in descending order of correlation with the music.

5. As far as possible, pair your students with someone who disagrees with them. Ask them to discuss how far they feel there are links between the paintings and the music as well as their reasons for thinking so.

6. Chair a general discussion to give the class an opportunity to share their ideas and learn something about painting and music.

Variations

i) In a particularly knowledgeable class, extend Step 1 by eliciting terms for different movements in painting (e.g. Realism, Romanticism, Impressionism, Expressionism, Cubism, etc.), discussing the movements and agreeing on a succinct chronology.

ii) Use photographs of sculpture or of buildings representative of different styles.

iii) If you use music which the composer intended to call particular images or kinds of image to mind (i.e. impressionistic and programme music), you can ask students to associate the subject of one of the paintings with your piece of music. For example, Hokusai's 'The Hollow of the Great Wave off Kanagawa' (Cologne, Museum für Ostasiatische Kunst) with instrumental music suggesting a rather pleasant mood such as Delius's *Aquarelle* No. 2, 'Gaily but not too quick', or Grieg's *Anitra's Dance* from *Pier Gynt/Suite No. 1*, Op. 46, or music actually originally linked with water or the sea, like passages from *Peter Grimes* by Benjamin Britten and Debussy's *Petite Suite* (1)*.

Suggestions for the choice of paintings and music

Choose paintings of very different styles, then choose a piece of music of the same style as one of the paintings.

- Expressionism. Paintings: Rottluf, Munch, Grosz and others to be used with music by romantic composers such as Wagner, Richard Strauss, Bartok when he was young. You can also try music by Alban Berg, Arnold Schönberg, Stravinsky or Webern.
- Impressionism. Paintings: Monet, Derain, Pissaro, Utrillo, Turner, Whistler. Music: Debussy, Ravel, Fauré.
- Abstractionism and Surrealism: Paintings: Mondrian, Appel, Braque, some Picasso, Magritte, Delvaux, Picabia, Miró, Dali. Music: Schoenberg, Stockhausen, Varèse, Boulez, Hamel, Zimmerman, Ligeti.

Similarly, people will generally associate 18th century music with a painting from the same period and so on for 17th century music and paintings, etc.

Also expect the subject and mood of the paintings to have an influence on students' associations.

Clem Laroy

---

* This has to be contrasted with music that expresses very different moods, e.g. Saint-Saëns' *Phaëton-Finale* (when the chase is over). Or music from a totally different culture can be introduced, for example: Francis Bebey: *Mopti* (OZILEKA) records – distribution sonodisc-LP:OZIL 3392.

10.8 Inside the painting

Level
Intermediate–Advanced

Time
30–40 minutes; or 60–70 minutes if
the writing is done in class rather than
at home

Focus
Conversation; writing

Materials
A reproduction of a painting (or colour
slide and projector); a musical excerpt

This activity blends storytelling, contemplation of a painting, music and visualisation to create very special results. Clem offers this quote as a hint: 'I believe one has never really penetrated a work of art until one has been guilty of the banal error of confusing fact and fiction.' (Lundquist 1967, p. 11)

Preparation

This activity works best with scenes (e.g. landscapes) rather than portraits. Settle on a suitable painting. You will need a slide or else a reproduction large enough for the whole class to see. Choose a musical excerpt that fits the atmosphere of the painting.

Procedure

1. The first time you do this activity with your class tell the Chinese legend given in outline below. Add embellishments to suit your students' level, interests and so on.

   The Chinese legend
   During the Tang dynasty, there was a painter Wu Tao-tzu. He spent his days painting on the walls of caves. One day, as he was examining a mural he had just finished, he suddenly clapped his hands. The door of the temple in the painting opened. He walked in through this temple door. It closed behind him. He never came back.

2. Allow about a minute for your students to discuss in pairs what they think the Chinese painter saw inside the temple and what happened to him.

3. Tell your students that they are going to enter a painting. Explain that you expect them to enter the painting at some point in it – a point of their choosing – so that they can visit the painting from inside.
4. Display the (reproduction of the) painting. Allow students time to look into it carefully. Encourage them to ask questions (e.g. about words for things and actions portrayed, who made the painting, when and where). Allow other students to answer if they can. Be wary of giving too much away just yet, as this can, to a certain extent, pre-empt later imaginative work on the part of the students.
5. Ask your students to relax and make themselves comfortable. Then play the music you have chosen.
6. Speaking in a calm voice, say something like the following: 'Look at the painting. Where can you get into it? Choose a point of entry. Go into the painting and close your eyes.'
   'Now ... what can you see, hear, smell, feel?'
   'Don't stop. Move on ... move farther into the painting. Let yourself be carried along by what you can hear and see and feel.'
7. Remove the reproduction or switch off the slide projector.
8. Continue speaking: 'Now, you are moving into another picture. Keep going. Where are you? Build the new picture in your mind. See it. Hear the sounds. What can you feel? Keep moving on. Notice what's there and what's happening. Remember this new scene.' Then stop talking and wait half a minute.
9. Tell your students to find a road, path, door, gate or other opening in their painting, one that leads back to the painting from before, the one they entered. From there they can come back to the classroom and then, slowly, open their eyes.
10. Ask everyone to jot down some notes and then tell at least two partners what they experienced inside their painting. Encourage people to draw speakers out by asking for elaboration and ask speakers to note down details that come out as a result of these questions.
11. Ask your students to write some kind of account of what they saw in whatever form they like (e.g. poem, short story, description).
12. Students read each other's writing.
13. Lead a discussion of the links between the initial painting, the music and what they wrote. If you know, perhaps add anything about what the painter had in mind to show or say in the painting. Or, if you can find anything the painter him- or herself wrote about this, read or hand it out to the class.

Extensions

a) Students research the life and times of the painter. They then rewrite their earlier text on the basis of any of this new information they want to include in it.
b) You can use the same painting again on another occasion. In a later lesson, show the painting and ask students to 'go into' it again, relive their earlier experiences but keep on going past where they were when you stopped them before. This time play different music. If you chose impressionist music before, this time play something dramatic. Students say this is like experiencing a dream in several episodes.
c) Students write essays in reaction to statements like these:
   - 'Art is only gold paint brushed over reality to fix it' (Lundquist p. 11)
   - 'I would like to paint a fabulous painting in which I could live' (Paul Delvaux, Belgian surrealist)
d) Read Lewis Caroll's *Through the Looking Glass.*

Variations

i) During the visualisation stage, put students in more unusual situations. For example, if you have displayed a pastoral scene, ask them to imagine they have become two inches tall.
ii) Experiment with different types of music for the same painting (e.g. playful, dramatic, pastoral . . .).

Clem Laroy

11 Not just for business people

The activities in this chapter are aimed primarily at mature students of more than elementary proficiency, especially students who are already working in business or a profession. However, these activities are often usable in general language classes comprising participants already in work, of whatever sort. It is, for example, not just business executives who rank the pros and cons of a job, as in Activity 11.2, or who participate in decisions about the purchase of a piece of equipment, the topic of Activity 11.4. The collocation learning and review activities (11.8–11.10) are also very usable in general language classes.

The activities that follow will not require you to act as an expert about any particular business or profession. On the one hand, if your participants are business and professional people, then, by definition, they do not need to be taught their trades by a language teacher. On the other hand, if yours is a general language course, the specialised knowledge and terminology of this or that business or profession is likely to be of limited interest to most of your participants. Accordingly, the activities in this chapter envisage different roles for a teacher than that of being an expert on everything. Chief among these roles are:

- Maximising participants' opportunities to improve their fluency and proficiency in listening comprehension.
- Encouraging the exchange of specialised information between and among participants (not from you to them) whenever appropriate. That is, given common interest in a topic, you elicit what various individuals in the group already know and spread it around so that afterwards, everyone is the wiser.
- Feeding in potentially useful elements of general language that your participants don't yet know.

The topics covered in this chapter are, in order:

- One's own job ('Advertise your own job', 11.1; 'The ideal job' (11.2); Marketing a new product' (11.3);
- who in an organisation takes responsibility for approving one-off purchases ('Decision makers' 11.4);
- factors in selling a product ('Selling power' 11.5 and 'Vendor analysis 11.6);

205

- things you can and can't do in meetings in different countries ('Bad meetings' 11.7);
- relations between clients and providers of a product or service ('Gifts to professionals' 11.11).

Activity 11.1 is a good course opener; 11.11 is a good course closer. Activities 11.4 and 11.6 form a suite.

Additionally, there are three activities designed to help participants learn collocations that occur with relatively high frequency in business-related contexts. 'Concept word pictionary' (11.8); 'Icon farrago race (11.9); and 'Market icons' (11.10).

11.1 Advertise your own job

Level
Intermediate–Advanced

Materials
A pile of broadsheet newspapers

Time
40 minutes

Focus
Jobs vocabulary; reading; writing

This is an effective exercise for early in a course. It stimulates participants to present their companies and their roles in their companies more deliberately than speaking activities typically tend to.

Preparation

Find a number of broadsheet newspapers with professional appointments sections – one or two per student. If possible, find issues specialising in the professional areas represented among your participants. (British newspapers tend to concentrate on a different area each day of the week; so for example on Tuesday *The Guardian*'s appointments section concentrates on jobs available in education.)

Procedure

1. Tell participants that they are going to write advertisements for their own jobs.

2. Ask them to read advertisements in the appointments sections of various broadsheet newspapers. Suggest that they pay special attention to the form or structure of the advertisements and note language that they think might be useful.
3. After they have read a few advertisements, ask participants to say what probably ought to go in a job advert. For example, an overview of the company, description of responsibilities, a short list of desirable personal qualities – all rendered in an upbeat tone.

Extension

If your students are interested in writing:
4. Ask them to write an advertisement for their job individually, or in pairs or groups as appropriate. When they finish, ask them to exchange advertisements and to correct language errors.
5. To complete the activity, display the finished advertisement for the whole class to read.

Marcus Child

11.2 The ideal job

Level
Lower-intermediate–Advanced

Materials
A class set of the worksheet (below)

Time
30–45 minutes

Focus
Discussion

The main instrument for stimulating discussion in this wide-ranging activity is the worksheets. Feel free to adapt and extend them.

Procedure

1. Ask students to think back to when they were children. What did they want to be when they grew up? Ask a few students what sort of job they hope (or hoped) to get after completing their studies/

apprenticeships. Ask for specifics – if a student answers 'lawyer', ask what kind (corporate, criminal, private practice, etc.).
2. Hand out copies of the worksheet. Explain vocabulary as necessary.
3. Ask students to place each element of job satisfaction into one of the categories according to how they perceive an ideal job (not necessarily their present job if they are employed).
4. Organise the students into groups of three to five and ask them to:
   – compare their classifications
   – discuss the characteristics of the ideal job
   – explain why they view these characteristics as ideal

Acknowledgement

The first part of the worksheet is an adaptation of one developed several years ago by a colleague at the Ecole des Mines in Nancy.

Denny Packard

The ideal job: worksheet

A recent survey posed the problem of people's (sometimes utopian) attitudes and considerations when looking for a job. They placed some of their requirements for a rewarding and satisfying job in order of importance. Here are most of the elements considered:
– a good salary
– good relationships with colleagues
– a good canteen/cafeteria
– variety and enjoyment in the work done
– contact with the public
– little work to do
– the opportunity to reduce other people's suffering
– flexible hours
– long holidays
– proximity to place of residence
– travel
– social activities at one's place of work (dinner dances, excursions, picnics, etc.)
– promotion prospects
– a pleasant and attractive place of work
– a clean and well-heated place of work
– the prestige of the company

- any members of the opposite sex working there should be attractive
- perks (company car, cheap loans, large discounts on company products, etc.)
- a feeling of making the world a better place to live in
- a smoke-free work area
- a crèche / daycare centre (for children)
- opportunities for continuing education
- an opportunity to initiate new products
- close supervision over you
- little or no supervision over you
- a strong union
- a tight organisational structure with a well-defined hierarchy
- loose organisational structure
- a democratic decision-making process
- lots of responsibility
- job security
- a feeling of being useful
- the opportunity to command other people
- a convenient place to park
- access to the out of doors

Classify each of the elements of the ideal job under the following four headings:

'ESSENTIAL' 'UNIMPORTANT' 'DESIRABLE' 'UNDESIRABLE'

© Cambridge University Press

11.3 Marketing a new product

Level
Intermediate–Advanced

Materials
None

Time
30–60 minutes

Focus
Discussion; creativity development;
marketing

This sequence of activities is a particularly neat blend of fantasy and realism. It culminates in useful and amusing practice of presentation skills.

Procedure

1. Ask the class to brainstorm a list of ten common objects. Have one student list these on the board.
2. Tell the class to forget this list for a moment and to brainstorm a new list, this one of ten materials that objects can be made of/from (wood, glass, etc.). These materials need not have any connection with the previous list. Have a different student write these on the board.
3. Ask everyone to consider the two lists and to speculate on the most unlikely combinations of materials and objects, for example, a wooden balloon.
4. After the class comes up with five or six suggestions, the whole class should discuss and then vote on the strangest combination of all those proposed.
5. Form groups of three to five students and ask each group to prepare a 15-second radio advertisement for this same product (i.e. the wooden balloon or whatever was voted the strangest combination). Set a 10- to 15-minute time limit. Ask groups that finish early to decide on the background music they would use in their advertisement.
6. Each group presents their radio advertisement to the class.

Variation

Ask business students and people in business to prepare a marketing plan rather than a radio spot.

Acknowledgement

I learned this marvellous idea from Jane Kendall, a management consultant specialising in human resources and creativity development.

Denny Packard

11.4 Decision makers

Level
Intermediate

Materials
A class set of the worksheet (below)

Time
20–30 minutes

Focus
Vocabulary; discussion

This exercise is a useful lead-in to the two following activities, 'Selling power' and 'Vendor analysis'. It works especially well if all the members of the class work for the same company.

Procedure

1. Ask students to bring to mind a recent large or small purchase made by their company – photocopying machine, desk, personal computer, etc.
2. Write all the suggestions on the board.
3. Ask everyone to list the people (by name / job title) who were involved in making the decision to buy 'their' item.
4. If your class has only a few members, hold the discussion as one group. Otherwise, put students in groups of three to compare and discuss; follow on with a stage where groups briefly report on their discussions to the whole class.
5. Give out the worksheet and ask students to work individually. Ask them to add onto the left column any items that are relevant to their job situation, either ones listed on the board or any others they might recall having been purchased.

211

6. Group the students in twos or threes to discuss the work done in Step 5.
7. Call the class together and ask for comments.

Satish Patel

Decision makers: worksheet

Item purchased	No. of people	Names / job titles	Other people not involved but who should be / should have been
OHP			
Photocopier			
Office furniture			
Portable PC			
Office phone			
Coffee machine			
A language course			
A holiday			
Gold watches			
Plants			
Car			
Car phone			
....			
....			
....			
....			
....			
....			
....			

© Cambridge University Press

11.5 Selling power

Level
Intermediate

Materials
A class set of the worksheet (below)

Time
20–30 minutes

Focus
Vocabulary; discussion

This activity serves as a useful lead-in to 'Vendor analysis'. It works especially well if all the members of the class work for the same company.

Procedure

1. Ask participants to draw up a list of factors that are necessary for success in selling their company's product/service. They may work individually, in pairs or in groups. See the worksheet for examples.
2. Ask them to call out their suggestions for you to write on the board.
3. Give everyone a copy of the worksheet. Ask students to add onto the worksheet any factors that are missing.
4. Working alone, students rank each factor according to its importance to their company.
5. In groups of three, students compare and discuss their rankings.
6. In plenary, ask groups to report on their discussions.
7. Lead the class into further discussion by saying something like:
   – 'We have now discussed your attitude to your own products. How do you think your ratings would differ if . . .
   i) you were buying a product from another company?'
   ii) you were buying or leasing a product that may occasionally/ often break down, a photocopier or a car, for example?' (In this case technical support might have greatest priority.)

Acknowledgement

This activity is adapted from the unit 'Organisational Markets and Buying Behaviour' in *Marketing Management Analysis* by P. Kotlers.

Satish Patel

Selling power: worksheet

Rate the following in order of importance for your company. Add any other factors you think are important.

____ company reputation	____ price
____ promptness of delivery	____ extension of credit
____ quality of product/service	____ skill of sales reps
____ completeness of product line	____ technical support
____ promptness of support, service etc.	____ personal relationships
____ manuals and other supporting literature	____ brochures and other promotional literature
____ company references (either word of mouth or instances of companies that lend their name to say they have been satisfied customers)	____ ....
	____ ....
	____ ....
	____ ....

© Cambridge University Press

11.6 Vendor analysis

Level
Intermediate–Advanced

Materials
A class set of the worksheet (below)

Time
30–40 minutes

Focus
Vocabulary; discussion; (extension) writing

This activity works particularly well if preceded by 'Selling power'.

Procedure

1. Give out the worksheet and explain vocabulary if necessary.
2. Ask students to extend the list of factors necessary for successful

selling of their company's product/service. (They can, of course, cross out any of the factors given which are not applicable.) Thinking of their own company, they rate the role of each factor from 1 to 5 by ticking the appropriate column. Note: A rating of '1' does not mean that a factor is of necessity insignificant. Instead, it means that this factor plays a role that is unacceptably below potential.

3. Ask students to form groups of three and to discuss their ratings.
4. Bring the class back together and ask the groups to report on their discussions.
5. Lead the class into further discussion by asking:
   - Can the rating of some of the factors be improved? Which ones? How?

Vendor analysis: worksheet

Factor	unacceptable 1	poor 2	fair 3	good 4	excellent 5
quality					
promptness of delivery					
technical support					
sales reps					
manuals					
brochures					
credit facilities					
price					
....					
....					
....					

© Cambridge University Press

Extension

6. Do one of the following:
   - Ask the students (individually or in pairs) to write a report of this lesson. They then give their reports to their managers who can then do something specific in order to improve the rating of that particular factor.
   - If you are working with a single company group, take the class's findings directly to the Managing Director of the company. If they are useful, he or she might decide to take part in the course too.

215

Acknowledgement

This activity is adapted from the unit 'Organisational Markets and Buying Behaviour' in *Marketing Management Analysis* by P. Kotlers.

Satish Patel

11.7 Bad meetings

Level	**Materials**
Intermediate–Advanced	None

Time
10–15 minutes

Focus
Discussion of cultural differences

This is a good way of rounding off a session on business meetings in which you have focused, for example, on useful phrases for interrupting, soliciting opinions, etc.

Preparation

Write a list of things which would be unacceptable to do or say in a fairly formal British or American business meeting. For example: smoking without asking, whispering while someone else has the floor, yawning, rocking your chair, getting too close, sitting with your arms crossed behind your head, sliding down low in your chair with your feet far out in front of you, fiddling with a pen or key chain, doodling, chewing gum or something similar, coming late and elaborately greeting everyone individually before you sit down, touching other participants when you speak to them, not making eye contact, eating something of your own (i.e. when no one else is eating).

Procedure

1. Display or hand out a copy of your list. Allow students time to ask you about items they don't understand.

2. Ask if these types of behaviour would be equally bad in their own culture(s).
3. Invite examples of bad behaviour in the students' own cultures.

Extension

4. Ask students if there are such things as informal business meetings in their country/culture where the rules of behaviour are more relaxed. Ask where these meetings might take place. Provided it is generally agreed that business meetings can be more or less formal, pair students up.
   - If partners are from different countries/cultures, ask them to tell each other which types of behaviour would be unacceptable even in an informal business meeting in their respective countries.
   - If partners are from the same country/culture, ask them to agree on what remains taboo.
5. If the pair discussions were lively, ask pairs briefly to report high points to the class.

Variation

Include a number of acceptable things on your list (e.g. 'passing someone a note', 'loosening your tie') and see if the class can spot them.

Chris Dalton

11.8 Concept word pictionary

Level
Lower- intermediate-Advanced

Materials
Several flash cards

Time
10 minutes

Focus
Collocations, conversation; team building

This lively activity is excellent not only for warming a class up and for vocabulary review but also for fostering the kind of relationships in class that make it easier for participants to work as teams.

217

Preparation

Prepare a set of flashcards, each bearing a different phrase or colloca-tion, e.g. 'go into receivership', 'friendly takeover', 'golden handshake' and so on.

Procedure

1. Divide the class into two teams.
2. Each team selects a representative who goes to the board and stands by it on one side or the other.
3. Show one of your cards to the two representatives, but not the rest of the class. Explain that it is the job of each of the two representatives to try to reveal to their team what your collocation is, not by speaking or writing, but by drawing and gesture only. The first team to shout out the collocation wins. (Add that it might be good tactic for representative A to stand so that members of team B do not have the easiest view of what representative A has drawn for the benefit of team A, and vice versa.)

Marcus Child

11.9 Icon farrago race

Level
Intermediate–Advanced

Time
20–25 minutes

Focus
Listening

Materials
A class set of sheets covered with small, clear images from the business world (icons, logos, etc.) (example below)

This is another high-energy activity for reviewing business vocabulary. Like 11.8 and 11.10, it exploits the mnemonic potential of icons and non-print symbols.

Preparation

1. Stick 70–100 black and white business related icons onto two or

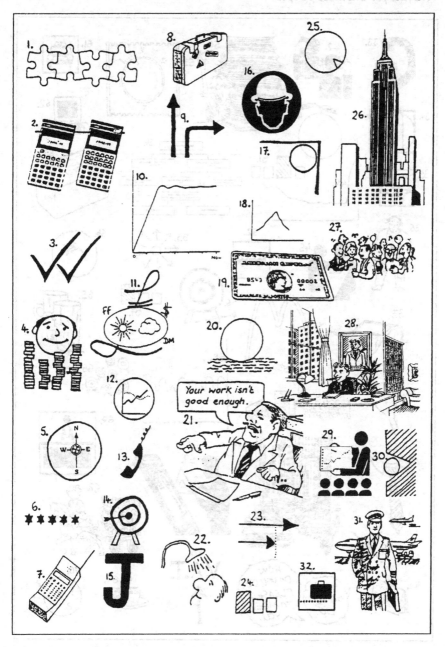

three sheets of A4. These can include company logos, simple graphs and directional signs.
2. Make a class set of each sheet.

Procedure

1. Divide the class into teams of three. Ask them to study the icon sheets silently for two or three minutes.
2. Say that you are going to read out a series of words and expressions each of which fits one of the icons, as its title perhaps. Add that as soon as they hear a word or phrase, they should scan the icons and shout out the number of the corresponding icon. Whoever shouts out the correct number first, wins a point for their team. Keep scores on the board. Tip: By periodically raising the number of points awarded for a correct answer, you can keep the energy of this activity very high.

Icon farrago race: key (Don't read the items out in the order given here!)

1.	Link up	36.	Recession
2.	Double check	37.	Speculation!
3.	"I totally agree"	38.	"I think we're missing the point"
4.	Profiteer	39.	White collar
5.	Market oriented	40.	I disagree
6.	Top quality	41.	Briefcase
7.	Mobility	42.	Contact-engaged
8.	Suitcase	43.	Natural market
9.	"To digress for a moment"	44.	Starting to pick up
10.	Levelling off	45.	Auditing
11.	Economic climate	46.	U.S. franchiser
12.	Market trends	47.	Production
13.	Off the hook	48.	Jam
14.	Realising objectives	49.	Making contact
15.	Jay	50.	Backlog
16.	Job security	51.	Australia
17.	To corner the market	52.	Shuttle/transit
18.	Peak	53.	Control
19.	Credit	54.	Organigram
20.	Buoyant market	55.	Delegation
21.	Authoritarian	56.	Below target
22.	R and R. Rest and relaxation	57.	Japanese
23.	"I agree with you up to a point"	58.	Fluctuation
24.	Italy	59.	Product design
25.	Market niche	60.	Tax rise
26.	Empire building	61.	For picking up and dropping off
27.	Conference (annual)	62.	Data processing
28.	Stressed management	63.	For recharging
29.	"Let's look at this diagram"	64.	Market forces
30.	Niche market	65.	"The next round is on me"
31.	High flier	66.	Target group
32.	Sales rep	67.	Check in
33.	Gee	68.	Disempowered team
34.	Captive market	69.	"How about a break?"
35.	Fresh air zone	70.	Market survey

Marcus Child

221

11.10 Market icons

Level
Intermediate–Advanced

Materials
Class sets of an 'icon sheet' (see below)

Time
45–60 minutes

Focus
Collocations with a collocationally versatile word such as *market*; conversation; writing

This highly interesting, reflective activity is a wonderful way to review and expand knowledge of collocations of key business words like 'market'.

Preparation

1. Write your key word, e.g. 'market', in a circle in the middle of the board.
2. Ask participants to go to the board and write as many words as they can think of that collocate with the key word. For example: 'flood the m', 'm research', 'overseas m', 'bear m', 'bull m', 'saturated m', 'active m', 'sluggish m', 'shrinking m', 'niche m', 'm niche', 'm economy', 'free m', 'restricted m', 'm share', 'domestic m'.
3. Elicit further collocations by offering verbal hints, e.g. 'What's the opposite of an active market?', 'If a company suddenly puts out a huge quantity of a certain product, we can say that it ...' Try to cover the board.
4. Explain that you wish to represent the key word with a circle – and that other concepts can then be represented by adding to this circle, for example:

$$\bigcirc = market \longrightarrow \bigcirc = market\ share$$

5. Ask everyone to work individually and draw representations, or icons, of six of the other phrases on the board. Each icon should include a circle (for the word 'market') as well as additional graphics to represent the collocating modifiers/nouns. They should not label their icons.

6. As participants finish their icons, they should each exchange sheets with someone else who has finished. Swappers sit next to each other and label each other's icons. Allow time for everyone to look at their partner's labels and, still in pairs, to comment as they like.
7. Call the class together and invite participants to present their favourite icons.
8. Hand out your sheet of icons (see example on next page). In pairs, participants try to label them.
9. Give the class some feedback about how they got on. Invite comments.
10. Participants use icons that have come up so far, along with others that they now invent, to compose longer phrases or sentences in a new iconic, or 'hieroglyphic' script. For example:

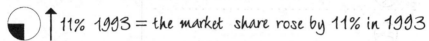

11% 1993 = the market share rose by 11% in 1993

Participants either label their creations and show them to others or they leave them unlabelled and invite someone else to guess the label intended.
11. Collect participants' work from Step 10 for display on a bulletin board in class.

Variations

i) This activity works with other key words too (mostly nouns, e.g. 'control', 'business', 'insurance', 'bank', 'government(al)', 'price', 'trade', 'economy'), though use of other symbols or icons than a circle might be appropriate. For example, the icon for 'trade' might be two parallel horizontal arrows, one pointing left and the other right; that for 'government' might be an upward pointing triangle.
ii) In the case of words having fewer common collocates than 'market', you can work with two at the same time.

Marcus Child

Expressions with 'market'

1.
2.
3.
4.
5.
6.
7.
8.
9.
10.
11.
12.
13.
14.
15.
16.
17.
18.

Key

1 market share
2 increased market share
3 market research
4 market penetration
5 money market
6 market trend
7 shrinking market
8 expanding market
9 flat market
10 market niche
11 niche market
12 market survey
13 active market
14 domestic market
15 overseas market
16 segmented market
17 flooded market
18 market leader

11.11 Gifts to professionals

Level
Elementary–Advanced

Materials
None

Time
30–40 minutes

Students
Working adults; see variation for teenage classes

Focus
Speaking; listening

This exercise is powerful at the end of an intensive course when people are preparing to return to their normal work. The stories from clients and the reactions to them can help students enter the 'transitional zone' between the course and their work.

Procedure

1. Suggest to the students that we are all clients/subjects of professionals, be they waste disposal experts, doctors, lawyers, librarians, managing directors or secretaries.
   Set the ball rolling by telling a story about yourself as the client/subject of a profession that is represented in the class. If you have a garage manager in the class, tell them about an incident connected with garages. Speak directly to them, making eye contact.
2. Ask if other members of the group have similar stories they can tell connected with garages. Some will, some won't. Again, people should tell their stories to the particular professional in the class, making eye contact with this person.
3. Offer the garage manager the chance to tell stories about clients or subjects.
4. Repeat the above three steps with each profession represented in the class. If you have a class of more than 12, form groups of six to eight students for this step; students then concentrate on the professions represented in their own groups.

Variation

With teenagers, ask them to describe their mother or father's job and to do the rest of the activity around these jobs.

Mario Rinvolucri

225

12 Grammar and register: practice, reflection, review

As the title of this chapter suggests, it contains activities which focus on some aspect of grammar – that is, 'grammar' in the broad sense of the form of words and the ordering of words in phrases, sentences and short sequences of sentences.

The first activity, 'The news in our town' (12.1), describes an activity you can do in every lesson, provided your course is taking place in your students' home town. It is unique among the activities in this chapter in that it is not only a way of encouraging students to use structures they have already met, but is also a way of introducing completely new ones.

The next four activities fit nicely into the 'use' phase of a classic presentation/practice/use grammar lesson. These are the activities 'I see ... You see' (12.2), 'Transposed questionnaires' (12.3), 'Crazy fortune' (12.4), and 'Gossips' (12.5). They can also work very nicely outside this classic framework – as fluency practice.

'Talking to the board' (12.6) and 'A translation task' (12.7) are useful for fostering the understanding of a number of grammatical and semantic issues in one lesson – whichever ones happen to be brought up by an earlier activity (12.6) or by a particular text (12.7).

'The register of replies' (12.8) concentrates on clarifying issues of register, or style levels.

12.1   The news in our town

Level
Beginner–low-intermediate

Materials
None

Time
10 minutes

Requirement
For courses taking place in students' home town

Focus
Discussion; exposing students to new grammatical structures; vocabulary

In every class I make a short break to talk about the news. Students enjoy this moment of relaxation. I have an ulterior motive though – to take advantage of the fact that students can pick up new structures and vocabulary items without these being explicitly taught. All that is necessary is that the new elements of language be comprehensible at the times students encounter them and that students have some reason to pay attention to the utterances that contain them. The key to making the most of this technique is to take information provided by the students as the starting point.

Procedure

1. Ask questions like 'What happened in our city yesterday?' As students answer, act as moderator and also as consultant, providing unknown words and correcting in a casual way, for example:

   S: Crashed two cars.
   T: Two cars crashed? Where?

2. After several pieces of news have been contributed and – if all goes well – discussed, elicit a summary of one or more of them and write it on the board. Guide the students so that the information provided is given in the order 'What?' 'Where?' 'When?' 'Why?'. Leave room under each statement for a paraphrase.

3. Add in your paraphrases. For example, under this student contribution:

   'Two cars crashed. The two drivers died.'

   you might write

   'Two drivers died in a car crash.'

227

As you think appropriate, use arrows and circles, etc. to highlight relationships between the student summary and your paraphrase, e.g.

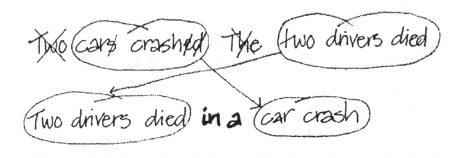

4. Ask students to read out each original summary and then its paraphrase. Then give them time to copy all the sentences down.

Variation

As students get used to this routine, try to elicit the paraphrases too, e.g.

S: A woman was with one of the drivers. She is in hospital.
T: Can you join the two sentences?

Here you might be aiming to elicit:

'The woman who was with one of the drivers is in hospital.'

Note

There are two important 'don'ts':
- Don't be afraid of using unknown structures in your paraphrases. Through comparison with the known (i.e. a sentence contributed by someone in the class), students can see what the unknown means.
- Don't try to teach explicitly the new structures and vocabulary that occur in the paraphrases. (As time passes, you'll be surprised to hear students use structures and words from these paraphrases despite their never having been formally presented.)

Viviana Valenti

12.2   I see ... You see

Level
Any, but especially elementary

Time
5–10 minutes

Materials
A varied assortment of interesting photos or similar, including landscapes and scenes with people

Focus
Writing; statements beginning 'I . . .' and 'You . . .'; conversation

At beginner and elementary levels this is a grammar practice activity with an unusual affective twist. At higher levels it works as a warm-up or filler, without losing any of its potential to produce interesting writing and conversation.

Procedure

1. Hand out your pictures and allow people time to sort through them and choose one each that they like. Meanwhile, write the following sentence starters on the board:

   'I am ...'
   'I can see ...'
   'I can hear ...'
   'I feel ...'
   'I ...'

2. Ask students to imagine they are in the pictures they have chosen and then to write five sentences. One starting 'I am ...', one starting 'I can hear ...' and so on.
3. In pairs, students swap papers. Each writes on their partner's paper three new sentences beginning 'You ...'.
4. Students swap their papers back, read and discuss.

John Morgan

12.3 Transposed questionnaires

Level
Elementary–Intermediate

Materials
A class set of questionnaires (example below)

Time
15–25 minutes

Focus
Depends on questionnaire; present simple
in the example below

You will sometimes throw interesting light on an area by using a questionnaire not designed for it. This activity describes a way of applying this insight to stimulate conversations in small groups.

Please mark X in the square which corresponds with what you consider to be the correct answer; the abbreviations are as follows:

EX = Excellent   VG = Very Good   G = Good
S = Satisfactory   U = Unsatisfactory

1. What is your opinion of:	EX	VG	G	S	U
(a) The family					
(b) The food					
(c) Your bedroom					
(d) Warmth					
(e) Opportunity to study quietly					
(f) Opportunity to watch television					
(g) Opportunity to speak					
(h) The journey to school					

Preparation

Select a questionnaire designed for one purpose and ask the students to use it for another. The one on page 231 is used by a language school in the UK to find out if students are happy in the families they are staying with.

Procedure

1. Give the students the questionnaire and ask them each to complete it, thinking about their own families *at home* (where they come from, not where they happen to be studying).
2. When they've finished, they cluster in threes and compare their thoughts about their families, explaining where necessary.

Acknowledgement

The mini-questionnaire (p. 231) has been used at Eurocentres in Cambridge, England.

Mario Rinvolucri

12.4 Crazy fortune

Level
Elementary–Advanced

Time
20–25 minutes

Focus
Conversation; use of 'will' in talking about the future

Materials
Optional: crystal balls, if you can get hold of any!

Units on horoscopes and fortune telling are routine in coursebooks, but none are as much fun to use as this ingenious activity.

Procedure

1. Introduce the activity by asking your students if they have ever had

their fortune told (When? Who by? How? etc.) and asking what they think of fortune tellers in general.

2. Ask everyone to write five questions on the left of a sheet of paper. These should be questions they would ask a fortune teller. Typical questions are: '(When) Will I get married?' 'How many children will I have?' 'How much will I earn next year?' 'Will I buy a new car?'.

3. On the right side of their papers they write:
   - three verbs
   - three nouns
   - three adjectives
   - three numbers between 2,005 and 2,050
   - three numbers between 5 and 15

   It is important that students write the questions first because this tends to lead them to write associated words or numbers on the left.

4. Students pair off and take turns roleplaying a fortune teller while the other asks their questions. But this is 'Crazy fortune-telling', so the fortune teller has to try always to give answers which are (a) positive in tone and which (b) include the words and numbers which the fortune tellers have written on the right of their own sheets. This produces really wild answers!

5. After about seven minutes – when each student in the pairs has had the opportunity of playing both roles – ask pairs to report on what they were told.

Extension

6. To round off the activity, put students in groups. Ask them to analyse the questions and make a list of 'common worries'.

7. Groups report to the class.

Variations

i) At Step 2, you can vary the parts of speech students need to write three of – for example, adverbs instead of adjectives.

ii) After Step 5, write several adjectives on the board (e.g. 'abrupt', 'sure of him-/herself', 'friendly', 'mysterious', 'hesitant', 'rude', 'well-mannered', 'sympathetic' ...) and elicit characterisations of the fortune tellers from their customers – that is, how they sounded, looked or acted.

Rationale

The first time I used this activity I became worried when listening to the questions which students asked (they were quite serious in tone). But when they received ludicrous replies, the students began to really enjoy themselves. It seemed that the ridiculous answers robbed the questions of seriousness. One of my students said (in Spanish), 'I felt better. It was as if I had been worrying too much about something which was not, after all, so important.'

Adriana Diaz

12.5 Gossips

Level
Intermediate

Time
30 minutes

Focus
Note-taking; speaking; speculating about past events (use of must/could/might/ may have, was/were probably, etc.)

Materials
At least half a class set of the worksheet (below)

This roleplay activity is a good prelude to recounting anecdotes about neighbours. (See 'Are you a worthy owner?', 7.5.)

Procedure

1. Introduce the activity by asking your students what they think about neighbours – if they are a help or a nuisance, what kinds of neighbours one can have, if neighbourliness is dying out and so on.
2. Form an even number of groups of from four to six members. Tell the class that half the groups are unsuspicious neighbours, people who tend to impute good intentions to others. The rest of the groups are typical gossips, people who like to spread rumours.
3. Distribute the worksheet. Explain that each item states something they happened to see in the neighbourhood. The group brainstorms the speculations their kind of neighbour might make about these goings-on. Each student keeps their own record, in note form. Circulate and make sure everybody is keeping a list. Call time when each group has at least a half dozen or more possibilities listed down.

233

4. Students now pair off, one unsuspicious neighbour with one gossipy one. If need be, remind students of the structure(s) they can use by writing it/them on the board. Stress that everyone should play their role – and not read off their list.

5. Students return to their original groups and share what other neighbours have told them. They choose the funniest speculations by other groups to report to the whole class.

Gossips

a) At 5 am you saw the McKennons' daughter come back home. A young, long-haired boy was with her.

b) At 7 you saw Mr Davis leave home. He was carrying two heavy-looking suitcases and he had a bandage over his forehead.

c) At 8 you saw a man entering the Davis' house. Mrs Davis looked very happy to see him. They hugged effusively on the doorstep.

d) At about 9 a police officer called at the Smiths'. He was inside for about half an hour.

e) At about the same time, Ms Browning, who lives alone and leaves for work at 8, took the rubbish bag out. She was wearing her dressing gown.

f) At about 10, when you were leaving home to do the shopping, the Wilsons' son bumped into you, didn't even say 'good morning' and ran on. A much older boy was chasing him. He was shouting something about a window but you didn't quite catch what it was.

© Cambridge University Press

Variations

i) In Step 4, students have more than one conversation.

ii) Instead of pairing off, students form new groups consisting of one member from each of the former ones. They pretend they have met at a shop. They all chat about the morning's events.

Adriana Diaz

12.6 Talking to the board

Level
Elementary–Advanced

Materials
20 to 30 slips of paper; Blu-tack or
Sellotape; a boardmarker

Time
15–30 minutes

Focus
Speaking; intensive reading; thinking
about grammar and word choice

This error correction activity works particularly well with groups of
10–15 students. It's not recommended for teachers who suffer from
claustrophobia!

Procedure

1. While students are involved in any speaking activity in small groups,
   you mingle unobtrusively with slips of paper in one hand and a pen
   in the other. Write down any sentences that you think are particularly good or bad – one sentence per slip, along with the speaker's
   name.
2. When the speaking activity has finished, hand your slips out.
3. Divide the board into two halves by drawing a vertical line down the
   middle. Write 'correct' as a heading in one half and 'incorrect' in the
   other.
4. Invite the students to stick their sentences in the appropriate half of
   the board. If they are not sure about a sentence, they stick it on the
   dividing line.
5. When all the slips have been stuck on the board, sit on a chair, kneel
   or squat directly in front of the board. Ask the students to gather
   round you. By standing as close as possible to you, they tower over
   you and it seems as if you almost disappear.
6. As the students focus on the board, start thinking aloud. Begin with
   sentences that have been placed in the proper half and do not have to
   be moved. For example, 'Oh, yes, that looks good. Everything looks
   in the right order'. Or, 'Yes, that's not right. The . . . should be . . .'
7. When the students have got used to you talking for the board, focus
   on the next slip and say something like, 'Well. I'm not sure about this
   one', and pause. Students will start giving their opinions to the

board, not to you. You speak for the board until the students are satisfied with what the board has said.

8. As far as the rest of the slips are concerned, you will only be needed to give the final verdict by moving the slips where necessary, ticking the correct slips and writing down the corrections under, next to or above the incorrect slips. The students argue it out with the board.

John Barnett

12.7 A translation task

Level
Beginner–Advanced

Materials
See 'Preparation'

Time
Varies with the length and complexity
of the text

Focus
Dictionary skills; vocabulary building;
motivated reading of authentic texts

This absorbing intensive reading and translation activity is for monolingual groups. You must have considerable knowledge of your students' mother tongue. Here it is assumed that the target language is English.

Preparation

1. Choose a text suitable for your group in terms of linguistic difficulty, topic and so on. Make a translation of it into the L1 (mother tongue) of your learners.
2. Prepare a class set of copies of each of the following: the L2 (English) original of the text (Sheet A), your translation (Sheet B) and a version of the original L1 text in which the lines are listed down the page in alphabetical order of the first letter of the first word (Sheet C). Note, these lines will not necessarily be sentences; in fact, they probably won't be.

Procedure

1. Tell your class that you're going to give them a translation exercise.

Divide them into twos and threes and make enough monolingual and bilingual dictionaries available.

2. Tell them that the text they're going to work with, which is in their own language, was originally written in English. Add that they are going to translate it back into English.
3. Give them copies of Sheet B (your translation of the text) and allow them a few minutes to read through it.
4. Then leave them to get on with their translation work. Answer questions and clarify any difficulties as they are working.
5. After they have finished, or gone as far as they can, hand out copies of Sheet C (alphabetical listing). Give them all time to read through this.
6. Tell the class to compare Sheets B and C and to try to number the alphabetically-ordered lines of Sheet C in the correct order based on their translation. Allow time for this.
7. As students finish, give out copies of Sheet A (the original text). Ask them to read it through carefully and try to resolve any misunderstandings that may have affected the accuracy of their earlier translations either in understanding the English original or in finding an appropriate (L1) translation. Encourage students to question each other or you if they can't work something out on their own.

Variations and Options

Some good sources of L2 texts are: students' own writing in previous classes; the coursebook(s) you are using; and English language coursebooks for other subjects your students might be studying.

This last option can be especially useful if you can liaise with a subject teacher, a history teacher for example, and get hold of a UK-published textbook from which you can take items that parallel texts currently being read by your students in history.

In advanced, linguistically sophisticated classes, texts on contrastive analysis can make for an interesting 'loop' since contrastive analysis is one of the things your students will be doing while reading, translating and discussing the text.

In addition to varying the source or topic of the text, you can also vary the type of text. If you choose a song or a poem, show your students the rhyme scheme at the beginning of Step 4. Make sure they understand how paying attention to the rhyme scheme can help them. Give an example or two, such as: 'costumbres', in line x, can be translated as 'customs', 'habits' or 'ways'. Which of these rhymes with 'days?'

A good source of poems are bilingual collections of verse. Working with teenagers, I have used current hit records as the source of original texts. I begin by saying that the original text is a poem (in order to keep the song a surprise for them). Then, at Step 7, I tell them they are going to hear a version of the original on tape and they should use this to check their final text. Once they have heard the song, I hand out copies of the lyrics.

Bryan Robinson

12.8　The register of replies

Level
Intermediate–Advanced

Materials
None

Time
30–40 minutes

Focus
Register; social/situational language

The 'register of replies' describes an ingenious way of helping students learn how to match language to situation.

Procedure

1. On the board or OHP write a starter phrase such as,
   'Make me a cup of tea'.
   Good starter phrases are ones that tend to invite a reply but not one or two in particular. Thus, 'How do you do?' isn't suitable while the following are:
   'Next please'.
   'I'm really zonked'.
2. Ask your students each to fold an A4 sheet in half, lengthwise, so that they have two long, narrow sides of paper to write on.
3. Ask them to work individually and write as many replies to your starter phrase as possible down the *left* side of the folded sheet (as in the figure at the top of page 240). Circulate helping out with language.
   Call a halt after 5 minutes or sooner if the majority are slowing down.
4. Arrange the students in groups of four or five. Ask everyone to

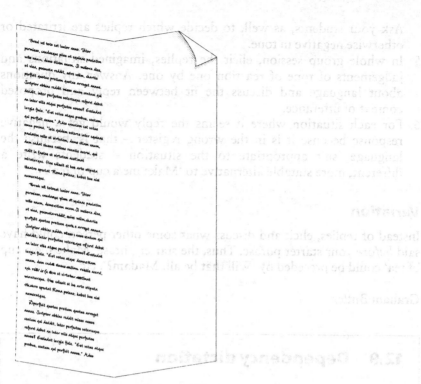

unfold their papers. The members of each group take turns reading out their replies. Working together, they agree on a plausible scene or set of characters for each reply to the original utterance (e.g. each reply to 'Make me a cup of tea'). They note what they decide about the settings and characters of each reply opposite it on the right half of the paper. As the discussion proceeds, each student should add to the 'reply column' of their own paper all the replies contributed by their colleagues in the group and, opposite each reply, all the situations, like this:

OK darling, just sit down

Wife returning from the supermarket, speaking to husband.

I'd rather not, if you don't mind.

A teacher talking to another in the staffroom, between classes

---

Ask your students, as well, to decide which replies are irritated or otherwise negative in tone.

5. In whole group session, elicit the replies, imagined situations and judgements of tone of reaction one by one. Answer any questions about language and discuss the fit between reply and proposed context of utterance.

6. For each situation where it seems the reply would get a negative response because it is in the wrong register – that is, because the language isn't appropriate to the situation – students write a different, more suitable alternative to 'Make me a cup of tea'.

Variation

Instead of replies, elicit and discuss what some other person could have said *before* your starter phrase. Thus, the starter phrase 'Make me a cup of tea' could be preceded by 'Will that be all, Madam?', etc.

Graham Butler

12.9 Dependency dictation

Level
Elementary–Advanced

Materials
None

Time
5–10 minutes

Focus
Review of previously encountered collocations

Preparation

Choose six to eight collocations. The examples below refer to adjective + preposition pairs such as *interested in*. (See the list below for examples of various kinds.)

Procedure

1. Tell students that:

- you are going to dictate several words, each of which is typically followed (or preceded) by a certain preposition.
- you will not say the preposition.
- they must write the preposition you don't say and not write the adjective (for example) which you do say.
- instead of writing the adjective you say they should write only one letter from it, but not the first letter.

Thus, if you say 'interested', your students should each write '____t____ in' or '____s____ in' or '_____d in', etc.

2. As you begin dictating, walk around and check that they are not writing out the adjective. Also, give examples of use as necessary but snap your fingers (or something) when you get to the preposition. For example, 'She's very good SNAP skiing' (i.e. 'good *at* skiing'). Dictate all your adjectives; students write just the one letter of each plus the missing preposition.
3. Now check by eliciting or calling out the correct preposition for each item.
4. Put students into pairs and ask them to try to remember each adjective and write it down.
5. Check that everyone has got all the collocations right.

Note

Either work only with 'post' prepositions or with 'pre' prepositions; don't mix them up in the same dictation.

Variations

i) You can make the activity much more challenging by telling students not to write any part of the longer word. You can make it easier by allowing them to write two interior or end letters.
ii) Use longer collocations, such as 'fed up WITH', 'IN an emergency', 'UNDER no circumstances', 'AT a glance/gallop'.
iii) You can use phrasal verbs too, provided you give them (orally) either a paraphrase (e.g. get SNAP ⟶ arrive) and/or a short example sentence ('We got SNAP London at 9'). This variation seems to work best if students do not note down any part of the verb and if you dictate no more than 6 items.
iv) This activity applies equally well to collocations of all sorts, for example: adverb + adjective clichés such as 'HAPPIly married' 'BITTERly disappointed', 'MORTALly offended', as well as adjectives which take *more* against ones which take -er in the comparative (i.e., students might write 'more ____t____', '____d____er' when you say 'interesting' and 'red'.

241

Rationale

Not allowing students to write out the adjective (etc.) in full is intended to foster long-term recollection.

Example collocations (choose ones suited to the level of your class)

ABOUT: sorry, anxious, angry, mad, furious, worried, concerned *about* (V + -ing) someone/something V + -ing someone/something; sceptical *about* something/someone (V + -ing); Verbs: worry *about* someone/something (V + -ing).

AT: bad, terrible, good, hopeless, brilliant, excellent *at* an activity/V + -ing; surprised, shocked, amazed, astonished *at* a person (V + -ing) a situation/event;

BY: fascinated, intrigued *by* someone/something (V + -ing) (see Note 2, below).

FOR: sorry *for* someone/V + -ing; famous, responsible, good *for* (V + -ing) something/someone; grateful *for* (V + -ing) something; Verbs: hope, long, yearn, pine, account *for* something; blame someone *for* (V + -ing).

FROM: different, absent *from* someone/something; Verbs: suffer *from* something.

OF: short, devoid, forgetful, mindful, full *of* something; fond, tired, capable *of* (V + -ing) someone/something; envious, jealous, suspicious *of* someone or someone's something; aware, conscious, mistrustful, proud, ashamed, frightened, fearful, scared, terrified, afraid *of* someone/something or someone/something V + -ing; Verbs: accuse someone *of* (V + -ing).

ON: keen *on* (V + -ing) someone/something; Verbs: depend, reply, count *on* someone/something (V + -ing).

TO: similar, different *to* (someone/something) V + -ing; married *to* someone/something; grateful *to* someone/something (for V + -ing); prone, liable, able, supposed *to* V; used, accustomed *to* someone/something (V + -ing); Verbs: object *to* something/someone (V + -ing something); agree *to* a plan/proposal.

WITH: crowded *with* people/things;

bored, fed up *with* someone/something (V + -ing);
angry, furious *with* someone/something (for V + -ing);
happy, pleased, satisfied, delighted, impressed, disappointed *with* someone/something (for V + -ing);
Verbs: cope *with* something/someone (V + -ing).

AT ____: least, first, last, times, random, war, peace, bay, risk

BY ____: accident, mistake, chance, right, heart, name, sight

FOR ____: sale (= buyable), rent, hire, good, example

IN ____: fact, general, love, practice, theory, principle, trouble, desperation, response, answer, reply, attendance, private, public, vain

ON ____: purpose, guard, duty, tap, sale (= unusually cheap), average, board, business, fire, foot, holiday, leave

OUT OF ____: control, order, danger, breath, date

UNDER ____: attack, way, suspicion, pressure, duress

Notes

1. In this list I have tried to include mainly highly predictable collocations rather than ones like 'on time' since 'time' may also be preceded by 'in', 'out of', 'before', 'through'.
2. 'By' commonly follows a word such as 'delighted' when it is not functioning as an adjective but is instead part of a passive verb construction, e.g. 'I was delighted *by* the news'. Such passives tend to refer to momentary emotional impact. If a different preposition is used, then the '-ed' word is an adjective, e.g. 'delighted *with* the news'. That is, it refers to a more long-lasting feeling.
3. Some adjectives ending in '-ful', like 'grateful' and 'mistrustful', may also be followed by 'towards' as well as 'by, 'of' or 'to'. There seems to be little difference between 'grateful to' and 'towards'. As for 'mistrustful', however, if you are mistrustful of someone, you may not actually show your feelings. If you are mistrustful towards someone, though, it may be that you let your feelings show.

Jon Carr

Bibliography

Bassnett, S. and P. Grundy. 1992. *Language through Literature*. Longman.

Brown, J. 1979. *Back to the Beanstalk: Enchantment and reality for couples*. Psychology and Consulting Associates Press (CA, USA).

Cranmer, D. and C. Laroy. 1992. *Musical Openings*. Longman.

Davis, P. and M. Rinvolucri. 1988. *Dictation: New Methods, New Possibilities*. Cambridge University Press.

Davis, P. and M. Rinvolucri. 1990. *The Confidence Book*. Longman.

Evans, C. 1993. *English People: The experience of teaching and learning English in British Universities*. Open University Press.

Evans, C., ed. 1994. *Developing University English Teaching*. Mellen Press.

Fanselow, J. 1987. *Breaking Rules*. Longman.

Frank, C., M. Rinvolucri and M. Berer. 1982. *Challenge to Think*. Cambridge University Press.

Höper, C. J. *et al.* 1975. *Awareness Games: Personal growth through group interaction*. St Martin's Press (New York). Original title: *Die spielende Gruppe*. 1974. Jugenddienst Verlag.

Kotlers, P. 1991. (7th edn.) *Marketing Management Analysis*. Prentice Hall.

Krashen, S. 1982. *Principles and Practice in Second Language Acquisition*. Pergamon.

Laroy, C. 1993. 'Using songs and music: an educative approach to language learning', MET. vol 2/2:7–13.

Lindstromberg, S., ed. 1990. *The Recipe Book*. Longman.

Lockspeiser, E. 1973. *Music and Painting*. Cassell.

Longman Dictionary of Contemporary English. 1987. D. Summers, ed. Longman.

Longman Language Activator. 1993. D. Summers and M. Rundell, eds. Longman.

Lundquist, S. 1967. *Myten om Wu Tao-tsu*. Bonniers (Stockholm).

Morgan, J. and M. Rinvolucri. 1983. *Once Upon a Time: Using Stories in the Language Classroom*. Cambridge University Press.

Morgan, J. and M. Rinvolucri. 1986. *Vocabulary*. Oxford University Press.

Moskowitz, G. 1978. *Caring and Sharing in the Foreign Language Class*. Newbury House.

Nattinger, J. and J. de Carrico. 1992. *Lexical Phrases and Language Teaching*. Oxford University Press.

Pfeiffer, J. and J. Jones, eds. 1975. *A Handbook of Structured Experiences for Human Relations Training*, vol 5. University Associates (La Jolla, CA).

Postman, N. and C. Weingartner. 1969. *Teaching as a Subversive Activity*. Dell.

Prabhu, N. 1987. *Second Language Pedagogy*. Oxford University Press.

Richards, J. and T. Rodgers. 1986. *Approaches and Methods in Language Teaching*. Cambridge University Press.

Rogers, C. 1969. *Freedom to Learn*. Charles E Merrill.

Serauky, C. 1986. *Der Streit mit Kalunga. – Märchen aus Angola*. Gustav Kiepenheuer.

Sion, C. 1985. *Recipes for Tired Teachers*. Addison Wesley.

Sion, C. 1991. *More Recipes for Tired Teachers*. Addison Wesley.

Soars, J. and L. Soars. 1992. *Headway Upper-Intermediate*. Oxford University Press.

Stern, H. 1992. *Issues and Options in Language Teaching*. Oxford University Press.

Strauss, E. 1994. *Dictionary of European Proverbs*, 3 vols. Routledge.

Woodward, T. 1990. *Models and Metaphors in Language Teacher Training*. Cambridge University Press.

Index

Most of the activities in *The Standby Book* include, to some degree, a listening/ speaking and vocabulary expansion component. Accordingly, this index only mentions these areas of work when they are quite prominent in any given activity. Similarly, because virtually all the activities are usable at intermediate level and many are usable at advanced level too, it is only usability at beginner level that is indexed below.

accuracy, 1.4, 1.8, 2.3, 2.8, 2.9, 3.4, 3.6, 8.10
see also grammar; translation
action and movement, 1.1–1.6, 1.9, 2.9, 10.2–10.4, 11.8

beginners / near beginners, 1.1–1.7, 2.4, 2.9, 3.2, 3.7, 3.8, 9.2 (Variation), 12.2
business and professional people, 8.1, 11.1–11.11

children, *see* young learners
classroom language, 2.2
collocations, 1.2, 11.8, 11.10, 12.9
conversation, 1.9, 2.3, 2.6, 2,7, 4.1, 4.3, 4.4, 4.7, 4.8, 4.10, 5.2, 5.4, 6.1, 6.5, 8.1, 8.2, 8.3, 9.7, 10.5–10.8, 11.1–11.7, 11.11, 12.4
coursebooks
    evaluating, Chapter 5 Introduction, 5.1
    planning use of, 5.2
    reviewing learning in, 5.4, 5.7
    supplementing, 5.3
    using more fully, 5.5, 5.6, 12.7 (Variation)
cultural differences, *see* topics

dialogues, 4.4 (Variation), 4.8, 9.1
see also writing, scripts

discussion (by whole class) of serious issues, 4.5, 7.3, 7.6, 7.9, 10.8, 11.2, 11.7 (for lighter discussion activities *see* conversation)
drama and roleplay, *see* mime for silent drama 4.2, 4.3, 4.8, 4.11, 9.1, 12.5

ending a course, 8.11, 11.11
English for Academic Purposes, 4.1, 4.5, 6.1–6.5, 7.8, 7.9, 8.7, 8.10, 10.8 (Extension)
error correction and other feedback to students, 4.5 (Step 10), 6.1, 8.3 (Step 7), 12.6

fillers, *see* warm-ups
film, *see* topics; video
fluency, *see* conversation
functional exponents, teaching of, 1.4 (Comment), 12.8

games
    competitive, 1.1, 1.2, 1.5, 4.7, 11.8, 11.9
    non–competitive, 1.3, 1.8, 1.9, 2.3
grammar
    practice (i.e., repeated use of one or more particular forms), 4.1, 4.9, 4.11, 8.5, 10.4, 10.6, 12.3–12.5
    teaching, 2.8, 12.1
    see also reviewing, grammar

ice–breakers, 1.1, 2.7

lesson planning, *see* planning
letters, *see* writing, letters
listening (other than participation in
   conversation and other normal
   classroom activities)
   listening to other students, 1.8, 2.1,
     3.6, 8.9
   see also reading aloud
   listening to a recorded text, 4,4, 5.3,
     7.2 (Variation 1), 9.6
   to teacher, 7.2 (Variation 2), 8.4,
     9.1, 9.5, 10.8, 11.9, 12.9
   see also literature, poetry;
     storytelling
literature
   poetry, 8.6, 9.1–9.10, 12.7
     (Variation)
   prose, 7.5, 7.9, 8.8, 9.4, 9.7
     (Variation)
   short passages, 9.2

mime, 10.2–10.4, 11.8 (plus drawing)
monolingual classes, especially for,
   6.3 (Variation), 8.6, 9.2
   (Variation), 12.1, 12.7
music or song
   about music, 2.7
   instrumental music, 8.4, 9.6,
     10.1–10.8
   music and poem, 9.6 (Extension)
   singing, 1.7
   songs, 8.2, 12.7 (Variation)

name learning/reviewing, 1.1
newspapers and magazines, 6.1–6.5
note–taking, 4.1, 4.6, 4.10, 6.1, 6.3,
   10.1, 12.5

planning courses and lessons, Main
   introduction, Introduction to
   chapter 5, 5.2
poetry *see* literature
project work, 5.8
pronunciation, especially rhythm and
   rhyme, 2.8, 2.9, 9.2, 9.3, 9.6
   see also reading aloud

proverbs, 2.8

reading (texts of more than a few
   lines)
   aloud, 6.4, 7.7, 9.2, 9.3, 9.8–9.10
   silently only, 3.2, 5.2, 6.1–6.3, 6.5,
     7.2–7.6, 7.8, 8.3, 8.6, 9.6, 11.1,
     12.7
register *see* style and register
reviewing
   collocations, 1.2, 12.9
   coursebook, material covered in,
     5.4, 5.8
   dialogues, 4.4 (Variation)
   flexible review activities, 1.1, 1.3,
     1.4, 3.7, 3.8
   grammar review activities, 1.2
     (Variation ii), 1.3 (Variation),
     3.6, 3.9
   proverbs, 2.8 (Ways to continue)
   vocabulary review activities, 1.2,
     1.5, 2.4, 2.5, 3.1–3.5, 11.8,
     11.9

rhythm *see* pronunciation
roleplay *see* drama and roleplay; for
   silent roleplay *see* mime

singing *see* music or songs
songs *see* music or songs
storytelling, telling anecdotes
   by students, 4.6, 4.7, 4.10
     (Variation), 5.6, 7.2, 7.7, 9.9,
     10.1, 10.2, 10.4, 11.11
   by teacher, 4.6, 4.9, 4.10, 7.1, 7.7,
     8.4, 11.11
style and register, 6.2, 7.8, 8.7, 8.10,
   12.8
summarising
   in speaking, 4.1 (Variation ii), 4.6,
     6.5
   in writing, 4.1, 6.2–6.4, 8.3

topics
   animals, 4.9, 8.7
   architecture, 10.5
   art/artists, 10.7, 10.8
   business topics, 11.1–11.7

Index

criminality, 7.4
cultural awareness, cultural
   differences, 6.5, 7.2, 8.9, 11.7
film, 4.7
homes, 10.6
horoscopes, the future, 4.11, 12.4
jobs, 8.1, 11.1, 11.2, 11.11
medicine, 6.2, 7.6
music, 10.7
the news, 12.1
ownership, 7.5
prejudice, 7.3
publishing, 8.3 (*see also* 4.1 which
   is about books and libraries)
translation, in writing, 8.6, 12.7

video
   making silent films, 10.4
   (Optional)
   watching silent films, 10.2, 10.3
vocabulary, teaching, 1.2 (Variation i),
   1.4, 2.4, 2.8, 8.10, 9.5, 11.10,
   12.1
   see also reviewing, vocabulary

warm-ups and fillers, 1.1–1.9,
   2.1–2.9, 11.8
writing
   in academic style, 6.2 (Variation),
   8.7, 8.10
   advertisements, 11.1, 11.3
   articles in various styles, 6.2
   biographical text, 10.8 (Extension)
   blurbs, 4.1, 5.1 (Variation)
   for children, 8.11
   comments, 6.1, 6.3

description, 8.7
dialogues, 9.1
essays, 10.8 (Extension)
exam tasks, 3.4
free form, 10.8
letters, 8.1, 8.2, 8.8
marketing plan, 11.3 (Variation)
narrative including stories, 4.6, 5.6
   (Variation), 7.1, 7.2, 7.4, 7.5, 8.3,
   8.4, 8.6, 9.9, 9.10, 10.1
paragraphs, 7.8 (Extension), 8.10
poems, 8.6 (Extension), 9.3, 9.5, 9.8
reports, 11.6 (Extension)
re–writing, 9.2
scripts, 10.3, 10.4
sentences, 2.8 (Ways to continue),
   4.9, 4.11, 8.5, 8.9, 9.4, 9.9, 12.2
summaries, 4.1, 6.2–6.4, 8.3
translations, 8.6, 12.7
see also note-taking

young learners (older teens are
   counted as adults)
pre–teens, 1.1–1.7, 2.4, 2.6, 2.9,
   3.3, 3.8, 5.7, 8.11, 12.1, 12.2
teens, early/mid, (depending on
   proficiency) 1.1, 1.2, 1.4, 2.1
   (but not large classes), 2.2
   (not monolingual classes),
   2.3–2.6, 2.8, 2.9, 3.1, 3.2,
   3.5–3.9, 4.1–4.4, 4.6–4.9, 4.11,
   5.1, 5.3, 5.5, 5.7, 5.8, 7.7, 7.9,
   8.2–8.4, 8.7–8.9, 9.1–9.3, 9.9,
   10.1–10.4, 10.6, 12.1–12.3, 12.5,
   12.6 (but not large classes), 12.7,
   12.9